IN SEARCH OF SCOTLAND

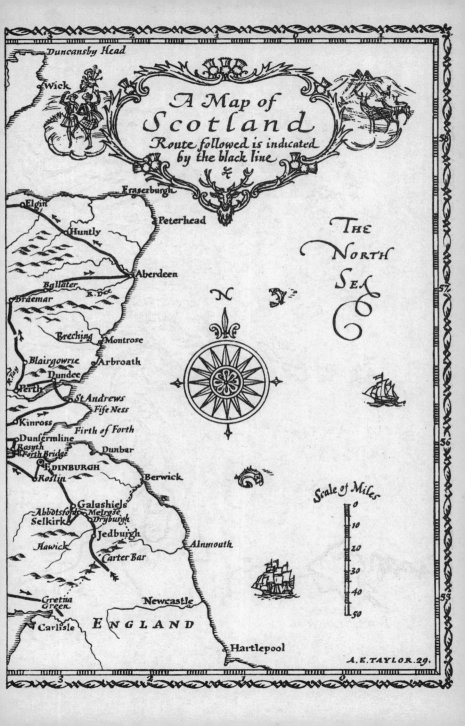

Books by H. V. Morton
published by Methuen

In Search of England
In Search of Wales
In Search of Ireland

IN SEARCH OF
Scotland

H. V. MORTON

Methuen

Published by Methuen 2000

1 3 5 7 9 10 8 6 4 2

First published by Methuen in 1929
This edition published in 2000 by
Methuen Publishing Ltd
215 Vauxhall Bridge Road, London SW1V 1EJ

Copyright © by the Estate of the late H. V. Morton

Methuen Publishing Limited Reg. No. 35431676

A CIP catalogue record for this book
is available from the British Library

ISBN 0 413 54480 x

Typeset by Deltatype Ltd, Birkenhead, Merseyside
Printed and bound in Great Britain by
Cox & Wyman Ltd, Reading, Berkshire

CONTENTS

INTRODUCTION

THE fat, second-hand book catalogues called by such imposing names as *Bibliotheca Scotica* suggest that only a fool would try to add to the books already written about Scotland. It is, however, a curious fact that no book quite of this scope and character has been written since the eighteenth century or, to be exact, the beginning of the nineteenth.

Bibliotheca Scotica contains, I would say, many thousands of works on county topography, hundreds upon hundreds of books devoted to restricted areas, countless descriptions of Scottish scenery, customs, traditions, folklore, and so forth; but you can look in vain for intimate personal records of journeys round Scotland.

England, on the other hand, and for obvious reasons, has been intimately explored and described from the time of the *Antonine Itinerary* to Cobbett.

When we talk about Scotland today we mean Lowlands and Highlands, with the accent (thanks to Sir Walter Scott) on the Highlands; but until as recently as 180 years ago Scotland meant only the Lowlands. The greater area of the Highlands was an unknown wilderness; in fact, as I suggest in this book, the Highlands of Scotland were discovered centuries after America!

Imagine, for instance, that Wales covered three-quarters of the area of England. Draw a line downward from the Wash to Weymouth, and imagine everything to the north of this line a trackless waste of mountains inhabited by armed tribes possessing nothing in common with the peoples of East Anglia, London, and the southern countries but a passion for their property, and you have something similar to the condition of Scotland until only a little over a century and a half ago.

In the days of Pope and Addison the Highlands of Scotland had as little interest for travellers as Afghanistan. Even

Scotsmen (Lowlanders) used to make their wills when forced to go there; and to Lowlander and Englishman alike the mountains were a wild, alien country – a country as distinct from the Scottish Lowlands as Wales from England – where the mountaineers pursued blood feuds in intervals of cattle lifting. It was the defeat of Prince Charles Edward in 1746 which broke up the clan system and led to the disarming of Gaelic Scotland and the consequent union of Highlands and Lowlands.

Writers began to explore Scotland soon after the claymores had been sheathed. Pennant made his tour in 1769; Boswell conducted Johnson through Lowlands and Highlands in 1773; then came a few forgotten inquisitives like Sir James Carr, who followed in 1809 on horseback and in coach much the same route as that taken by my motor car in 1928. But such books are few and far between. The roads a century ago were bad. Accommodation – read Boswell's *Tour* – was so foul that only a madman or an author would voluntarily have endured such an ordeal. Nevertheless, Scotland was to attract travellers; but not by road.

Sir Walter Scott, born at the psychological moment, created the modern conception of Scotland. He it was who ennobled the clans and made the kilt, hitherto an unpopular garment, aristocratic and romantic. Queen Victoria carried on the good work, and by going to live on Deeside in the autumn proved that the Highlands were not only high-minded but harmless. So the tourist's Scotland was born.

The railway and the Caledonian Canal now took travellers through Scotland. They offered an easy and a comfortable escape from the fatigue of travel in a mountainous country, and it is to this fact, coupled, of course, with the weakness of human nature, that we have no record of a circuit of Scotland since the day of the horse and coach.

Now, with the motor-car we have returned to road travel, so that once more books will be written from the standpoint of Pennant, Boswell, and Carr by men able to move freely about the country in touch with the inhabitants.

IN SEARCH OF SCOTLAND

This book is not primarily a book about Scotland: it is an account of a journey through Scotland. It has all the defects of such books, all the omissions and the other sins, and I am too close to it at the moment to say whether it has any of the vital virtues. The skeleton, on which I have put an enormous amount of flesh, was a series of articles written in the *Daily Express* when that newspaper opened its printing office in Glasgow in 1928; but with the exception of the chapters on Edinburgh, Glasgow, and Skye it is really a new book.

There is, I think, something to be said for books written by an explorer who admits frankly, as I do, that he knew nothing about Scotland when he set out, because then commonplace knowledge comes freshly with an air of discovery, and those readers who are also ignorant are possibly stimulated to go forth and perform the same trick of progressive absorption. The knowledgeable reader, on the other hand, will gain a certain amusement as he watches how a fresh mind approaches an old story; he will also perhaps enjoy quite a lot of fun as he notes how many good things a stranger can miss by a hair's breadth. The less a man knows at the start of such a journey as mine the better. All he needs is restless curiosity.

I enjoyed Scotland and I loved the Scots. If something of that enjoyment and affection has found its way into the story of my journey I am inclined to look at my critics and say:

> Here's tae us,
> Wha's like us?
> De'il the yin.

If you don't know what that means you must go to Scotland and find out.

LONDON
June 1929

CHAPTER ONE

I go in search of Scotland. Describes how I leave London, cross the Border, explore Border towns and Border abbeys, how I stand beside a haunted burn, visit the home of Sir Walter Scott and meet a moss trooper

I

EARLY on an autumn morning a small but experienced motor-car moved out from a London square on its way to the Great North Road.

The London square looked as innocent as only a London square can look in the early morning. The sinful old houses which had known so much of life since the time of Queen Anne stood behind their prim iron fences with veiled windows.

Autumn and sleep were over them.

In the still moment soon after sunrise when a city has obviously been forgiven all its sins a man can actually smell autumn in the very heart of London. This warm earthiness, with its suggestion of heavy orchards and corn piled up on stubble-fields, hides in the central trees and in the tangle of grass and shrubs, that rather pitiful patch of country which the Anglo-Saxon bears with him like a captive into cities. It is an appealing, lazy smell. It suggests peace and inactivity as surely as hawthorn inspires movement and adventure.

The early sunlight flung those strange shadows which are known only to milkmen. Everything looked snug and languid, and here was a man in a small car isolated by an adventure from his recumbent fellows going on alone into Scotland.

What would he find there? What new friends would he make? What new songs would he sing? Over what graves would he stand a moment in thought?

There was a night at York in a majestic room once

I

occupied by Queen Victoria. It still rustles furtively in the small hours, as with black silk.

There was an early start.

Newcastle.

And a road going on and on: the road into Scotland.

2

The road, flinging itself round the shoulders of hills, rises and falls, running on in bleak solitude. It narrows to a pass; it opens out into moorland wine-dark with heather; and there is no sound over it but the bleating of sheep and the whistle of wind in the telegraph wires.

The clouds sail in close communion with the hill-crests. Crows like scraps of burnt paper, buffeting the upper air, cry harshly as they are blown downward to a distant valley. Here and there man, exercising his amazing sense of property, has painfully built stone walls, breast-high and brown, to include a few steep acres of tough and soggy grass where black-faced sheep, perpetually optimistic, seek scattered nourishment as they wander, shaggy and unkempt, their long, limp tails swinging in the wind.

This is the Border.

Over it is the loneliness of the sea; the rise and fall of its hills are as the sweep of frozen billows, and the eye, like that of the sailor, searches the solitude for a sign of humanity: a shepherd with his flocks, a farmer in his field, or, best of all, a little white house with a curl of smoke from its chimneys which suggests the presence of the three advance-guards of civilization: a woman, a fire, and children.

As I go on I feel that every bend of the road will bring me face to face with the promised land. A wilderness cannot continue for ever. In the desert you can smell the oasis long before its palm-trees break the sky-line. So it seems to me as I mount hills and descend into valleys, cross streams and skirt the shoulders of hills, that I can feel Scotland round the next corner. But how wrong am I! The Border – that No

Man's Land between England and Scotland – is a wide and persistent wilderness. It has a spirit of its own. These very rocks thrusting their sharp jaws from the brown moorland sheltered the Picts, who sat in the heather listening to the bees that made their honey-wine as they gazed southward to the far smoke and the occasional heliograph of a brazen shield which marked the western limit of the Roman world. This side of the Wall was never tamed. It has known many playmates but no masters. It has made many songs but no laws.

I stop my car. I take out a map. I climb a stone wall and strike off over a field to a high waste of heather; and there I discover my bearings. What names men have given to these hills! How snugly they fit! To my left is Corby Pike and Windy Crag, Dour Hill and Hungry Law; miles away is Bloodybush Edge and Beefstand Hill. Six names as right and racy as a ballad! On my right looms the bulk of Blackman's Law and beyond it the height of Oh Me Edge. It is almost too good to be true! What, I wonder, is the origin of the name of Oh Me Edge? Is it, like Weary-all Hill, near Glastonbury, a tribute to the effect of this ridge on the limbs of its victims?

The heather bends back before the wind until the smooth, smoke-grey stems shine like satinwood. Little pools of peat-brown water gather in my heel-marks, for the sun is shining after recent rains. Each footfall crushes from the wet moorland the rich smell of autumn. From the wind, the heather, the peat water, the line of hill against hill, the bleating of sheep, the drone of insects in the heather, the trilling of larks, and the utter solitude of earth and sky is distilled a powerful emotion that soothes while it excites me; for behind this visible world is an invisible but immortal host. I have not read my Border balladry in vain.

I seek a patch of dry heather and lie reading my map and watching the smoke of my pipe going down the wind. A name leaps out at me. What a fool I am! I passed this place without stopping, and in ignorance, fifteen miles back along the road. Shall I go back and look at Otterburn? Here at the very gates of Scotland is the first milestone of romance:

> *It fell about the Lammas-tide,*
> *When the muir-men win their hay,*
> *The doughty earl of Douglas rode*
> *Into England to catch a prey.*
> *He chose the Gordons and the Graemes,*
> *With them the Lindesays, light and gay,*
> *But the Jardines wald not with him ride,*
> *And they rue it to this day.*

I remember the words of Sir Philip Sidney: 'I never heard the old song of Percy and Douglas that I found not my heart more moved than with a trumpet.' All the chivalry of ancient warfare flowered in that fight. To read Froissart's account of it – such a careful, authentic piece of description – is to feel the ache of having been born in an inferior age. I like, even better than the ballad-monger's story of the death of Douglas and the hiding of his body in the brier bush until the fight was won, the account by Froissart of the pursuit by the Scots knight, Sir James Lindsay, of the English Sir Matthew Redman, governor of Berwick. I know of few incidents which illustrate more vividly the gallantry of that wild time.

After the battle Sir Matthew claps spurs to his horse and takes the road to safety – and Newcastle. The Scotsman, Sir James Lindsay, gallops after him crying: 'Ah! Sir knight. Turn! It is a shame thus to fly! I am James of Lindsay!' But Sir Matthew has had enough! He declines the challenge and, spurring his horse again, tries to fling off his pursuer. The chase continues for three miles. Suddenly Sir Matthew's horse stumbles and the Englishman takes a toss. Lindsay, lance in hand, is on him. Sir Matthew draws his sword and prepares to put up a fight against the mounted man. Lindsay drives at him with his lance. Sir Matthew parries the thrust, and in doing so severs the lance with one mighty sweep of his sword. First blood to the Englishman! Lindsay leaps from his horse and, grasping the short battle-axe which he carries slung at his back, sets about his adversary with great fury. So they pant and gasp, thrusting and cutting until Sir Matthew, who had obviously seen quite enough fighting before the tenacious Scot came after him, puts down his sword and surrenders to Lindsay. Now what happens? After this blood-thirsty combat the two knights talk together like old friends! All their animosity vanishes. I will modernize Froissart:

'Well, what do you want me to do now?' asked the vanquished Redman. 'I am your prisoner. You have beaten me.'

Then he adds, in a matter-of-fact way for a man who has been so near to death's door:

'I badly want to go to Newcastle, but I will within fifteen days come to Scotland and surrender to you.'

Lindsay is content to let him go on the word of one gentleman to another.

'I am content,' he says. 'Promise by your faith to come to me at Edinburgh within four weeks; but wherever you go let it be known that you are my prisoner.'

The enemies part on these friendly terms: Lindsay back to the Border; Sir Matthew to Newcastle. Now occurs what Froissart calls the 'strange chance of war' which gives piquancy to the story. Lindsay gallops into four hundred horsemen. He thinks he has come up with the Scots. But it is the English reserve led by the Bishop of Durham. They capture him, and in a few minutes he is following his recent captive along the road to Newcastle! They place him in the Bishop's lodgings. The first person he meets is his prisoner Sir Matthew, who finds him 'in a studye lying in a windowe'.

'What are you doing here?' asks the astonished English knight.

'I rather think,' replies Lindsay, 'that you will not now come to Edinburgh to surrender to me. We will exchange one for the other!'

'Well, sir,' says Sir Matthew, in the words of Froissart,

'we shall accord ryght well toguyder; ye shall dine this day with me.'

(How perfectly English of him! He might almost have been educated at Eton!)

'I am content to dyne with you,' says Lindsay.

Thus the desperate encounter of the morning, the exchange of knightly trust, ends at evening over a dinner-table in Newcastle. How dearly would I like to have listened to their talk that night!

Is there a more perfect cameo of the Dark Ages or a more charming prophecy of the friendship, then so remote, between two nations?

So I look back to Oh Me Edge, remembering more than meets the eye. This is the spell of the Border. It grips you from Otterburn onwards: the spell of a country wild and untameable, whose every nook and corner is marked down on the map of romance. There can be no wild place in the world which men have embroidered more richly with daring deeds. It shares with all places in which generations of men have loved or hated an arresting importance, almost as if some part of their passion had soaked itself into the grass and into the hard surface of the rocks, making them different from other grass and other rocks.

And now I take to the road again, still feeling the nearness of Scotland, still expecting at every bend the wilderness to unfold, as unfold it must, towards the frontier of another country. Suddenly the road sweeps upward to a ridge. At last! They call this place Carter Bar. Below me lies Scotland. . . .

3

There are certain views in all countries which must quicken the heart of the man who sees them again after an absence. Such is the sight of Scotland from Carter Bar. It is a tender, lovely view. This is not 'Caledonia stern and wild'; it is

Scotland in a homely, gracious mood with a smile on her lips, a welcome in her eyes, a cake on the girdle, a kettle on the hob. It is a view of Scotland which burnt itself into the brain of that greatest of all Borderers – Walter Scott. It would be impossible, I think, for any Scotsman returning home by Carter Bar after years of foreign places to hold back a shout or perhaps a tear. It is so authentically Scotland and could be nowhere else. It seemed to me, as I stood there looking down into the valley, that here is something as definite and unmistakable to a Scotsman as the white cliff of Dover to an Englishman.

The heathery moors slope down to a distant valley. The sun is setting. The sky above the Lammermuirs is red and troubled. The wind drops. The autumn mists far below are creeping from wood to wood. The smoke from chimneys hangs motionless in the air. Thin veils of grey wrap themselves round the foot-hills. Faint white serpents of mist twist above the greenwood, outlining the course of stream and river. It is a study in blue. In the foreground, like a promise of the Highlands, and as notable as a ship at sea, rise the tall peaks of the Eildon Hills, blue as hothouse grapes, standing with their feet among the woodlands of the Tweed. To the far sky lie hills, always hills, fading in graduated subtleties of blue; ahead the long slopes of the Lammermuirs merge westward in the outline of the Moorfoot and the Pentlands. And it is quiet and so still. I can hear a dog barking miles off in the valley.

I am all alone at the Border, one foot in England, the other in Scotland. There is a metal post with 'Scotland' written on it. It is a superfluous post. You do not need to be told that you have come to the end of England. Carter Bar is indeed a gate: the historic barrier between Celt and Saxon; it is the gateway of Scotland.

I sit for a long time watching the light fade from the sky and the mist thickening and the blue deepening. In the hush of evening, with the first star burning above the Eildon Hills, the mystery of the Border winds itself round me like a spell. How can I describe the strange knowingness of the Border? Its uncanny watchfulness. Its queer trick of seeming still to listen and to wait. I feel that invisible things are watching. A blown tree against the sky looks like a crouching man. Out of the fern silently might ride the Queen of Elfland, just as she came to Thomas of Ercildoune in this very country with 'fifty silver bells and nine' hanging from her horse's mane.

Likelier still, it seems as I look down over the moorland stained with heather like blood, that suddenly this land might leap violently to life in pin-points of fire from tree-top to peel tower, from ridge to ridge, filling the dusk with the sound of swords and the mad gallop of horses and the wild clamour of a border raid – 'A Scott! A Scott!' 'An Armstrong!' 'An Elliot!' – as a dark horde sweeps on under the 'lee licht o' the mune'.

The border is haunted still. It sleeps, but – with one eye open! And it is growing cold. I dip down into Scotland.

It is that time ''twixt the gloaming and the mirk'. Smoke is rising from the chimneys of small border villages, grey and stone-built, flush to the street, stern and uncompromising. I stop my car to get the smell and the sound of it. The smell is the comfortable, warm smell of smoke and homes with just an honest hint of cow byre; and the sound? A man and a woman are talking on a doorstep. Their voices ring out in the stillness:

'I canna tell ye,' says the woman. 'Gang tae Maister Armstrong doon the road.'

'Aye,' says the man.

'Should he be oot, gang tae Mr Ferguson next door tae the manse.'

'Aye, I mind it fine,' says the man.

Another figure passes and sings out:

'A graund nicht!'

'It is that!' says the woman.

It is nothing, yet to me it is much: it is the voice of

Scotland. The rich Border tang sinks into my mind. I say the words to myself as they had pronounced them. A 'hoose' is prettier, more lovable than a 'house'. You could not be uncomfortable in a 'hoose' – or it would be more difficult.

In the dusk of a lane I meet a shepherd with his sheep. A small dog with the expression of a professor of mathematics does all the work. She is a little beauty – white muzzle, white chest, paws, and tail tip, but otherwise as black as night. She never barks like the sheep-dogs of the South Downs. She just cruises noiselessly round the flock with the precision of a presiding deity, and if she wishes to rebuke some woolly laggard she gives him a gentle nip in passing and continues, silent and efficient, on the flanks of the trotting grey wave.

That flock of sheep, that dog, and that bent, sandy-haired shepherd could not happen in an English lane.

'A fine nicht,' he says to me.

'It is that!' I reply.

They press past me, a perfect vignette of the Lowlands, towards the stone village, the little lit windows, the warm smell of home. . . .

I go on in the deepening dusk to hilly Jedburgh, where a ruined abbey lifts its broken nave to the stars. The streets are full of life. I note little Scotticisms. A butcher is called a 'flesher'. A chemist hangs an enormous mortar and pestle above his door. I buy an evening paper in which the most interesting items are 'In Memoriam' notices – a whole column of them at 1s. per line, minimum 3s. – which strike me as peculiar. They remind me of Ireland. It is only in Celtic countries that the grief-stricken break into song. Yet how certainly the simplicity of grief is annihilated by the preposterous verses:

> *The call was sudden, the shock severe.*
> *You're not forgotten, Willie, dear,*
> *Nor ever will you be;*
> *For as long as life and memory last*
> *We will remember thee.*

Again:

> *Today we are thinking of someone*
> *Who was so loving, kind, and true,*
> *Whose smile was as dear as the sunshine.*
> *Dear Agnes, that someone was you.*

How strange to discover all this salt heartache expressed in the sugar of the drawing-room ballad.

4

I went to bed in Jedburgh in a room which was prim and bare. An experienced iron bedstead shared the chief honours with a hideous yellow wardrobe of generous proportions. There was a table, a chair, and a dressing-table which during a useful past had been the parking place for many cigarettes. One picture illuminated the hungry walls. It was a Marcus Stone idyll in which an ardent young man backed by a baronial hall bends over a rustic bench towards a coy and frilly maiden with an expression like a confectionary exhibition.

I am keenly sensitive to bedrooms. I wish I were not. They are so personal, and they pretend to be impersonal. I can never rest on an alien pillow but I wonder what head rested there last night and what strange dreams came during that alarming imitation of death which we call sleep. The influences in this room were commercial and romantic. In a drawer was a half sheet of business paper on which a vanished commercial traveller had started to type out an order for galvanized iron dustbins; in the wardrobe lived that faint scent of departed women, always to the lonely and thoughtful traveller the most provoking ghost in a strange room.

There is one way only to bring a reluctant smile to the face of a bedroom which looks as though it doubted your ability to pay the bill – smother it in books! Pile them on chairs, tables, washstands, on mantelpiece and, if possible, on the floor. The most bitter and resentful room is flattered if you try to turn it into a library. Books and a fire can humanize any room, so that if you travel, as I do, with more books than clothes you have nothing to fear from any hotel. And this hotel was a good, solid country town hostelry which, I imagine, in its time had welcomed many a coachload of frozen adventurers after that which, in days before the railway, must have been one of the most trying ordeals in the British Isles.

But, alas, I had to ring for a bedside light. A maid with red hair and a freckled nose entered bearing a candle in a stick of blue and glossy enamel. For one reason only would I enter Parliament: to draft a Bill making it compulsory for every hotel to fit a good light over every bed, which light must be extinguishable from the aforesaid bed. How agonizing and infuriating to the reader-in-bed is that loathsome python composed of ties, braces, leather straps and string, which in a mood of half-optimistic pessimism he attaches to the light switch in the hope that when the time comes a strong upward heave of the variegated cable will fulfil the laws of mechanics necessary to extinguish the light from the bed. Why, in a world that teems with useless and maddening inventions, has no one invented a long-distance electric light extinguisher?

In bed I became filled with that delicious drowsiness which is the half-way house to sleep. I watched the fire flickering over the ceiling, and now and then the sound of Jedburgh came to me from the street below, the hail of belated wayfarers, the striking of a clock, the horn of that lineal descendant of the stagecoach, the big, smooth Pullman omnibus on its pneumatic way to Newcastle, or even, perhaps, to London.

Through the night came the beat of hooves, and I knew that I was listening to Mary, Queen of Scots, riding to Bothwell's bedside in Jedburgh. It was a gallant ride, and her enemies made the most of it; and it was in Jedburgh that she lay ill – so ill that they opened the windows for her soul.

'Would that I had died that time in Jedburgh,' she said later in life.

The steps of the last wayfarer go down the street and silence comes to Jedburgh.

5

On a sunny morning I took the road to Kelso over Jedfort Bridge. One glance at Kelso, and I held my breath in amazement! Surely I was in France! An enormous *grande place* paved with whinstone forms the heart of the town. Round it rise those tall, demure, many-storied houses which – anyhow in France – seem to know almost as many secrets as a concierge. Wooden shutters only were necessary to complete the illusion.

I asked one of several loungers about it. He regarded me with deep distaste and said briefly:

'It's Sco'land!'

But it is not! It is as foreign in appearance as Boston in Lincolnshire or Bradford-on-Avon in Wilts. And it is surely strange that one of the most French-looking towns outside France was one of the towns in Scotland which gave no recruits to Prince Charlie in '45. All he received were the smiles and tears of Kelso women.

It was late afternoon. I went to an enormous hotel in the *grande place*, an hotel with a great arch for stagecoaches, and here, without any surprise, I found myself in the atmosphere of eighteenth-century France. The inn yard was just the sort of place in which Sterne found the carriage for his sentimental journey after his discovery of the perfect chambermaid.

Up dark stairs, in a tremendous dining-room overlooking the square, a girl, as neat as a French maid, with a white cap on her hair, was placing before a solitary commercial traveller that amazing meal known in Scotland, with unconscious humour, as 'tea'.

I tried my theory on the commercial traveller, and he, to my satisfaction, responded:

'You've hit it!' he said. 'Kelso is like a French town, especially when the sun is shining as it is today. I've often thought so!'

We leaned out of the window and admired the splendid square, brilliant in the sun. How strange the good Border names looked over the shop fronts!

'It's so like France,' said the commercial traveller, 'that you expect to see *Estaminet* and *Brasserie* over the shops and a gendarme with baggy blue trousers smoking a cigarette in the middle of the square!'

The man was a thought-reader! No ex-soldier in Kelso would, I think, be surprised to see a battery of artillery come rumbling over the whinstones, or to be pulled up by an inquisitive military policeman in the shadow of the 'Queen's Head'.

While we were talking the neat, small maid had covered my table with a Scottish tea. No southerner can conceive the reckless generosity of Scottish teas. They are of two calibres: heavy and light, but known technically as high or plain. There is nothing you cannot eat at high tea in Scotland. You could order ham and eggs, half a cold grouse, with outriders in the form of bannocks and cakes and many varieties of bread. I think the Scots are, with the Viennese, the best pastrycooks in the world.

This particular tea was, however, plain. There were hot cakes and butter, white and brown bread, currant bread, some relation to a plum pudding called a 'Selkirk bannock', girdle cakes, a loaf of gingerbread, and a plate of claret-coloured apple-jelly. The table looked like the prize stall in the bakers' exhibition.

'Would ye no' like a boiled egg?' asked the girl softly. And she was serious!

No; it was the last thing I could have 'liked'.

Full of apple-jelly, oatcake, bannock, and Selkirk currants I walked slowly down the generous stairs of this hospitable inn to take stock of Kelso. I found that the Frenchness ended as if cut off with a knife at the stone bridge over the Tweed.

A little way up the road over the bridge is a view of Kelso which must be among the most lovely in all the Borderland. You look over meadows and see the Tweed running under a bridge which is exactly like a little brother of Waterloo Bridge in London. Behind, bowered in trees, rise the roofs of Kelso, the spire of a church, and, higher than everything, the pink sandstone Norman tower of the ruined abbey.

It is a perfect sight. It reminded me of Wiltshire as much as the square reminded me of France. It is not typically Border; all the gentleness and the sweetness of the Scottish Lowlands seem to have come to rest in Kelso.

The resemblance of Kelso Bridge to Waterloo Bridge bothered me. I find that it was built by Rennie in 1803, some say as a model and a 'try-out' for his famous bridge over the Thames.

In the *grande place* of Kelso I found my car. The sun was low. In this square James Stuart was proclaimed James VIII in 1715, and in this square thirty years later came Charles Stuart with his army. Perhaps the square has never recovered from the French it heard in '45!

As I swung round and out of Kelso I could not resist the temptation of saying '*Au revoir*' to the policeman: a remark which I fear he misinterpreted.

6

On these Border hills, or lying beside the troutful waters of these Border burns, or full length in the stubble of a Border harvest, what dreams come to a man as a book falls from his hand. And the book? There is for me one book only in this land – Walter Scott's *Minstrelsy of the Scottish Border*. Had

Scott done nothing but gather these deathless ballads he would have placed us for ever in his debt. They are to poetry as the wild pink is to the carnation, or, to mix metaphor, as the rude handshake of the peasant to the cultured greeting of the scholar. No one should explore this country without this book. The Border ballads come down to us with the wind and the rain in them, with some quiet, approving gleam of firelight over them, and between their lines the thin echo of a harp. We cannot fail to recognize in them the authentic gateway to another world. They are so naked. They are so unashamed. They are so sincere. They are as real as a sword dug up on a battlefield. I do not concern myself with the arguments of those meticulous ones who would tear a rainbow to pieces in the interests of analysis – the higher critics. They may take these ballads word by word and say 'Scott put in this or that'; they may examine them line by line and turn them over just as furniture dealers go over every inch of a Queen Anne chair in search of false walnut; it is enough for me that these songs recreate the spirit of their time so deftly that, as I read them, I can feel a horse under me and a spear beside me at the saddle-bow.

In the Border ballads the peel towers rise whole again from Berwick to Carlisle. The night is alive with riders. Through the gloom of green woods comes the knight in search of love or pain, or both. The Queen of Elfland rides silently out of the fern to claim a soul. There are wild hammerings on door and wild shoutings at casements; over the edge of the hill come the freebooters driving their startled kine. Many a host strikes its pallions on hilltop and moves down to battle; many a daring band slips over the boundary line to singe the beard of the March Wardens; many a fair maiden listens the long night through for the returning beat of hooves. It is all sublimated journalism. Most of it happened. It is the history of a vanished age, refined in imagination and preserved by the approbation of generations who knew that it was true. To read these ballads once is to be haunted by them for ever. 'Verses and snatches of these ballads are continually haunting and twittering about my memory,' wrote Alexander Smith, 'as in summer the swallows haunt and twitter about the eaves of my dwelling.' How true this is and how vivid they are:

> *About the dead hour o' the night*
> *She heard the bridles ring;*

and

> *O there was horsing, horsing in haste.*
> *And cracking of whips out o'er the lee;*

and

> *The King sits in Dunfermline town*
> *Drinking the blude-red wine;*

and

> *They lighted high on Otterbourne*
> *And threw their pallions down;*

and

> *He belted on his gude braid sword,*
> *And to the field he ran;*
> *But he forgot the helmet good*
> *That should have kept his brain;*

and

> *They swakked their swords, till sair they swat,*
> *And the blood ran down like wine;*

and

> *It fell about the Martinmas tide,*
> *When our Border steeds get corn and hay,*

and

> *They shot him at the Nine-Stone Rig,*
> *Beside the Headless Cross,*
> *And they left him lying in his blood*
> *Upon the moor and moss.*

For sheer savage realism give me 'The Fray of Suport'. I know of nothing like it in English. It is a Red Indian war-dance! It is the cry of an enraged English Borderwoman whose 'gear', or goods, have been plundered in the night by a band of Scottish moss-troopers. Each wild verse ends:

> *Fy, lads! Shout a' a' a' a' a',*
> *My gear's a' gane!*

As she rouses the reivers to pursuit and vengeance she describes what happened to her. The Scots came and drove off twenty-four head of cattle and all her horses. She cries:

> *Weel mey ye ken,*
> *Last night I was right scarce o' men:*
> *But Toppet Hob o' the Mains had guestene'd in my house by chance.*
> *I set him to wear the fore-door wi' the speir while I kept the back-door wi' the lance.*
> *But they hae run him through the thick o' the thie and broke his knee-pan,*
> *And the mergh [marrow] o' his shin-bane has run down on his spur-leather whang:*
> *He's lame while he lives, and where'er he may gang.*
> > *Fy, lads! Shout a' a' a' a' a',*
> > *My gear's a' gane!*

If poor lame Toppet Hob o' the Mains came back to life he could tell us no more of Border raids than we know from this. And the fearful things that happen in these ballads might have happened on any moonless night in the old days. Read 'Jamie Telfer' and 'The Lament of the Border Widow' and 'Kinmont Willie', whose release from Carlisle Castle in April 1596 was one of the most daring deeds of the Scottish Border.

And as you go through this haunted country, now so peaceful, where the gaunt outline of the peel towers rises up from field or wood, you may see in imagination a solitary horseman, the presiding genius of this Borderland, reining in his horse to gaze round him with eyes which see more of Scotland than any man has ever seen – Walter Scott.

Every unresisting visitor to Scotland finds himself in Abbotsford, the home of Sir Walter Scott, and the scene of the greatest financial drama in the history of literature. Scott found himself at the age of fifty-five faced by a financial crisis which might have driven many a man to suicide. His co-partners failed for £117,000. There was no such thing in 1826 as a limited liability company. Now, Scott was at the height of his powers. He was making from his novels an income of £10,000 a year: and this in days before film rights and big American royalties!

This middle-aged man decided to devote his life to paying off the debt. It seems as though Fate was determined to test a brain whose fertility can be compared only with that of Shakespeare's. In six years Scott wrote himself into the grave; but in those six years his amazing effort resulted in the payment of £80,000.

The last six years of Walter Scott's life were as heroic as any of the knightly deeds in the pages of his novels.

Abbotsford is a many-turreted mansion standing among trees and built on rising ground which slopes gently to the Tweed. It looks as though it has been composed by the author of *Ivanhoe*. As you skirt the high walls that surround it and observe its towers, its air of having descended from Border keep and baronial castle, it would appear only right that a herald should ride to the sound of trumpets and inquire your status in Debrett. Unfortunately, such thoughts are not of long duration; visitors go in by the tradesmen's entrance!

A guide takes you up back stairs to the entrance hall. Here you find yourself in a museum. It is exactly as Scott knew it: an incredibly Gothic apartment, almost as though the novelist had tried to pack the entire Middle Ages into one room. Crowds of Scottish and American visitors stand gazing doubtfully at the rich harvest of medievalism, thinking that it would be a difficult place to live in; as, of course, it would. It fitted Walter Scott's mind as his clothes fitted his body.

There are queer monastic carvings, suits of armour, grim relics of Border raids, bloodthirsty mementoes of Old Edinburgh – jail keys and executioners' swords – battle-axes and all the rough material of the romantic novel. It is like nothing so much as a studio; these were the lay figures from which Scott drew inspiration.

'Say, guide,' said an American, 'Scott must have had a lot of money to build this house and buy all this junk.'

'He built it bit by bit,' replied the guide, 'as the money came in from his books.'

This also is an interesting side to Scott's character. When he began to make money he started with a more than feminine intensity to buy a beautiful frame for his personality. Abbotsford was to be his darling, the ideal background, the complete expression of himself.

He built it by instalments. When Washington Irving visited him in 1817 he found him living in a small cottage on the estate, watching the lordly turrets of Abbotsford rise up under the hands of workmen. He wrote for ten years to make Abbotsford; and Abbotsford is, I am inclined to think, one of his greatest historical novels. Each new success meant an addition to the house of his dreams, a new room, a new ceiling, a new area of panelling, a few stalls copied from Melrose Abbey or some other extravagant fancy which ministered to his atmosphere.

No man has ever worked with greater intensity to build the perfect home. When the crash came, he looked at the baronial mansion in which he had sunk capital and income, and, with grim pathos, he called it his 'Delilah'.

I am no Scott expert. I have not even read his *Journal*; it is many years since I read Lockhart; but it seemed to me as I explored Abbotsford that the only pleasure of his later years must have been the fact that he was permitted to live and work in the sanctuary he had made for his imagination.

The reality of Scott's race to make £117,000 before he

died must appeal with force to every person who goes to Abbotsford. Every day visitors stand in his small, book-lined study with its gallery and its little monastic door leading to his bedroom. How many of them see him coming along the gallery in the early morning and to his desk? It is easy to imagine that fine head bent over papers, dreaming of knights entering the lists of chivalry: himself a knight in the lists of honour.

His royalties were enormous. This age, which considers itself to be the age of colossal literary rewards, will perhaps be astonished to know that for his *Life of Napoleon* – a work better known in Edinburgh than in London – Scott received, in advance of future royalties, the sum of £19,000. Other advances were £6,075 for *Woodstock*; £11,400 for *Chronicles of the Canongate*; and £4,200 for *Anne of Geierstein*. The creditors were certainly on a safe proposition.

Many a modern 'best seller' will open his eyes at these figures; but they are by no means a record. In those days, before Hollywood and New York piled up the rewards of popularity, Macaulay received (nine months before it was due, and in advance of money still to come!) £20,000 for his *History of England.*

I left Abbotsford with the firm determination to re-read some of the books with which Scott repaid the debt.

Every room of Abbotsford holds something of a presence so strong that even one who imagined that his interest in Scott evaporated at school must feel the awakening of an old loyalty.

Facing the Eildon Hills on Bemersyde is 'Sir Walter's View'. It is perhaps the loveliest view on the Border. Here Scott used to drive in his carriage and sit silently for half an hour gazing over the land whose people he loved and whose legends were in his blood.

It was evening when I stood there. The sun was sinking above Melrose, and the smoke from the distant farms lay in the air and drifted in thin banks to lie over the waters of the Tweed. It was so still that I heard dogs barking far down in the valley; and as the sun sank the grey mists grew denser between the hills, outlining the valleys and lying like grey veils in the hollow places.

And I met an old man returning from work. I talked to him. His mind was full of a recent fishing competition in the Tweed, and he talked freely about baskets of 'troot'. Gradually I led him to Scott, and found, as I had imagined, that he had never read a line of him! But you must not imagine that he did not admire Scott! He had been brought up on the Border! He told me the story of 'Sir Walter's' funeral, how the long line of carriages was held up on Bemersyde because Scott's carriage horses, drawing the hearse, stopped at the view he loved so well and stood patiently there for half an hour, as they had done so often.

'Aye, he was a graund man!' said the old fellow who had never read a line of Scott!

And I thought that this perhaps was the greatest tribute ever paid to a writer by one of his own people. Scott was no mere author. He was a Border chief and a prince of ballad-singers; and something of his quality found its way into the hearts of men who worked around him with scythe and spade.

8

I saw marked on the map, and not far from Melrose, a small stream called the 'Bogle Burn'. Who could resist such a name? I set out to find it.

A 'bogle' is an evil spirit. It is no relation to the English 'bogey', which was originally 'Boney', and dates only from the Napoleonic wars, when mothers frightened their children with threats of Bonaparte. 'Bogle' is, to my mind, much more fearful than 'bogey'. It has a goggle-eyed horror about it. There is an icy, graveyard wind round it. To meet a 'bogle' would be, I feel sure, to meet the real thing!

Now the Bogle Burn runs under the road midway between Melrose and Newtown St Boswells. It trickles beneath thick banks of undergrowth. I climbed a wall and followed the little stream for some way, breaking through the dense bracken and shrub. It was the ideal fairy glen. In parts you lose the burn, but you can always hear it rippling over the stones beneath its screen of leaves.

I broke through to a field in which an old man was working.

'What is a bogle?' I asked him.

'A ghaist,' he said.

'And is this burn haunted?'

'Och, no, maun; it's juist some auld wives' tale of a ghaist. . . .'

It is difficult to make people talk about local legends. They think you are laughing at them. I have spent days wooing old people in Cornwall and Somerset until they melted into narrative. This old man was, however, tougher than anything I have met in Somerset. He had a red face, a jaw like a steel trap, and two of the most challenging blue eyes on the Border. Och, no; he'd forgotten the blather. . . .

However, just as I was relinquishing him as hopeless he melted, and, sitting beside me on the wall, told me a typical Border legend, bit by bit.

'Ye see,' he began, 'in auld days there lived over at Earlston a man called Thomas the Rhymer. . . .'

Light broke over me, and I settled down to listen. His story was not correct in all particulars, but I have checked it with a ballad book.

Thomas the Rhymer was Thomas of Ercildoune, or Thomas Learmont, who lived in the shadow of the Eildoun Hills in the thirteenth century. His fame throughout the Border as a rhyming prophet was rather similar to that of Mother Shipton in England. It was Thomas who made the prophecy printed all over the world when Earl Haig died:

> *'Tyde what may betyde,*
> *Haig shall be Haig of Bemersyde.*

This was a terribly rash statement to make in the thirteenth century, when men were cut down in war and Border fray like corn in autumn; but it held good. No matter how many Haigs were slain there was always a laird to succeed to Bemersyde. The reputation of Thomas seemed to be in peril in the eighteenth century, when a Haig had twelve daughters! But, lo, the Border prophet was right: the thirteenth child was a son!

But the great event of Thomas's life was meeting with the Queen of Fairyland, who dared him to kiss her, and he, being a reckless Scotsman, up and kissed her before the words were out of her mouth. Then, for seven years, he vanished into Fairyland.

'Aye, 'twas in this glen he met her,' said the old man, 'and beside this very burn, the Bogle Burn. . . .'

And as he told me one of the prettiest legends of the Scottish Border we could hear the little stream slipping away through its green tunnel, tinkling and laughing, over brown stones.

The ballad book says that Thomas was sleeping under the 'Eildon Tree' when a 'ladye bright' in a 'shirt of grass green silk' came silently riding up to him on a milk-white horse. At first he thought she was the Blesed Virgin, but she, hurriedly denying this, told him that she was the Queen of Elfland:

> 'Harp and carp, Thomas,' she said,
>   'Harp and carp along wi' me;
> And if ye dare to kiss my lips,
>   Sure of your bodie I will be.'
>
> 'Betide me weal, betide me woe,
>   That weird shall never daunten me.'
> Syne he had kissed her rosy lips,
>   All underneath the Eildon Tree.

This, of course, was exactly what the queen desired. 'Now ye maun go wi' me,' she told Thomas, 'and ye maun serve me seven years, thro' weal or woe as chance to be'. She mounted her milk-white steed and took Thomas up behind her, and together they galloped swifter than the wind into the land of faery.

During the seven years which he spent in Fairyland True Thomas received his gift of prophecy. The queen pulled an apple from a tree and gave it to him as a reward: it endowed him with a 'tongue that can never lie'. Thomas, realizing how awkward it would be to have a tongue that could never lie, attempted to decline the doubtful blessing, but the queen was an insistent and determined lady:

> When seven years were come and gane
>   The sun blinked fair on pool and stream;
> And Thomas lay on Huntlie bank,
>   Like one awakened from a dream.

He had returned to astonish Scotland with his prophecies. They are remembered to this day. But the ballad suggests that Thomas was not happy. He had known true love. He had lived in Fairyland. He went dreaming of 'rosy lips all underneath the Eildon Tree'. But it was a hopeful misery. He was pledged to return to his queen whenever she called him. And the call came suddenly.

One night when Thomas was holding a banquet in his Tower of Ercildoune, a messenger rushed in to say that a hart and a hind had come out of the forest and were walking together down the village street. The guests were astonished, but Thomas of Ercildoune rose up from the feast and went without a word. The cottagers saw him go, between the hart and the hind, down the street and up the hill behind, and so into the green shade of the forest. He was never seen again.

I stood for a long while beside the Bogle Burn listening to the sound of water, the rustle of leaves, and the piping of birds. . . .

Is there a more perfect fairy tale?

I felt that an enchanted country had drawn aside her veil and had let me look for a moment into the reality of her eyes.

In this queer compromise between fairyland and battlefield which is the Border, the lowland abbeys stand with their shattered naves in green grass. Where the Tweed makes wide loops through meadow and woodland the monks, who always recognized a desirable building site, built their churches to the glory of God. Like islands these abbeys rode for centuries above the rough seas of Border battles. They belonged not to Scot or English but to Mother Church – therefore, in a sense, to both of them. Their bells rang out over a land so often scarred by war and pillage; matins and vespers followed one another in calm procession down their chaste aisles, and many an abbot at High Mass must have smelt the pungent incense of Border wrath going up before the high altar with the incense of the Church.

So these abbeys – Kelso, Jedburgh, Dryburgh, and Melrose – as close together as the abbeys of Yorkshire, preached the gospel of love in a land of hate. They were situated gallantly in the front line like four *padres*, helpless to stem the tide of war, nevertheless a comfort to friend and foe.

When you see them one after the other in a day, as I did, you appreciate the horror that must have swept through the Lowlands when men ran panting with the news: 'Melrose is burning! Jedburgh's afire! Kelso's no more!'

It must have seemed the ultimate blasphemy even to a land brought up on curses.

It should ease Scotland's conscience a little to realize that England saved her the sin of destroying these glories of the Border. How the storm broke seems to me one of the saddest, yet most inevitable, chapters in the history of the two countries.

Perpetual peace between England and Scotland had been proclaimed in Edinburgh! Henry VIII, like an enormous ogre, sat in Westminster, rubbing his impatient hands with delight, or possibly in that acute Tudor brain lurked the knowledge that after all his scheming and bribery his dream was not to come true. However, his boy, Edward, was pledged in marriage to the infant Mary, Queen of Scots. The Treaty was concluded at Greenwich on July 1st 1543. The Catholic party in Scotland, backed by the nation, favoured the French alliance, with the result that in December Scotland tore up the Greenwich Treaty and recklessly flung down the glove to the nation which had already given her Flodden. This part of history has more than one good question mark. How, I wonder, would the course of events have been altered had Mary gone to England as the future Queen, and had the lovable prince, Edward, lived long enough to have married her? It is as provocative, and as useless, a speculation as: what course would the Reformation have taken had Prince Arthur, the elder brother of Henry VIII, lived to wear the crown of England? Henry VIII was a second son, destined for the Church!

However, when Henry knew that his plans were frustrated and that the Scottish Parliament had cancelled the Greenwich Treaty he did not delay his vengeance. Then began the 'rough wooing'. He tried to force Scotland into the betrothal with a drawn sword as a go-between. As the Earl of Huntly said, he 'disliked not the match but he hated the manner of wooing'. An English fleet appeared in the Firth of Forth in May 1544. The Earl of Hertford landed with a great army of assorted aliens. He sacked Edinburgh and destroyed the Abbey of Holyrood. His forces marched on the Border, laying waste, looting, murdering, giving no quarter. The sight of an abbey in flames was no novelty to English eyes. Over the Border, in fair Yorkshire dales, in the rich lands of the midlands, and wherever the monks and friars had established their houses, 3,219 abbeys lay in ruins, and His Majesty had increased his income by £161,000.

What more natural than that Hertford – afterwards the Protector, Somerset, whose sole legacy to posterity is the association of the name with the headquarters of the Income-tax – should put a brand to the Scottish abbeys, and, incidentally, light a fire which was not destined to go out. At this time, when many a good Scottish Catholic shook with horror at the deed, a middle-aged priest, chaplain and tutor to the Kers of Samuelston, may have heard of the burning with grim satisfaction. In two years the priest, on fire with the new doctrine, was to go round East Lothian with the Protestant martyr, George Wishart, carrying a great two-handed sword. So John Knox is seen, rather vaguely but already armed, through the prophetic smoke of the Border abbeys.

Three years later the English armies returned on a second 'wooing' and took what little they had failed to appropriate on the first occasion. Those three years of growing Protestantism in Scotland needed no assistance from English incendiaries. While the English were training their guns for the second time on the ruins of the Border abbeys, John Knox was chained to an oar in a French galley, called, rather grimly, *Notre Dame*, where, with other Scottish Protestants, he had time, but no leisure, to contemplate a future that seemed to hold no hope. He did not know, perhaps, that Fate was keeping him out of trouble until his time should come.

And while the Border abbeys were hardly cold from their burning, England still made love to Scotland on behalf of the boy King Edward. A prayer used in England at this time ran:

Ye shall also make your hartie and effectual prayer to Almighty God, for the peace of all Christian regions, and especially, that the most joyfull and perpetual peace and unity of this realm and Scotland may shortly be perfected and brought to pass, by the most Godly and happy marriage of the King's Majesty and the young Queen of Scotland. And that it would please the Almighty to aid with strength, wisdom and power, and with His holy defence, all those who favourith and setteth forward the same, and weaken and confound all those which labour- eth or studyeth to the interruption of so godly a quiet

whereof both these realmes should take so great a benefit
and profit. . . .

A good prayer; but it was not granted.

10

I was sitting on a stone in the grass beside the broken north
aisle of Melrose Abbey. Birds were singing; and I had just
drunk a glass of beer with a bow-legged man who told me
endless, and probably aprocryphal, stories of the Duke of
Buccleuch's hounds. If I was thinking of anything it was that
Melrose is the most beautiful of Border towns. It must have
improved since Walter Scott's time, because he states that
Kelso is the most beautiful, if not the most romantic, place
on the Borderland. I cannot think that anyone would prefer
Kelso to Melrose. Melrose is just as Scottish as Kelso is
French.

I became aware of a strange scratch and rustle on the
other side of the wall. Someone was trying to walk along
the narrow ledge and turn the corner without falling off.
Then – such strange things do occasionally happen to the
traveller – a remarkably long, slim leg in a brown silk
stocking appeared round the corner of the wall and felt
blindly for a foothold. Lower and lower it felt, revealing
itself with the generosity of authentic beauty.

My intention, which was to spring forward helpfully and
guide the foot to a stone, was arrested by the sight of a
narrow tartan garter. The next instant a girl with very blue
eyes was pulling her skirt down over her knees.

'My!' she said, 'you bet I wouldn't have done that fool
thing if I had known there was an audience.'

'Boston!' I said to myself.

I assured her that I had been fast asleep. American girls
of this type go round the world in ecstatic troops attended
sometimes by a slightly older girl even more lovely than her
charges. I looked round for the rest of the college.

'I guess you haven't seen a guide-book lying around?'

'No,' I replied, hastily making a search among the daisies.

'Darn it!' she said. 'I've come back for it. I want to read about the Heart.'

'Bruce's heart?'

'Sure.'

'Shall I tell you?'

'Why, certainly, if you know the story.'

'Have a cigarette?'

'Well, yes, I guess I will.'

I told the story, which, I suppose, every Scottish school child must know, for it seems to possess every sign of being the Scottish equivalent of England's story of Alfred and the cakes. When Bruce was dying he ordered that they should cut his heart from his body, place it in a casket, and take it on a pilgrimage to the Holy Land. The Douglas took it, but, being a good Scotsman, got into a fight in Spain, where he was slain in a battle with the Moors. The heart of the Bruce, denied greater sanctuary, was brought home and buried before the high altar of Melrose Abbey.

'I think it is a perfectly horrible story,' said the girl. 'Those old boys did some awful things with themselves alive or dead.'

She smoked reflectively.

'I suppose it's true?'

'In 1920, I am told on excellent authority, the Office of Works, discovered, during excavations here, a casket containing a heart. It was said to be Bruce's heart. Then someone found that it was not buried in the right place, so they concluded that it must have been the heart of a monk.'

'You don't say so!' she said, which is American for our equally idiotic 'Not really!'

I looked at her critically as she sat with her superb legs crossed, flicking cigarette ash on the daisies. She was a perfect flower of the New World. All this was to her improbable and unreal. She was slightly contemptuous. It was rather stimulating. Most American girls of her age are generally so eager to absorb the history of a new country that their brains are frequently a chamber of horrors in which Edward the Conqueror and William the Confessor chase one another through labyrinths of wild inaccuracy. This brain was beautifully free from history.

'Do you like Scotland?'

'No, I like Paris.'

I wanted to ask her why she wore tartan garters, but at this point a sallow American wearing horn spectacles came round the corner and said:

'So there you are! Ma and I have been bawling the place down.'

'Hallo, Daddy! I've been learning things.'

Her father was one of those middle-aged Americans with eyes of steel and a heart full of queer hooks and crannies of emotion. As soon as I saw him I knew that he was embarked on one of those sentimental journeys which happen to all successful Americans. I do not know whether Polish Americans, German Americans, Czecho-Slovakian Americans, Italian Americans, or all the other kinds of Americans, are to be discovered pervading the churchyards of Europe with an air of wistful uncertainty; but I do know that every American with English, Scottish, or Irish blood in him comes back at some time to find his roots. They drift about unlikely towns and villages like prosperous ghouls, poring over old parish registers with expectant fingers, and standing for a long time before half-obliterated tombstones. This, I think, is the most lovable trait in the character of the American.

Scotland was, to this man, a tremendous romance. I was inclined to think that his daughter's diffidence was a barrier which she had erected as a protection against his enthusiasm. In level tones, like a strong man sawing a gigantic tree, he spoke to me shyly of seeing Scotland for the first time, of finding all kinds of memories awakening in him – memories of his father and, more dimly, of his grandfather. And as he talked his steely eyes softened and belied the matter-of-factness of his words.

'We came from Perth in the 'forties, I guess,' he said. His eyes kindled. 'We are a sept of the Clan Macdonald.'

'A nice bright tartan,' I said, with a glance at the girl.

'Beast!' she said quickly.

'But, I guess,' his voice sawed on, 'there are none of our family here now; but I do remember my father said that my grandfather was buried in Perth. It is just fine to be here at last.'

He smiled. I liked him. It was a pity he could not have left his women in Paris. Somewhere deep down in him his Scots blood was stirring, puzzling him a lot, I think. I wondered how many of these wanderers really find their roots or know them when they see them.

They got into an enormous car and exploded away in the direction of Edinburgh.

The sun was still over Melrose Abbey. It is finer than Jedburgh or Kelso, probably because there is more of it. In the churchyard I met a man addicted to the most melancholy of all hobbies – the collection of epitaphs. He led me to an old red tombstone which, with his help, I spelt out:

> The earth goeth on the earth,
>   Glistring like gold;
> The earth goeth to the earth
>   Sooner than it wold,
> The earth builds on the earth
>   Castles and towers;
> The earth says to the earth,
>   All shall be ours.

§ II

Most beautiful of all four abbeys is Dryburgh. It lies in a loop of the Tweed. The broad, brown waters ring it round, and I am sure that the monks never went short of trout. Round the abbey rise gigantic cedars of Lebanon which were brought back from the Crusades. There is also a magnificent English yew which I am told is 750 years old.

There is always a Scottish pilgrimage to Dryburgh. Here lies the soul of the Border – Walter Scott. England has no literary loyalty like that felt by Scotland for Scott. It was through this man's imagination that all things dearest in the memories of his countrymen found expression and received immortality.

When I hear people talking about 'Wordsworth's Country' or the 'Doone Country' I want to push them into the nearest pond; but there *is* a Scott Country. It is a reality. Walter Scott was, and is for ever, the King of the Border. No man can see the Eildon Hills or look at the long sweep of the Lammermuirs without remembering him; no man can hear the gurgling of a Border burn or watch the river mist lift in the morning from Teviot or Tweed with no thought for the man who knew this country better than any before or after him.

Near the tomb of Scott lies Earl Haig, a ring of red Flanders poppies on the new turf, and in the centre the standard pattern 'war-grave' headstone bearing his name, just like that of a private soldier.

Over Dryburgh lies indescribable peace, only the throstle piping in the yew-trees, the slow murmur of the Tweed, and the simple sounds of open country that drift through the trees from Bemersyde.

12

I came into the busy town of Galashiels as the last flush of sunset was dying in the west. Dusk had fallen. The lamps were lit. The streets were full of neat, small girls. Here and there a mill chimney lifted an ugly finger to the sky.

I came in this hive of woollen mills on a thing of such supreme beauty and strength that it might have been the vision created by a mind obsessed by the history of the Scottish Border. . . .

A perfect peel tower rises up in the night, a building of grey stone crowned with a triangular roof. There are narrow slits in the walls. The stone is new. The building is modern, but it is so good a reconstruction of a Border keep that it seems at first sight as though one of the many ruined towers along the Scottish Border had come suddenly to life and had marched into the square of Galashiels. Cut in the front of the tower is a shrine lit by concealed lights which cast a golden flush over a bronze tablet containing the names of the men of Galashiels who died in the war. By some strange freak of light and shade two shadowy wings rise from the shoulders of the sculptured figure of a woman who stands above the roll of honour bearing in each hand a laurel wreath.

But, magnificent as the tower is, strong and arresting as it is, the figure of a horseman on a plinth, set just far enough from the main building to form a silhouette against the dimly-lit shrine, simply takes away the breath. He is a Border 'reiver' in helmet and breastplate. An English eye would find him like one of Cromwell's Ironsides; a Scot's eye sees in him the ancient knight of the Borderland round whose daring deeds fully half the songs and stories of the Border have been sung and written. A sword hangs from his left thigh; a long lance is carried over his right shoulder. He has just reined-in his horse, almost on its haunches. He sits, a perfect, lifelike thing, his body easy in the saddle, his mind alert and his eyes fixed on the distance. He is vivid: he is alive! As you look at him you half expect him to leap from the plinth towards the thing he sees so far off, or else suddenly to wheel his horse about and disappear in a waste of heather.

This superb inspiration is the tribute which the town of Galashiels has paid to the 'braw lads' who did not come home.

If there are still towns in England engaged in planning war memorials I suggest that committees should visit Galashiels and learn a lesson. This memorial is the most imaginative I have seen, and I have inspected, with varying emotions, hundreds from one end of England to the other.

Although I have seen little yet of Scotland, it seems to me

that this country is fortunate in its freedom from the third-class war memorial – such as Sir Edwin Lutyens' railway obelisk at York, and the confused 'cenotaph' in Manchester – and, so far, I have not encountered in Scotland that type of memorial which can, perhaps, and most charitably, be described as ninety-nine per cent emotion and one per cent execution.

If a Scottish village cannot afford a large memorial it is content with a simple tablet; and it is noteworthy that even the most modest shrine is invariably a beautiful thing.

But Galashiels has surpassed itself. If a vote were taken for the most perfect town memorial in the British Isles mine would go to the peel tower and the horseman of Galashiels. It is so good that it should put this town, which has nothing to offer the inquisitive traveller except woollen mills, right on the tourist map. No one motoring into Scotland over the Border should miss this memorial; and it should be seen, as I saw it, at night.

How easy it would have been to have placed on that plinth a Scottish Borderer in steel helmet and a rifle in the defiant South African war tradition; how splendid to have led the ghostly column of those Border lads with a figure who stands in Scottish history and legend as the symbol of all Border men who have gone a-roving for hearth and home.

I had some food and met a man, an ex-soldier, an Edinburgh man and now a commercial traveller. He was as enthusiastic as I about the Galashiels memorial. Naturally we lapsed into war talk.

'Scotsmen are clannish,' he said. 'Touch one and you touch all. I remember . . .'

He then told me, in crude, naked sentences, full of army slang and war profanity, a story that made me see Vimy Ridge in the wet spring of '16, the chalk hells of trenches, the sappers driving their mines under the enemy lines, the bleak nights lit by Verey lights, the tangled mass of wire, the horror and stench of the beastly mud and filth which the Germans pumped from their own hell into that of the Canadians.

'I was attached to the Canadians for intelligence, ye see,' he said. 'One o' those buckshee experts no one loved! I was not on the ration sheet. I had to scrounge food in the line. Oh, man, it was awfu'! Well, after twelve weeks of it I got out of the line, and set off to find Oubigny. Ye see, that was where the Canadian headquarters were. I was an awful mess! I could just crawl. Ye see, I was wearing two left-foot gumboots! I found them sticking out of the mud in the parapet. I had to clean one out, but – well . . .

'My feet were like pulp, and, ye see, I was starving too. Well, I thought to myself, being an old cavalryman and a good scrounger, "There's always a Scotsman in charge of stores!" so I tried to find the horse lines to get a bite to eat and perhaps a blanket, for, ye see, I was wet through and my clothes sticking on me and verminous as hell. I came to a bivouac. It was night, ye see, and inside a big Canadian was making cocoa over a spirit lamp. Oh, man! I shall smell that cocoa until the end of my days! I was so weak I could hardly stand. I put my head inside and began to ask if the quarter-bloke could find me a blanket or perhaps a horse-rug. The big Canadian looked up.

' "Whaur d'ye come frae?" he said.

' "Edinburgh!" I said. "Where do *you* come from?"

' "Gala'," he said; and as he said it he held his can of cocoa towards me and "Come in, Jock, and have a drop o' this," he said. Man, I could have cried! I just fell in. He hadna been in Galashiels since he emigrated; but that didna matter; Edinburgh's not far off! He scrounged four horse-rugs for me, and he fed me. Man, d'ye know, I've often wondered what he'd ha' said had I told him I came from Gala'. He'd have scrounged me a horse and a G.S. wagon, for, ye see, when ye touch one ye touch all. . . .'

Another man at the next table who had been pretending not to listen to this story smiled and came up.

'I couldna help hearin',' he apologized. 'I once found masel' in a scrap wi' Australians oot i' France. Ye ken, nae doot, what kind o' a scrap it was. We were in rest billets, and I don't mind tellin' ye we were no' teetotallers! Weel, I met wi' a great yaird o' pump water who said something tae me which I considered no' a thing ony man could pu' up wi' and keep his self-respect. So – although I'm no' a great fighter, not being what ye might call verra big – I up wi' ma fists and hit him a grand crack on the jaw. Noo there was aboot ten Aussies present. They saw me and came at me wi' a rush! Man, I thought ma last hour had come! But – what d'ye think? – five oot o' the ten formed a ring roond me. "Come alang, Jock!" they shouted. "We're here, Jock, and we'll stand by ye!" An' they began tae scrap wi' their pals! Man, it was an awfu' bloody evening . . . Ye see, in hittin' the big Aussie I must ha' said something which gave awa' ma nationality, and every Scots Australian i' that bunch came over and sided wi' me!'

Then, turning to me, the stranger explained, as if any explanation were necessary:

'That's how clannish we are!' he said. 'Ye've only to raise a voice and a brither Scot will turn up fra somewhere. . . .'

And the horseman of Galashiels stands guard over the Border men. Go and see him. He is the perfect sentinel for those lads who carried their love of Scotland and their passionate devotion to the Borderland, their splendid pride, and their fine gallantry into the Valley of Death.

CHAPTER TWO

I explore Edinburgh, learn something in the house of John Knox, visit Holyrood, discover a 'poet', also a mystery, and stand bereft of words in the most beautiful War Shrine in the world

§ I

WHEN I went to bed in Edinburgh a mighty wind was roaring in the chimney. It was a wind such as I have heard only at sea, howling round a ship, but the gale must have blown itself out in the night. I awakened to a still, autumn morning.

Princes Street has been called the finest street in the kingdom. There are shops on one side only; the other side runs along the edge of a deep ravine, planted with gardens, above which rise the Castle Rock and the high roofline of Old Edinburgh. On a calm autumn morning the ravine is filled with mist. The shops of Princes Street stand with their doorsteps against a grey wall, dense as the greyness that blows in from the Atlantic at Land's End. If you did not know that there are shops on the north side only, you might be excused the belief that, a landslide having occurred in the night, the south side had fallen into the grey abyss.

It is still and breathless, but overhead is just the faintest smothered flush in the greyness, a promise that the sun will break through in his due time. Then, imperceptibly at first, begins one of the most beautiful atmospheric phenomena in the British Isles. Vague shapes are seen in the mist, or rather you imagine them from a hint here and there of far-off shadows. You realize that something tremendous is hiding there in the immense impenetrability. The mist thins in patches, and again comes that shadow of a shadow, as though some mighty Armada is lying becalmed at anchor in the grey sea.

But the shapes in the mist are not masts and cross-trees.

37

Bit by bit an unbelievable vision uplifts itself, at first like a mirage which hangs uncertain in the air over a desert, and then, etched in toneless grey, as if painted in thin smoke against the sky, a phantom city emerges spire by spire, pinnacle by pinnacle, tower by tower; a ghostly city on the edge of a steep ravine: a Camelot, a Tintagel; a city turreted and loopholed; a city that seems to spring from the mist to the sound of horns; a city that seems still to grasp a sword.

So Old Edinburgh looks down in these autumn mornings over a grey mist, and over many centuries, to New Edinburgh.

I had the strangest feeling as I saw this. It was unreal. It was ghostly. Round me was New Edinburgh lying on level land, a city of rectangular streets, excessively modern in parts; and in parts as solid and leisurely as a man in a bag wig leaning on an ebony cane.

There were tramcars and the bustle of a new day, the opening of shops, the shaking of mats, the letting forth of cats, the cleaning of steps, the sound of motor-car horns. And, away up there, intangible and remote on a hill, flat as if cut out of cardboard and pinned to the sky, hung this other Edinburgh like a spectre.

Is there another city in the world which marches hand in hand with its past as does Edinburgh; which can look up from its modernity and see itself as it always was, upon a hill intact, impregnable and still in arms? Salisbury could have done so had the hill of Old Sarum not been ruined; but I know of no other.

My heart went out to this craggy ghost, so wise with living and perhaps a little weary, so self-assured and so unselfconscious, so lost in the memory of important things, and so removed from the shallow and the cheap that when men decided to make money, and to be successful in the way of money, they had to climb down out of it and build their city on a plain.

It hung half-seen for a while, like a city of the dead until the sun dispersed the last pale veil and then, splendid in its strength, Old Edinburgh rose out of the mists of morning, stern in majesty, like a king upon his throne.

And I knew at once that while I could admire New Edinburgh I could love Old Edinburgh.

There is a touch of royalty about certain cities. York has it; so has Winchester. No matter how quiet they are today there is still an air of temporal power over them. You feel that courts were held there. That kings rode in through the gates. Their stones mean something in history. Dublin lacks authentic regality, but Galway, impoverished and deserted as it is, seems to me to possess it in some queer, unhappy way.

Edinburgh is obviously regal. She is plainly a capital. She has the superiority complex of a capital, which is openly reviled, and secretly admired, by all provinces. Her exclusiveness is the exclusiveness of the aristocrat who has tried out most things and knows exactly what she does not wish to do. Such snobberies as she may possess – and what city does not possess them? – have little to do with money. It would be, I feel, more difficult for a man of no quality to buy himself into Edinburgh than into any other city, with possibly the exception of Dublin.

I have used the wrong pronoun to Edinburgh. This city is 'he', not 'she'. Edinburgh is as masculine as London. The three great feminine capitals are Paris, Vienna, and Dublin; the first two have all the lure of woman, and the last has all her charm and all her spite. But Edinburgh, London, Berlin, and Rome are as masculine as a herd of steers. I am told that New York is feminine; but I cannot say.

The air of Edinburgh seems to demand a viceroy. You feel that there should be a throne somewhere. The shuttered windows of Holyrood affect me rather as the drawn blinds of Buckingham Palace when no standard flies from the mast and the guard is changed in St James's. No matter how unpalatial Holyrood may be it is still tremendously a palace.

You feel that in the throneroom, to round off Edinburgh's appearance of coronation, should be a Prince of Scotland.

I suppose every able-bodied visitor to Edinburgh goes, or is driven by some enthusiastic native, to the top of Arthur's Seat, there to brood like Ashmodeus over the city that lies spread at his feet.

I climbed this hill, and there in the late afternoon recaptured the thrill of early morning. Edinburgh is one of the few cities which cannot be exaggerated. The sun was sinking. Away to the right hand shone the blue Firth of Forth and the 'Kingdom' of Fife; below lay Edinburgh under a blue cap of smoke. From such a height the rocky contour was smoothed out; but how easy to pick out the Castle Rock which brought Edinburgh into being as inevitably as the Thames brought London.

'Why is it called "Auld Reekie"?' I asked a man who shared the hill with me.

'There was a man in Fife yonder – a laird called Durham of Largo,' he replied, 'who regulated evening prayers by the smoke of Edinburgh, which he could see from his own door. When the reek grew heavy as Edinburgh cooked its supper he used to call his family into the house with: "It's time, noo, bairns, to tak' the buiks and gang to our beds, for yonder's Auld Reekie, I see, putting on her nichtcap!" '

It was not quite prayer time, but the lums were reeking gently, sending up a thin haze of blue, while above it the Castle Rock rose clear and strong in sunlight. I could trace the Royal Mile from the Castle to Holyrood and radiating from it the straggling streets of the old medieval town; and northward of the gap where the railway now runs was new Edinburgh, trim and rectangular, almost American, with Princes Street a long straight line drawn on the edge of a cliff. What a frame for a city! To the south the Pentlands and the Moorfoots; to the east the Lammermuirs and those prominent humps, North Berwick Law and the Bass Rock;

to the north the Kingdom of Fife over the blue water of the Firth, on which many a slow ship steamed towards the clustered roofs of Leith. But look westward, where in graduated blueness are mountains, refined by distance, some the colour of hothouse grapes, some almost mauve, some faint and thin like shadows against the sky: the Highlands! A friendly direction-finder tells me that the king of the western hierarchy is Ben Lomond dreaming above the 'bonny, bonny banks' of his loch.

When darkness comes walk into Old Edinburgh, down the ancient Royal Mile, out of Castle Hill into Lawnmarket, past St Giles' and into Canongate.

Here are the ghosts of Edinburgh, here in these old stone courtyards, in these dim wynds and closes where pale, significant lamps hang above flights of grey steps, the mighty history of this city stirs a little in its sleep. It is grey, sinister, medieval. The harmless figures who lean carelessly at the entry to queer quadrangles, silhouetted against the stairway lamps, seem to be waiting for fellow conspirators, and when they move it seems that they should be easing a dagger in its sheath.

In the stillness of night you stand in Canongate aware of many things: of those ill-fated, sallow Stuarts with their melancholy eyes, of that unhappy, lovely queen who still stirs men's hearts, of John Knox, with his denunciatory finger – a legacy which he has bequeathed to all argumentative Scotsmen – Bothwell, Darnley, and the wild men of that tempestuous court.

The Royal Mile is a mile of memories. There comes a skirl of pipes, a shaggy crowd in torchlight, the glitter of steel, and somewhere in the midst a fair young man on his way to seek a crown. . . .

As you go past the dim wynds, peeping here and there, a man with a limp and a fine high brow goes with you. Walter Scott! And it may be, if you are lucky, that you will see

Stevenson in a black velvet jacket, bearing an armchair on his head to the old infirmary where Henley lies ill.

There are too many ghosts in Old Edinburgh. They crowd round you, pulling at your memory with their eager fingers, trying to drag you into dark, uncomfortable places, attempting to lure you all night long with their story. You must not give way to them as they press round you. So turn about as a bell strikes midnight and bid farewell to the amazing host: to the pale kings and the one dear, misguided queen, to the saints and the sinners, the men of the sword and the men of the pen, and leave them to the old grey courtyards which they knew so well, to the darkness and the stars.

2

The white spats of a kilted sentry twinkle before the main gates of Holyrood. The sentry guards, presumably, the ghost of Mary, Queen of Scots, for there is now nothing else in Holyrood except the worst picture gallery in the world.

I have encountered few things so fascinatingly bad as these alleged portraits of 110 Scottish monarchs 'who,' said Sir Walter Scott, taking the words out of the mouths of later critics, 'if they ever flourished at all, lived several hundred years before the invention of painting in oil colours.' When I saw these pictures for the first time I was unwilling to believe them; a second visit gave me, perhaps, too high an opinion of the artistic sensibilities of Hawley's dragoons, who, embittered at having been routed by Prince Charlie's Highlanders at Falkirk, got their own back with sabres on the picture gallery of Holyrood. But a third visit – and now I was under the influence of a morbid fascination – led me to a more sympathetic point of view, and to a remarkable story.

These 110 monarchs were executed – that seems the right word – by a Dutchman living in Edinburgh named James de Witt. The period was the time of Charles II, when

Holyrood, battered by tragedy and pushed into the background by Whitehall, suffered a much-needed spring-cleaning.

How is it that Stevenson and other writers of Edinburgh have failed to notice James de Witt? I recommend this unfortunate artist to the attention of those with the time to dig his story from the records in which it may lie embalmed. No artist since the world began signed such a contract as that drawn up on February 26th, 1684, by Hugh Wallace, His Majesty's Cashkeeper: a most just title! James de Witt bound himself to paint and deliver within two years from the signing of the contract, and for a salary of £120 per annum, 110 portraits 'in large royall postures' of all the kings, mythical and actual, who had reigned over Scotland 'from King Fergus the First to King Charles the Second, our Gracious Soveraigne'. It was also part of the compact that de Witt had to find his own paint and canvas, and inscribe each portrait with the name of the subject – 'the names of the kings most famous in large characters and the remanent lesser characters'!

This extract reads like the beginning of the Aberdeen joke!

So the awful race began. De Witt turned out Scottish monarchs at the rate of one and a fraction a week for two years, and at an all-in price of a little over forty shillings per royal head. I do not know whether he was the same de Witt who at this time decorated several fireplaces in Holyrood and also turned a chimney marble colour. If so, perhaps he did that in his spare time!

History is silent about de Witt. But can the Canongate in all its long and adventurous history have seen anything more desperate than his studio? Who were his friends? Who sympathized with him in his travail? Who gave him the courage necessary to complete his task? While Whitehall echoed to the notes of viol and pipe, while the second Charles enjoyed his restoration, while Mistress Gwynne smiled her auburn way westward from Covent Garden, and while the one and only Samuel Pepys followed his observant path through life, poor de Witt, buried in the Canongate – and probably by this time a confirmed Bolshevik – unconscious, no doubt, of the world's events, strove to complete the 110 'large royall postures'!

This picture gallery is, to me, full of human interest. There is nothing like it on earth. Did de Witt work with his tongue in his cheek as he churned out his catalogue of Scottish royalty – all the earlier portraits and even many of the names are pure fiction – or did he take his job with the dreadful solemnity of a small man fulfilling a large task?

As I look at the amazing collection of kings, real and apocryphal, I want to know whether there was a Mistress de Witt to console him and support him in his reckless ordeal, to burst in on him at night with:

'Now, James, you *must* go to bed. . . . Who's that supposed to be?'

De Witt runs his finger down a long list:

'Fergusius the Third – no, sorry, Thebus the First.'

'But, my dear, you *must* go to bed. You're overdoing it; you've given him exactly the same face as Eugenius the Seventh. . . .'

'Oh, well, I can't help it! I'll give him a squint! Do you think the milkman would come in tomorrow and sit for Corbredus the First?'

'But you had him for Caractacus!'

And, once a week for two years, the greatest sight in Edinburgh must have been that of a man in a cloak and a Socialist tie going down the Canongate to Holyrood with the weekly monarch under his arm! My heart bleeds for de Witt! How did he hand over the result of his artistic debauchment:

'Here's old Corvallus the Third – damn him!'

'Right you are, laddie; fling him on the pile. How many to come now?'

'Sixty-eight!'

'Are you on time?'

'Yes; I'm winning by two lengths – William the Lion and Macbeth. . . .'

'Good egg! Then you'll be able to paint a chimney next week, just to keep your hand in. . . .'

Instinct tells me that there is a great story in poor de Witt. He was the Henry Ford in oils of the seventeenth centuty!

A guide rescued me from de Witt and led me to those grim, panelled rooms which give Holyrood its intense sentimental interest, the rooms in which Mary, Queen of Scots, played a little, loved a little, and wept often.

Every visitor to Edinburgh tries to reconstruct the murder of Riccio. The wretched Italian dragged from the skirts of his queen to meet his death is to thouands the most famous scene in Scottish history. It was a horrible deed, but, as Sir Herbert Maxwell, president of the Society of Antiquaries of Scotland, says in the best guide I have ever read (issued at 6d. by the Office of Works), the murder of Riccio was merely 'a stroke in the strife of party, little more reprehensible according to sixteenth-century ethics and practice than a "snap" division might be reckoned in the twentieth century'.

'Aye, it was here that Riccio was supping wi' the queen,' said the guide, 'when a knock came to the door and in walked the murderers. . . .'

The room is incredibly small, a mere panelled cupboard. How Mary, Riccio, and the Countess of Argyll managed to dine in comfort there is a mystery. Arthur Erskine, captain of the guard, and Lord Robert Stuart were also in the tiny room on that dreadful March night in 1566.

As the guide talked I tried to get beyond his words to the tragedy of that supper party. Many men have reconstructed the scene, and certainly every one who visits the room tries to do so. It would have been quiet in Holyrood that night: perhaps a March wind at the windows, and rain. The Earl of Morton had secured all the doors and passages. The conspirators, led by the drunken young king, were creeping towards the little room; Darnley with Ruthven by the narrow, spiral, stone stair that opens directly into the supper room; Morton and his band by the main stairs, through the audience chamber and the queen's bedroom.

Darnley was there first, and Ruthven, deadly pale from his recent illness. There would be a second's awful silence while the terrible thing that was to happen took shape. No need for Ruthven's drawn dagger. Riccio's quick brain must have known at once. There would have been questions and the crash of smashed glass as he tried to put the table between himself and the murderers, the falling of candles, and then only one light in the room held by the Countess of Argyll. Things must have happened quickly – the ring of spurs outside as Morton and the other conspirators tramped in; the small room packed with armed men; faces at the doors; angry voices; the young king flinging foul insults at his queen; Riccio's scream of terror and his frantic clinging to her skirts; the wild scramble at the small door as they dragged him out; the struggle with him in the queen's bedroom; the final scuffle in the audience-room beyond as they worried him like hounds; and then the sound of his stabbed corpse bumping softly from step to step.

Ruthven, who was ill, went back to the small panelled room and asked for a cup of wine. . . .

'Years ago,' said the guide, taking me to the audience chamber, 'they used to put raddle down here at the head of the steps and tell people that Riccio's blood would never wash away; but now we have a brass plate.'

Holyrood has fewer brilliant memories than perhaps any palace in the world. I would like to have been there the night that James VI (and the First of England) was surprised by a band of armed men, escaping down the back stairs 'with his breeks in his hand'. James was a welcome touch of comedy to Holyrood. How splendid to have seen him, still holding his 'breeks', accepting the repentance of Francis, Earl of Bothwell!

And it must have been a great Saturday night in

Holyrood in March 1603 when Sir Robert Carey, who had ridden 400 miles from London in sixty-two hours, came, mud-spattered, demanding an immediate audience with the King of Scotland; and James, again 'breekless', heard that Elizabeth was dead and that he was King of England.

Carey's ride to Edinburgh from London must surely be the most remarkable in the history of horsemanship. He had relays of fresh horses all along the road, but even so his average speed of six and a half miles an hour for sixty-two hours is an astonishing feat of endurance. The highwayman Nevinson, who did the ride from Chatham to York, thanks to Harrison Ainsworth, inaccurately attributed to Dick Turpin, covered the 230 miles in fifteen hours, with an average of fifteen miles an hour; but this cannot be compared with the much greater distance covered by Carey, the more difficult roads, and the month of March. Nevinson set out on a fine May morning. . . .

I would like to have been in Holyrood, too, that night in September 1745 when a young man wearing a light-coloured periwig with his own hair combed over the front, a tartan short-coat without the plaid, a blue bonnet, and on his breast the Star of the Order of St Andrew, rode thoughtfully – the Duke of Perth on his right hand, Lord Elcho on his left – to take possession of Edinburgh in the name of his father, James VIII. The royal salute was a hostile round-shot from the Castle which hit the north-west tower, sending a cloud of plaster and brick down into the courtyard. Bonnie Prince Charlie dismounted while James Hepburn of Keith, who had been 'out' with the 'Old Pretender' in 1715, drew his sword and led the way up the grand staircase. A window opened. Prince Charles Edward – 'Prince of Wales, Regent of Scotland, England, France and the Dominions thereunto belonging' – stood bowing and smiling to the crowds. Below him, in the courtyard, vivacious Mrs Secretary Murry, a drawn sword in her hand, sat a horse and distributed white cockades! What a perfect scene; what an operatic prelude to a tragedy!

Holyrood that night was more brilliant than at any time since Mary, Queen of Scots, held her masques by the light of many candles. There was a ball which must have stirred the old, uneasy echoes of this palace. Lights shone in every window. The old palace had been dragged into history again, slightly incredulous perhaps and a little fearful: its shadows remembered so much. One may fancy that had a man mounted the stairs that night to those dark rooms which need no other name he might have seen, pale as a flower, the face that loved music and the sight of a brave young man. But none thought of failure or defeat that night as Prince Charles Edward moved through his tartan court in a pretty lane of curtsys.

After his victory at Prestonpans the Prince held court in Holyrood for nearly five weeks. He dined in public with the Highland chieftains. He 'touched' for the King's Evil, he reviewed his troops, and in the evenings he picked a 'too chaste' way through adoring drawing-rooms in the court dress of France or Italy. When reproached for his neglect of the ladies he said, pointing to a hairy Highland sentry: 'These are my beauties!' Alexander Carlyle, the divine, when a boy went down to Holyrood to see the Prince:

'I went twice down to the Abbey Court,' he wrote, 'to wait till the Prince should come out of the Palace and mount his horse to ride to the east side of Arthur Seat to visit his army. I had the good fortune to see him both days, one of which I was close by him when he walked through the guard. He was a good-looking man of about five feet ten inches; his hair was dark red, and his eyes black. His features were regular, his visage long, much sunburnt and freckled, and his countenance thoughtful and melancholy. He mounted his horse and rode off through Ann's Yard and the Duke's Walk to his army.'

This brief glory ended, Holyrood sank again into a silence as deep as that of the palace of the Sleeping Beauty until the Wizard of the North, waving an astounding wand

and administering a tremendous kiss of friendship, awakened the tired old place to a Hanoverian *bal masque*. It was mainly owing to Scott's popularity that the visit in 1822 of George IV to Edinburgh was such an unqualified success. It was an incredible affair. How those same old ghosts who nodded sadly in 1745 must have rubbed their eyes in 1822! There had been nothing in Holyrood to make a ghost laugh since poor James became King of England minus his trousers. But now, lo, at the waving of Scott's tartan wand all the Gaelic glory which the House of Hanover had stamped out with dragoons and Acts of Parliament was revived in honour of the House of Hanover. When George IV held his first levee in the slightly bewildered halls of Holyrood 'the full extent was realized,' says Sir Herbert Maxwell, 'to which Sir Walter Scott had Celticized the sober Scot, for here was his Majesty arrayed in the garb of Old Gaul, as interpreted by a nineteenth-century tailor, glowing in royal Stuart tartan from head to foot, barring the orthodox interval in the region of the knees'. Nor he alone, for, rivalling his Majesty in stature and bulk, came a London alderman, upon whom Byron has imposed immortality:

> He caught Sir William Curtis in a kilt
> While thronged the chiefs of every Highland clan
> To hail their brother — Vich Ian Alderman.

It is recorded that during the evening whenever the King caught the eye of Sir William Curtis neither could refrain from smiling. 'Probably,' says the scribe – and 'probably' is quite good – 'at the singularity of their appearance in the garb of "the Tartan Confederacy".'

I have been entertained by a long and fulsome account of the levee, written too near the event to permit any humour to break through, in David Beattie's *Scotland*. I cannot decide from the following description whether the young ladies of Edinburgh were blinded by the appearance of the King or whether they still retained Jacobite sympathies and had to be dragged struggling before him:

'The demeanour of the Scottish ladies, says an observer, was extremely characteristic as they moved towards the state apartments – their eyes motionless yet keen with intelligence – dignified but betraying by the timidity of their advances the invincible modesty of their nature. . . . The tartan plaid and sable plume of the North were never displayed to greater advantage. The ladies, attended by their fathers, their husbands or brothers, advanced with delicate but proud submission to receive the royal token of recognition on their blushing cheek. The young and timid shrinking insensibly back as they approached the Sovereign, required the repeated promptings of matronly reminiscence to entice them forward into the circle. But, this important step once achieved and the stated number of courtseys performed, with what pleasure (says a lady) they opened their eyes upon the mighty Rubicon they had just passed!'

It is curious that their grandmothers exhibited none of this shrinking in the same room seventy years before!

But what was going on in Scott's mind as he moved through the adulation of that evening? Surely the irony of it sunk into him! It is an excellent thing to bury a hatchet but it is never necessary to extend full military honours to it. Let me quote Beattie once more:

'As the old Celtic chiefs, in plaid and philabeg, and flowing tartan, passed in review – each with the badge of his clan – the dress that had distinguished his name for centuries – colours that had been so oft paraded in those very apartments – the picture was full of martial show and animation. The basket-hilted sword – the *Ferrara* of other times, the hereditary palladium from father to son – recalled the party feuds and patriotic struggles in which it had been so often displayed as the sole arbiter from which there was no appeal. The richly inlaid pistols, generally of the famous Doune manufactory, and the dagger of Damascus metal – all arranged in the girdle, gave the wearer more the aspect of a corsair prepared for a cruise than of a courtier in the presence of his sovereign. But the native beauty on which they were here only as knight-attendant, threw a hallowing lustre over the scene, and where wounds were to be inflicted reserved that privilege to itself.

'A profusion of military, and other orders sparkling on the scarlet and tartan uniforms, told many a tale of service done "i' the deadly breach", the morning and the midnight bivouac. Family badges that had not seen the light for centuries were here made available. *Bijouterie* that had been worn, perhaps, to welcome the first James, were now burnished up for the reception of George IV. Some, while they offered their meed of loyalty to their lawful sovereign, thought with bitterness on that unhappy prince who, in the last generation, had here received their family allegiance, and in his own ruin involved so many illustrious followers.'

It is rather strange to realize that we of this age are more distant from George IV than he was from Culloden, which makes it all the more difficult to explain how people so near to the world's last romance could play at charades. But there was wizardry in it, or it could never have happened! Anyhow, it was an excellent idea – and everyone had a jolly time!

On such a happy event the visitor may leave Holyrood to its brooding.

3

On a fine morning if the sun is out it is a good plan to leave Scotland and sit on a wall in Nova Scotia waiting for Edinburgh Castle to open, which happens sharp at 10 a.m. By one of those charming parodies of fact which occur in all old countries the Esplanade – the wide parade ground before the Castle gates – is legally on the other side of the Atlantic. It was declared Nova Scotia territory in the reign of Charles I in order that newly made Nova Scotian baronets might 'take seizin' of their lands! This decree has never been annulled, and is there a lawyer in Edinburgh who will deny the fact that in the eyes of his profession this bit of Scotland is really in Canada?

As you sit on this wall in Nova Scotia, gazing thoughtfully down into the distant chimneys of the Grassmarket, you will attract the attention of numberless small children who are dancing about, crying in shrill voices a rhyme which resolves itself, if you listen carefully, into:

> *Nievie, nievie, nick-nack*
> *Which hand will ye tak'?*
> *Tak' the richt, tak' the wrang,*
> *I'll beguile ye if I can. . . .*

The child who sings this holds his hands behind his back while the others guess in which hand he is holding the nick-nack. However, as soon as they observe the lonely figure in Nova Scotia this game ceases and they advance in disorder – little girls in tartan skirts and boys in torn breeks – and begin, three or four speaking together, a long, shrill, and monotonous history of the Castle complete with dates. Their voices are so soft and their accent, mostly, so attractive that one is inclined to commit the error of enriching them with a few pennies; it is also rather difficult to resist the sharp blue eyes of small girls with hair like blazing thorn bushes and noses as freckled as cowslips. If you give them money they will tell their friends that a stranger worth knowing has come among them; if you do not give them money their friends will appear just the same! The only sure way to disperse them is to turn round suddenly and, with pointed finger and the air of a schoolmaster, put them through a history examination. This they heartily detest. They much prefer the indifference of the aloof Englishman or the sphinx-like immutability of the Japanese tourist, but it is perhaps nationally characteristic that, while the main body may decamp, at least one dogged, determined, red-polled youngster will remain and wrestle with your unfair queries. He deserves, and so far as I am concerned always receives, that coin which seems to have migrated in its millions to Scotland – the three-penny bit.

But we linger in Nova Scotia! Behold, the Castle of Edinburgh flings wide its gates, and, beneath that experienced postern, an unmistakable Cockney in a mauve shirt is offering to sell a guide-book in the accents of the Whitechapel Road. . . .

Edinburgh Castle is more like those up and down fortresses which small boys receive at Christmas than any castle I can call to mind. Its first builders saw a formidable rock rising conveniently up and said:

'Aye, maun, it's a bonny spot for a wee bittie peace!'

Whereupon they climbed up and built a castle which became the despair of their enemies. They tunnelled down like moles, they threw up ramparts, they adapted a crag to civil and military life. Everywhere this rock asserts itself. It springs up into view in the most unlikely places.

Most glorious is the view of Edinburgh from the Argyle Battery. You look over a gorge right down into the distant windows of Princes Street and, beyond, over massed roofs to the blue Firth and the green hills of Fife. High up above Edinburgh is a beautiful Norman chapel. It is one of the smallest churches in Great Britain – only seventeen feet by eleven feet. I suppose an intelligent survey of Edinburgh would start at this small stone church, for it was built to the orders of the Saxon Margaret, wife of Malcolm Canmore, who was driven to the coast of Scotland by a storm four years after William the Conqueror had invaded England. She was the first and last good gift England was to send to her sister nation for many a long year! As the guide-book says, 'She did much to introduce civilization and the beginnings of refinement into Scotland.' Her little chapel has withstood the storms of eight and a half centuries. It is in a sense the real germ of Edinburgh. It was Margaret who persuaded the King to move his capital from Dunfermline, and we may imagine that the pious lady signalled her arrival by founding this small sanctuary. Below it on the ridge Edinburgh must have grown almost at once, for do we not read that good Queen Margaret fed 300 beggars daily?

The Crown Room of Edinburgh Castle is not perhaps so dazzling to the eye as that in the Tower of London. I stood against the plate glass with an American who said:

'They look worth about ten cents.'

'You have seen the Crown Jewels in London?'

'I'll say so! They're an eyeful. . . .'

He was surprised to know – and few English people, I think, know it – that the 'Honours of Scotland' are older than the Regalia in the Tower. After the execution of Charles I the English Regalia was destroyed by the order of Parliament. The only objects saved were the Black Prince's ruby, the ampulla and spoon, and Queen Elizabeth's salt-cellar. If you take the trouble to hunt up documents in the Record Office in Chancery Lane you will find a list of all objects broken up or destroyed, with their estimated value. Perhaps the most senseless act of sabotage, a deed which even now makes the antiquary boil with anger, was the destruction of King Alfred's crown 'of goulde wyer worke sett with slight stones', as the records have it. That such an object should have been broken up or cast into the melting-pot is a national loss: the crown of Alfred the Great: the Crown under which grew the English State. After the Restoration Charles II ordered a new Regalia. These are the objects which glitter so dazzlingly in the Tower of London, none of them, with the few exceptions noted, are earlier than the Restoration.

Scotland is luckier. The Crown of Scotland is said to have been used at the Coronation of Bruce. (The concentric arches are obviously of much later date.) It was last used when Charles II was crowned at Scone in 1651. The sceptre, with its crystal globe, is sixteenth-century work, and the great sword of state is that which Pope Julius II presented to James IV.

I wandered away round the ramparts, heard them discharge the gun that startles a stranger in Edinburgh at 1 p.m., and found myself in what is perhaps the most generally interesting room in the Castle. It was here, as an intelligent guide in uniform will tell you in the crisp phrases of an old soldier, that Mary, Queen of Scots, gave birth to the son who became James I of England and VI of Scotland. It is a small room. There is hardly space in it for a four-poster bed. It is almost as small as her supper-room in Holyrood. And the window of this room looks down on the face of the cliff to the distant earth. The guide will repeat the traditional story that the infant was let down in a basket from this dizzy window in order that he might be christened in the Catholic faith. Is not this a confused memory of the removal of the infant James II of Scotland from the custody of the Chancellor Crichton?

'Is there a story that an infant's body was discovered in these walls some years ago wrapped in cloth of gold?'

'Aye, there is so! The body was put back and is in the walls now.'

The guides in the Castle know this story well. It is one of the mysteries of Scottish history. For many centuries a tradition has persisted in Scotland that the infant born to Mary three months after Riccio was murdered as he clutched her gown died at birth or soon after, and that, in order to avert a political crisis, a changeling was substituted who later ascended the thrones of England and Scotland as James I and VI. It has been remarked that James was never sure of his legitimacy and that he rewarded those who reassured him. This, however, is no evidence.

The legend gained new importance in 1830, when after a fire in Queen Mary's apartments a small oak coffin was discovered behind the wainscoting in a recess measuring about two feet six inches by one foot. This coffin contained the bones of an infant wrapped in a richly embroidered silk covering. Two initials were worked on this shroud and one of them was clearly the letter J. Was this the body of Mary's infant and the rightful heir to the throne. If so, who was James VI?

This legend was examined in some detail by the Dowager Lady Forbes in an article entitled 'The Mystery of the

Coffin in the Wall' which appeared in *Chambers's Journal* for October 1st, 1923. The writer supported the theory that the changeling was the infant son of Lady Ryves, the wet nurse to the royal infant. A new speculation, or rather an old one supported by new evidence, is that advanced by Mr Grant R. Francis in his book (published in 1928) *Scotland's Royal Line*. His is the most plausible theory so far advanced, and quite the best account of a problem which will, there seems no doubt, never be solved.

Mr Francis notes a fact, frequently commented on, that James VI departs from the facial characteristics of the Stuarts. Compare him with any of his ancestors: he is different. But he bears an astonishing resemblance to John second Earl of Mar, whose lifelong friend he was, whose mother, the Countess of Mar, took charge of Mary's child soon after his birth and until his christening. Did the countess substitute her second child for that of her royal mistress? If so, James VI was the younger brother of John, Earl of Mar.

Such is the tradition which has existed for centuries in the Erskine family. The author approached the present Earl of Mar and Kellie on the subject, and received the following letter:

'I have no objection to your mentioning, as a possible reason of the change of type in the Stuart family, my family tradition that one of Lord Mar's sons was substituted for the infant King. I think that it is possible and even probable that some child *was* substituted, but we have only a shadowy family tradition and the really extraordinary likeness between James and John, Earl of Mar, to go upon. In a magazine article I read some time ago, the Dowager Lady Forbes argues that a son of Lady Ryves was the child in question. In any case, for those times the secret must have been extraordinarily well kept, as Mary herself had no suspicion that James was not her son.'

It is historically proved, as the Earl of Mar and Kellie states, that if the substitution took place, Mary never knew. It is also, I suggest, equally certain that the royal child was not stillborn. In the next edition of his book Mr Francis might, in order to demolish this theory, quote the touching scene in Edinburgh Castle on June 19th, 1566, when Darnley came to see his son two hours after birth. Mary took the child in her arms and held him towards Darnley with these words:

'My lord, here I protest unto God and as I shall answer to Him at the great day of judgment, this is your son, and no other man's son; and I am desirous that all here, both ladies and others, bear witness, for he is so much your son that I fear it may be worse for him hereafter.'

Darnley kissed the child and was silent.

'This is the prince,' said Mary to Sir William Standen, 'who, I hope, will first unite the two kingdoms of England and Scotland.'

That has the ring of truth in it and the pride of motherhood. That was in June. In October Mary set out on her famous progress through the Border. She did not return to Edinburgh until December 2nd. For about two months the child was apparently in the charge of the Countess of Mar either at Stirling Castle, of which the earl was hereditary governor, or at Alloa House.

'If Mary's child had died after her departure,' writes Mr Francis, 'and been buried in the wall of the royal apartments at Edinburgh, and if, as has been suggested, the Countess of Mar had meanwhile given birth to a child, nothing could have been more easy than to present the latter at the font at Stirling on December 17th as Mary's child; no one except the English and French Ambassadors appears to have seen him until the christening. . . . Once christened, the infant Prince was often to be seen at Mar's house at Alloa in his nurse's arms, and he remained in the custody of the Earl and Countess of Mar thereafter; while the solicitude of the Countess for the infant Prince has been commented on by several historians.'

If this is something more than an ingenious theory, may it not explain the friendship of James for the second Earl of Mar, his elder brother? Did Mar owe his immunity from the royal displeasure for the part he played in various plots, notably the Gowrie conspiracy, to the knowledge, shared by the King, that James was his brother?

The strongest point in the argument is the evidence of physiognomy. Mr Francis reproduces two paintings, one of James and one of the Earl of Mar, which show an almost exact facial resemblance. The likeness is so startling that the pictures might be of one man. A weak point is the hazy knowledge of the skeleton found in Edinburgh Castle. Whatever the truth there is no shadow of doubt that Mary believed to her dying day that James VI was her son. She knew him only as a child. It is said that the boy found means to communicate with her during her captivity. After years of imprisonment she is said to have declared: 'As for my son, nothing can sever me from him, for I live for him and not for myself.'

Those who support the substitution theory might, however, find an argument in his cruel behaviour to her when he was nineteen years of age. Did he know the secret of his birth when he wrote that letter, which must have nearly broken her weary heart, telling her that 'as she was held captive in a remote place he declined to associate her with himself in the sovereignty of Scotland. . . .'

That was either the voice of his advisers or the voice of a son who no longer felt any love for his mother.

Somewhere in the walls high above Edinburgh there may be a clue to the mystery. The body was replaced as it was found by order of the colonel commanding the garrison. Perhaps some day it may be submitted to a scientific and archaeological post-mortem.

On Castle Rock is the Scottish National War Shrine, one of the greatest sights in the British Isles.

4

I find it more difficult to write about Scotland's National War Shrine than about anything I have ever attempted to describe. There is nothing like it in the world: it is the Soul of Scotland.

We are perhaps too close to the war to interpret it. We have not achieved that tranquillity in which emotion is refined and remembered. The war has produced no epic. It has crystallized nowhere in an everlasting thing. It has produced a number of emotional anchorages, such as the Cenotaph in Whitehall and the graves of the Unknown Warriors in Westminster, Paris, and Washington; but these, mighty as they are in the hearts of this generation, are for our time only. They will not bring tears to the eyes of our grandchildren. Future ages will reverence and cherish them; they will not pray before them.

The immense Canadian memorial on the crest of Vimy, which I have seen in the course of construction, magnificent as it is, beautiful and full of humility as it is, will, nevertheless, in time become a gaping place for the next generation.

Scotland alone of all the nations who suffered in the war has visibly, and with pride, placed her emotion like an offering on the Knees of God.

It is strange, too, that the land of John Knox should have conceived and carried to a triumphant fulfilment a work of faith which can be compared only with the undying achievements of the Catholic Middle Ages, when men, working anonymously, strove not for personal credit, but for the sake of the faith that was in them. Scotland's Shrine is the only great thing born out of the travail of war which is cosmic in its conception and still personal in its appeal. It is as coldly dignified as Hardy's *Dynasts*, and as warmly emotional as the Unknown Warrior's grave in the nave of Westminster.

The philosopher of the future standing in this, the only

cathedral which Scotland has built since the Reformation, will see war not as a tragedy or an epic, but as a strange adventure of the soul. He will, if Anglo-Saxon, marvel that men who lived through, and perhaps fought in, the war could in their own time have mounted mentally so far above the tragedy of death to a vision of the splendour of sacrifice. This Shrine seems to have been designed from the crest of the Grampians.

In England the phrase 'the Glorious Dead' has tears in it. Even as we say it our subconscious mind weeps a little, thinking: 'Had he lived he would now be thirty-five years old'; and we remember all the things he meant to do, and all the things he should have done; and in our secret hearts the glory of his death is something very like a phrase.

Scotland's shrine is a requiem and a hymn of praise. Yet a Scottish mother today, unconscious, perhaps, of these things, can stand on Castle Rock and feel herself in the presence of one of those 100,000 lads who lie in soil which is for ever Scotland.

There is more pride and less regret in this than in any war memorial in the world.

The Shrine is the highest building in Edinburgh. It rises from virgin rock. Its walls spring from jagged ledges. In shape it is a sanctuary facing north with an east and west transept.

You enter under a great porch and come into a dim place of tinted light. Left and right lie the transepts divided into bays, each bay lit by a window of stained glass, but pale enough to allow you to read the regimental memorials in each bay and the names of Scotland's 100,000 dead in books placed on bronze lecterns. The keynote of the building is harmony. It is difficult to believe that it is not the work of one genius able to work with equal ease in stone, bronze, paint and glass. Such exquisite artistic discipline for the sake of a unified scheme has not been achieved for centuries.

The arches in which each regiment is enshrined differ

one from the other, but blend together; and beside each hang the colours of the regiments commemorated.

The windows paint the picture of the war. They are amazing windows. They are full of the Gothic spirit; but look into them and see subjects never before interpreted in glass. The Women's Window shows land girls gathering a war harvest; it shows a woman machinist sitting with bound hair in the grim reality of a shell factory; it shows the Red Cross woman at work in the field and the nurse bending over her patient in hospital. There is no aspect of war forgotten in these windows; we see anti-aircraft guns defending a city from Zeppelin and Gotha, we see mine-sweepers at sea, we see troopships, we see airplanes, horse, foot, and guns.

In no window has the artist permitted himself an opinion. There is nothing here of the beastliness and horror of war. Cold, refined, and dispassionate as a saint in glass, these scenes shine out from the windows of Scotland's soul.

And the eye, moving over it, marvels at its completeness.

Even the smallest of God's creatures has been remembered: the mice – 'the tunnellers' friends' – the carrier pigeons, and even that trial of war, the sullen and reluctant mule.

You pass from this Hall of Honour into a place for prayer. Bronze gates divide it from the main building. Outside is the place for record and remembrance; within is that holy of holies designed for the secret places of the heart.

The light is soft and tinted. The fan vaulting sweeps up above you like solemn music, and from the stone vault hangs the mighty figure of St Michael in full armour, the cross upon his brow and his feet trampling the Spirit of Evil. Round this Shrine is a miracle in bronze; every type of Scotsman and Scotswoman who took part in the war has place in the long procession. They are seen as they fought, neither glorified nor debased, but with a kind of dispassion-ate clarity. The surgeon is there, his field boots beneath his overall; the infantryman in his war kit; the cavalryman; the gunner; the airman; the sailor; the nurse; the W.A.A.C.; the V.A.D.

Nothing that has been done to commemorate the war can compare for poignancy and exactitude with this parade of Scotland's sons and daughters.

But beneath the window where the Spirit of Man hangs triumphant on a Cross, his hands free and unpierced, is an outcrop of the virgin rock of Edinburgh. It looks as though it had burst its way through the smooth, costly granite with which the Shrine is paved. It stands in all its native roughness, jagged, hard, immovable, magnificently right.

Upon it is an altar; on the altar, guarded by four kneeling angels, is a steel casket lined with cedar wood in which lie the names of those hundred thousand Scotsmen from every part of the world who died in the war.

As I stood inarticulate before the Shrine a thought came to me which was like a light. I was, not long ago, in Ypres at the opening of the Menin Gate. It was a fine day with a wind blowing over the old front line. When the gate was declared open Scots pipers mounted high on the ramparts played the 'Flowers o' the Forest'.

No man at that moment dared to look into another man's eyes. It was one of life's terrible moments. The lament sobbed its grand way out along the road to Hooge, it wailed its way, sobbing, sobbing, 'the flowers o' the forest are a' wede awa'' into every little dip and hollow where the corn now grows. . . .'

It seemed to me, as I stood in Scotland's Shrine, that the sound of this lament had flown home to crystallize in stone upon the rock of Edinburgh. The Shrine is a lament in stone, the greatest of all Scotland's laments, with all the sweetness of pipes crying among hills, with all the haunting beauty of a lament, all the pride, all the grandeur.

I think the Cenotaph in London and the National Shrine in Edinburgh are the most remarkable symbols in existence of the temperamental difference between the two nations. One is Saxon and inarticulate; the other is Celtic and articulate. Grief locks the English heart, but it opens the Scottish. The Celt has a genius for the glorification of sorrow. All his sweetest songs are sad; all his finest music is sad; all his greatest poetry springs from tragedy.

That is why Scotland has built the greatest war memorial in the world.

The 'Flowers o' the Forest' have all turned to stone.

5

'I assure you the voice of this one man, John Knox, is able in one hour to put more life in us than five hundred trumpets continually blustering in our ears.'

Thomas Randolph, the English Ambassador to Scotland, wrote these words in the year 1561 to Sir William Cecil (afterwards Lord Burghley), Queen Elizabeth's chief Secretary of State.

John Knox and Mary, Queen of Scots, are Edinburgh's most famous ghosts. The least imaginative visitor to the city must take away with him the mental picture of stern, fearless Master Knox, on fire with his Calvinism, expounding the broad basis of Scottish Protestantism to the indignant young Catholic queen. The memory of Knox broods over the Canongate. You cannot take a walk past St Giles at night without meeting, in imagination, that wizard-like man, severe of face, sallow, long-nosed, full-lipped, his black beard threaded with grey and fully a span and a half in length, his keen blue-grey eyes, heavy lidded, burning beneath a rather narrow brow and under a black velvet bonnet. Or you may visualize him during that surprising but successful domestic experiment, his second marriage at the age of fifty-nine to seventeen-year-old Margaret Stewart, riding home up Canongate with his bride, mounted on a trim gelding and followed by a great crowd. There was nothing of the priest or prophet in his bearing at that moment. He had rather the air of a princeling. His 'bands of taffetie' were fastened with golden rings and precious stones.

It is to me surprising that in spite of the fact that John Knox stood over the religious life of his time like a colossus, the people of Edinburgh forgot his grave. A small brass plate with the initials 'J. K.' and the date 1572 set into the road in Parliament Square marks the approximate site of his burial. Visitors walk over it every day unconscious of it and more interested in the big lead statue of Charles II, mounted on a most authentic stallion, which the urchins of Edinburgh – always ready to attach themselves to profit-able-looking strangers – call the 'two-faced king', because the royal armour is fastened at the back with a queer little human face in the form of a clasp.

Edinburgh has, however, made up for its neglect of Knox's grave by devoting much interest and argument to the marvellous old house in Canongate, approached by an outside flight of steps, called forestairs. Tradition claims this house as John Knox's manse, but up-to-date critics appear to agree that it was merely the lodging to which he came to live, broken down in health, for those last two or three years before his end.

The house is packed with objects all bearing a more or less remote connexion with the great reformer. It is a splendid example of a medieval dwelling. It is oak-panelled, much larger than it seems; and if I could have my choice of houses in Edinburgh I would rather live in this than in the finest Adams mansion behind Princes Street.

But the objects which interested me in John Knox's House have nothing to do with John Knox. The first is a 'tirling pin'. Thousands of English people must have encountered this word and, if curious, may still be wondering what constitutes the act of 'tirling'. The word occurs in the proper version of 'Wee Willie Winkie', which is sung in English nurseries every night:

Wee Willie Winkie rins thro' the town,
Upstairs and downstairs in his nicht gown,
Tirlin' at the window, crying at the lock:
'Are the weans in their beds, for it's now ten o'clock?'

The word also occurs in the third and seldom-sung verse of 'Charlie, He's my Darling':

Sae light he jumped up the stair,
And tirl'd at the pin:
And whae sae ready as hersel'
To let the laddie in?

Willie Winkie, it will be noticed, 'tirled' on the windowglass, but Charlie 'tirled' at the pin. Both, however, made much the same sound. Willie Winkie made a trilling sound on the window by drumming with his fingernails; Charlie made a trilling sound by taking up a ring of metal and running it rapidly up and down a 'tirling pin'; which is a strip of iron with blunt teeth along its outer edge, the method and the sound produced being similar to that produced by running a stick along an iron railing.

The 'tirling pin' has now, I imagine, vanished from the doors of Scotland, but in earlier times it was commonly used to attract the attention of people; and a much gentler and more musical method than the villainous wire bell of Victorian times or the unpleasant electric bell of today.

The phrase 'dead as a door-nail' is also explained once and for all in John Knox's House. This expression puzzled Dickens, who had quite the wrong theory about it. On the first page of *A Christmas Carol* you will find the following:

'Old Marley was as dead as a door-nail. Mind, I don't mean to say that I know, of my own knowledge, what there is particularly dead about a door-nail. I might have been inclined, myself, to regard a coffin-nail as the deadest piece of ironmongery in the trade, but the wisdom of our ancestors is in the simile. . . .'

Dickens would never have written this had he first visited the old house in Canongate. Here, fixed to an oak door, is an old Scottish 'door-nail'. It is a rough-cast, heavy chunk of iron with a small hammer-like head. In repose, the hammer rests against a metal boss. When lifted and dropped against this boss the 'door-nail' makes the deadest of all dead sounds: it is a chill, unechoing crash. Another phrase which everyone uses – burning the candle at both ends – is illustrated on the mantelpiece of Knox's dining-room. The ancient candles were long, flexible tapers held in a kind of metal rushlight holder. By bending the taper and lighting both ends you got double the illumination, but you exhausted your taper in half the normal time – an act which impressed itself on the economical Scottish mind!

But to return to John Knox. It is not known, and will probably never be known, whether he preached to the crowds from the projecting window or whether he was sitting in this house when a musket shot missed him and lodged in the candlestick which is now, I believe, in Perth Museum. There seems no doubt, however, that in this house were acted the final scenes of his life.

It was from this house that James Melville used to see him led, a feeble old man, walking slowly 'with a furring of martricks about his neck', a staff in one hand, and his secretary, Richard Bannatyne, supporting him under the left arm. He had to be lifted into the pulpit, where he leant exhausted for some time until his spirit conquered his infirmity. Then, as Melville has said so vividly, 'Ere he had done with his sermon, he was so active and vigorous that he was like to ding that pulpit in blads and flee out of it!'

How many Englishmen can translate 'ding that pulpit in blads'? This vigorous phrase defeated a French translator of Melville who, having no Scotsman to help him, rendered it as 'he broke his pulpit and jumped into the midst of his auditors'. The words mean that he seemed about to 'break his pulpit in pieces'.

In this house took place that death scene which Ballantyne has drawn with such simple care: the feeble old man, lying still, bidding them to wet his lips with a little weak ale, and then lapsing into a coma which was plainly the shadow of the end. They asked him if he heard the prayers they had offered for him, and they struck from him the last spark:

'I would to God,' he answered, 'that you and all men heard them as I have heard them. . . .'

He gave one long sigh. Those round him asked him, now that the hour had come for which he had so often called to God, if he would give them a sign that he had hope. He could not speak. He lifted up his one hand and 'rendered the spirit'.

6

Every man who writes about Edinburgh is compelled by a regrettable sense of decency to deal at some length with her literary giants. I will not mention one of them: they are too well known. Every other shop in Edinburgh is a bookshop; and they seem to thrive. It is the most intellectual-seeming city on earth. Paris is, by comparison, almost illiterate.

Instead, however, I will remind Edinburgh of a poet who seems to have in some unaccountable way escaped recognition – Sir Topaz McGonagall.

I am a reluctant sleeper. When I go to bed all the past rises up before me, all the things I have done badly and all the things I have not done come and sit on the pillow like the germs of some disease, infecting me with vivid wakefulness. I carry round the world with me such opiates as Thackeray, and Harvey's *Circulation of the Blood*, and books called, goodness knows why, 'bedside', obviously written or compiled by people who sleep soundly in order to keep other people awake. Not one of them works. I find myself worrying about omissions in anthologies, becoming furious about inclusions, and, worst of all, I find myself taking an intelligent interest in Thackeray and Harvey. And the clock goes on striking.

The ideal bedside book is one like *Alice in Wonderland*, which first obliterates the world in which we live and secondly induces a placid, soporific smile. 'Alice' obliterates the world, but she makes me laugh! A laugh is as fatal to sleep as a smile is its forerunner. The quickest path to dreamland is the slide into unconsciousness on a smile. Such a lullaby is Sir Topaz McGonagall, born in Dundee, and lately of Edinburgh, poet!

The few who still remember McGonagall refer to him as the world's worst poet; but in this I cannot agree. He was perhaps merely in advance of his time. In his works we find that splendid disregard for the decencies of literary formulae which has in recent times made many large fortunes, coupled with a gay and cavalier-like habit with the English language – a kind of chuck under the chin – an indignity tolerable only in a great lover or a great master.

McGonagall was at the height of his powers during the South African War. He was, I gather, one of those eccentric characters thrown up now and then by great cities. London was full of them in the time of Dickens. McGonagall wrote poems about anything and everything. National events, natural phenomena, shipwrecks, the birth and death of princes, all fired his muse. His haunt was the magnificent Parliament Hall, where, I am told, he found a ready market for his broadsides among the foremost lawyers in Edinburgh.

He printed them with the Royal Arms above in black type! At some period in his career a band of students held a mock levee and gave him an exotic title from which he never recovered. He then began to sign his work 'Sir Topaz McGonagall, Kt of the Order of the White Elephant'.

In the archives of a Government department in the shadows of St Giles is a staff magazine which contains a priceless selection of his work. I am indebted to the courtesy of this department for many dreamless nights. Take, for instance, his poem on Glasgow:

> *O wonderful city of Glasgow, with your triple expansion engines,*
> *At the making of which your workmen get many singeins;*
> *Also the deepening of the Clyde, most marvellous to behold,*
> *Which cost much money, be it told.*

O beautiful city of Glasgow, I must conclude my lay
By calling thee the greatest city of the present day;
For your treatment of me was by no means churlish,
Therefore I say, 'Let Glasgow flourish!'

There is a lot more; but I have picked out the two best verses.

Another little masterpiece is his poem 'Baldovan Mansion'; in which the following occurs:

Stately mansion of Baldovan,
Most beautiful to see,
Belonging to Sir John Ogilvy,
Ex-M.P. of Dundee.

In sterner vein McGonagall could lash out at social evils:

Oh, thou Demon Drink, thou fell destroyer,
The curse of Society and its greatest annoyer,
What hast thou done to Society, let me think?
I answer, thou has caused the most of ills, thou Demon Drink.
Thou causes the mother to neglect her child,
Also the father to act as he were wild,
So that he neglects his wife and family dear
By spending his earnings foolishly on whisky, rum, and beer.

McGonagall would have made an excellent reporter. Nothing escaped his imagination. When the Duke of Albany died in 1884 he wrote eighteen stanzas about it, concluding with a remarkable reference to the grief of Queen Victoria:

Her Majesty was unable to stand long, she was overcome with grief,
And when the Highlanders lowered the coffin in the tomb she felt relief.
Then the ceremony closed with singing 'Lead, Kindly Light',
And the Queen withdrew in haste from the mournful sight.

He exercised his turbulent muse on 'The Attempted Assassination of Queen Victoria', which begins:

God prosper long our noble Queen,
And long may she reign.
Maclean he tried to shoot her,
But it was all in vain.

> *Long may she be spared to roam*
> *Among the bonnie Highland floral,*
> *And spend many a happy day*
> *In the Palace of Balmoral.*

Some of the rarest collectors' items – McGonagalliana, I suppose, booksellers would call them – deal with ancient battles, Tel-el-Kebir, Majuba Hill, and so forth, and with national sorrows such as the death of 'Chinese' Gordon. Unbelievable as these epics are, I much prefer McGonagall when he is interpreting the beauties of his native land, or such remarkable happenings as the Tay Bridge Disaster and the whale that was washed up at Dundee. Take his eulogy of Nairn:

> *All ye tourists who wish to be away*
> *From the crowded city for a brief holiday,*
> *The town of Nairn is worth a visit, I do confess,*
> *And it's only about fifteen miles short of Inverness.*
> *And in the summer season it's a very popular bathing place,*
> *And the visitors from London and Edinburgh find great solace*
> *As they walk along the yellow sand beach, with spirits light as air –*
> *Besides, there's every accommodation for ladies and gentlemen there.*
> *Then there's a large number of bathing coaches there,*
> *And the climate is salubrious and very warm the air.*

McGonagall was, it seems, the butt of many a rather cruel joke; but, on the other hand, I wonder to what extent he pulled the legs of those who professed to admire him? His vanity appeared to be without limit. He became the licensed buffoon of legal and academic Edinburgh. Men who remember his spare, uncouth figure in a long barn-storming coat tell how they used to hire a room and get 'the great' McGonagall to give a reading from his dreadful works, every one, of course, keeping a solemn face.

Once a member of the audience assumed the name of a noted playwright and told the poet that he had a brilliant future on the stage. McGonagall set off for London to interview Sir Henry Irving. This unlucky journey explains the inclusion in his works of a poem called 'Descriptive Jottings of London', which begins:

As I stood upon London Bridge and viewed the mighty throng
Of thousands of people in cabs and buses rapidly whirling along,
All furiously driving to and fro,
Up one street and down another as quick as they could go.

Then I was struck with the discordant sounds of human voices there,
Which seemed to me like wild geese cackling in the air;
And the River Thames is a most beautiful sight,
To see the steamers sailing upon it by day and by night.

And the Tower of London is most gloomy to behold,
And the Crown of England lies there, begemmed with jewels and gold;
King Henry the Sixth was murdered there by the Duke of Gloucester,
And when he killed him with his sword he called him an impostor.

He was also 'struck' by Trafalgar Square, and the fountains 'where the weary traveller can drink when he feels dry'. On Sunday he went to hear Mr Spurgeon preach, and he ends his assault on London with the withering remark: 'Mr Spurgeon was the only man I heard speaking proper English, I do declare.'

Perhaps I have given a sufficient taste of McGonagall to explain why I regard him as the perfect bedside book. Someone should sweep up all his mighty conflicts with scansion and put them between covers for the benefit of the sleepless.

He was a genuine relic of Old Edinburgh. He made a mysterious visit to New York, but I can find no one who remembers how and why he went. As far as I can gather his patrons subscribed for his absence. But in an alarmingly short time his gaunt figure turned up in the Law Courts again and his misguided fingers held a new broadside beginning:

Oh, mighty city of New York, you are wonderful to behold!

Nothing, apparently, could stop him! Poor, relentless Sir Topaz!

Some day I will return to Edinburgh unencumbered by a pen, to spend my time nosing round the queer closes and wynds of the Canongate. But nothing less than a cloak of invisibility would be a protection against the Canongate's vivid children.

I went to a mean house in the Canongate. Children were playing on the floor. A line of washing hung from one end of the room to the other. The place smelt of intensive habitation and food, but over the fire, carved in stone, was the coat of arms of a Scottish earl! I have seen much the same thing in Galway. The great houses in which so much of Scotland's history was nursed have been handed over to families which in Glasgow or Manchester would be living in flats or tenements. They camp out in them, unconscious of their past, like bands of Arabs among the ruins of a previous civilization. When exploring the streets of Old Edinburgh I came to a place which should be visited by every golfer. This is the Mercat Cross erected by W. E. Gladstone on the site of that Cross which in ancient times was the focus of Edinburgh's street life. Round this Cross the caddie first enters history.

The dictionary traces this word to the French 'cadet'. The caddies, or 'cawdies', of Old Edinburgh were a peculiar institution. They hung about the Cross in the hope of attaching themselves to bewildered strangers, and anyone who has spent a day wandering through the rabbit warren of Old Edinburgh will realize that in times before a police force or a street directory Edinburgh must have been one of the mysteries of Europe.

The caddies were a wild, villainous-looking species of street lounger; but they had a remarkable code of honour, rather like the secret society of the Berbers who form the servant class in Cairo. They were a community within a community. They paid deference to a Chief Caddie, who imposed fines and punishments if any of his band committed an offence. They had also a common fund out of which any traveller who happened to strike a thieving caddie was reimbursed.

They knew everything about Edinburgh. Every scrap of gossip found its way immediately to the caddies. They knew every address in the city. They knew the haunts of every citizen, and when one attached himself to you he would in a few hours know more about you than you knew about yourself.

They could guide you through the maze of huddled houses to an address which you could never have found without assistance. It must have been almost impossible for a stranger to keep an appointment in Old Edinburgh without the help of the encyclopaedic caddie.

Major Topham, writing of the Edinburgh of 1774, says that the caddies were 'the tutelary guardians of the city, and it is entirely owing to them that there are fewer robberies and less housebreaking in Edinburgh than anywhere else'.

There is a legend that a judge with original ideas on education turned his sons loose on the streets of Edinburgh as caddies in the belief that the insight they would gain into human nature and the mental agility necessary to their calling would be invaluable to them in later life.

How did the caddie associate himself with the golf course? I do not know whether the literature of golf provides a definite answer. I have certainly been unable to find one.

It seems fairly obvious that the caddie, the general handyman of his time, would naturally hire himself to carry a man's clubs round the course. Golf was played in Edinburgh as early as 1457. It was, in fact, played too frequently, because an Act of the Scottish Parliaments was passed in that year to suppress 'the golf' in the interests of 'schuting' at the butts. Mary, Queen of Scots, is the first recorded woman golfer. She played a round on the links at Seton a few days after the murder of Darnley, a game which her enemies were not slow to notice.

The first caddie whose name is known was Andrew Dickson, a golf club maker of Edinburgh, who in his young days used to caddie for the Duke of York, afterwards James II. We can be sure that when a brilliant company left Holyrood to play a round on Leith links the Cross at Edinburgh would know all about it, and the caddies would set out in the hope of an afternoon's employment.

Another landmark in Edinburgh, of peculiar interest to golfers, is that building in Canongate known as 'Golfers' Land', a house which was built on the proceeds of the most profitable amateur golf match ever played. It is a high stone house, with an excellent motto over it: 'I hate no person.'

The story is that when James, Duke of York (afterwards James VII of Scotland and the Second of England), was at Holyrood he became a keen golfer. There must have been with him at that time the first keen English players, for a discussion arose – a rather absurd one and probably a joke – whether the game of golf was an English or Scottish one! In order to settle the question it was agreed to hold the first Anglo-Scottish championship match. James – and this is evidently the only humanly interesting thing he ever did – agreed to pick a Scottish player and uphold the national title against two English players. A large sum of money was placed on the winners.

James craftily inquired for the best player in Edinburgh. Here one may possibly see the finger of the ubiquitous caddies! News was rapidly brought to him that a shoemaker, a John Patersone, could beat anybody in the city. The heir to the throne and the shoemaker set off for Leith links, and there they 'put it across' the English players in great style. History does not, I think, record details of the match, which is a pity! The entire Court trooped off to Leith to witness the game, and Patersone was rewarded with half the wager.

He spent it, the story goes, in building 'Golfers' Land', the stylish house in Canongate. . . .

It is untidy to leave the subject of golf without quoting Smollett. In *Humphrey Clinker*, which was written in 1770, is the following:

'Hard by in the fields called the Links, the citizens of Edinburgh divert themselves at a game called Golf, in which they use a curious kind of bats, tipped with horn, and small elastic balls of leather, stuffed with feathers, rather less than tennis balls, but of a much harder consistency; this they strike with such force and dexterity from one hole to another that they will fly to an incredible distance. Of this diversion the Scots are so fond, that, when the weather will permit, you may see a multitude of all ranks, from the senator of justice to the lowest tradesman, mingled together in their shirts, and following the balls with the utmost eagerness. Among others, I was shown one particular set of golfers, the youngest of whom was turned of fourscore; they were all gentlemen of independent fortunes, who had amused themselves with this pastime for the best part of a century, without ever having felt the least alarm from sickness or disgust; and they never went to bed without having each the best part of a gallon of claret in his belly.'

8

I remember many things about Edinburgh. There was an evening in a high flat in the centre of the city where a grey-haired lady played songs of the Western Isles and a tune the seals know; there was a rather different evening in the Royal Scots Club and much talk of Ypres and Vimy; and, again, there was night in Glencorse Churchyard and no moon, owls calling and bats flickering, and a young man of mournful disposition solemnly calling on the spirit of Robert Louis Stevenson to appear beside the witch elm where the burn crosses the road.

But always will I remember Old Edinburgh in the evening. The sun goes down and dusk falls. I feel conscious that I should descend to fashionable Georgian levels, but that, to me, is an unreal Edinburgh. I like to linger on the hill in the dark, where winds whistle like swords and darkness creeps with an air of conspiracy.

CHAPTER THREE

I see the Castle of Roslin, cross into the Kingdom of Fife, see the end of the German Fleet, and go on to the town of Andrew Carnegie, to Linlithgow, and so to the beauty of Stirling, where I remember a Queen

I

I SET out from Edinburgh with the intention of crossing over into Fife. But I had gone no more than a mile or so when I remembered that among the 6,082 things which I had not done in, or in the neighbourhood of, Edinburgh, was to see the Castle of Roslin. Why do beautiful hostesses extort from the innocent wanderer his word of honour that he will go to such and such a place and in the fullness of time write to her about it, or, at least, send her a post card? This love of sending men on inconvenient journeys is a peculiar trait in the mentality of women. It is probably a survival from days when every girl in every bower took a singular delight in sending reckless young men to obtain impossible gifts or to encounter appalling dangers. I suppose there was no other way of weeding out suitors in the Middle Ages.

However, a promise is a promise, and it is, in addition, the worst kind of bad luck to break faith with a beautiful hostess. So, sighing, I turned south and came in a short time to Roslin.

I saw, sitting on the edge of a crag above a woody ravine, all that is left of a noble castle. I crossed what was once a magnificent drawbridge and met a man who offered to rent me the whole place for £120 a year. The idea went to my head. It seemed incredible that for less than the price of a third-rate Kensington flat I could live on this cliff and write to all my friends on notepaper stamped 'Roslin Castle, Scotland', or, even better – the old spelling – 'Rosslyn'. Yes, there was a bath (h. and c.), four bedrooms, and a dining-

77

room with windows flush with the gorge; and among the fittings is 'Fair Rosamund, the White Lady of Roslin', who, alas! no longer walks as well as she used to do.

I have often wondered what Dick Turpin and Company mean when they advertise an 'ideal residence for a literary gentleman'. My own belief is that the ideal residence for a 'literary gentleman' should be mortgaged up to the hilt and provided with a view of a soap factory. The handmaids of literature are necessity, discomfort, and a wife who is always 'in rags', but house-agents, having at some time seen 'Patience', visualize a kind of Bunthorne as the victim for the decayed barns, the mews, and the desiccated cottages which are too full of 'atmosphere' for normal people. Roslin Castle advertised by a London agent in a fit of congenital lyricism would most certainly become the home of all inspiration. And in the ghost of Fair Rosamund what a pleasingly elusive pretext for a fat premium!

Strangely enough, the agent would be speaking the truth! Roslin is the ideal place for the writing of a humorous novel. The 'literary gentleman', concentrating against his dungeons, would seek refuge in a Wodehouse hero, or, removing his desk to a torture-chamber hacked with axes in the solid rock in the time of Robert the Bruce, he might write a rollicking revue.

Perhaps the greatest attraction in Roslin for a 'literary gentleman' is the legend of the buried millions said to be lying in a vault beneath the courtyard. The only person who knows the hiding-place is a lady of the house of St Clair, now inconveniently dead. If, however, a trumpet blown in the upper apartments is heard in the dungeons, she will appear and lead on to the gold. (Who more likely to awaken her than a 'literary gentleman' accustomed to blowing his own trumpet?)

In the ancient dining-hall are the arms of that St Clair who restored the castle in 1580. Above are four bedrooms with a fine view of the mess Monk's cannon made of the keep in 1650, but below in the rock are the chain of passages and the dim caverns lit by holes as small as your hand, in which, if I rented Roslin, I would give my dinner-parties – a thin trickle of water down the slimy rock as an orchestra. By the way, a dinner-party in these dungeons would establish the reputation of any Mayfair hostess.

The present tenant, who shows visitors over the castle, is the best guide I have met in Scotland. He knows the castle from the rock upwards. He has a marvellous trick of projecting himself back in time, so that when he is talking you can positively feel what it was to take a spar of wood and push a scaling ladder from the ramparts, and then leaning over, to watch your enemies tumbling and turning in the air, on their way to the glen beneath.

'Do you mean to tell me you have never dug for the treasure?' I asked him.

'I have that!' he admitted, with a grim smile. 'I've dug everywhere, but I canna locate it.'

There is a possibility, I understand, that Roslin Castle may be taken over by the Office of Works as an ancient monument. If so, a professional excavation will be made, with perhaps exciting results. But they will find nothing in the dungeons. The hardy Scots who built the first castle cared nothing for difficulties. They just hacked rooms in the rock. There is a dungeon in Roslin (no one knows where it is) known as 'Little Ease'. It was merely a pit. The prisoner was thrown into it, or, if his captor was in a kindly mood, let down on a rope. Here hopelessness closed over him as he lingered, growing blind and insane.

There are other dungeons quite as horrible. You stand in them, and there is no sound, but the slow drip, drip, drip of one spot of water on a stone. It is outside the dungeon, so that if you were dying of thirst you would beat your bleeding knuckles on the stone door to get to it. If not, you would just sit there year after year counting the drips, waiting for them, and probably in time talking to them.

The finest room in the rock is a kitchen with a gigantic fireplace. There is a gutter round it, hacked in the rock, so that the fat from a roasting ox would run away into a receptacle placed for it. When St Clair gave a dinner-party in the Middle Ages this place must have been chaos, black with smoke, loud with shouts and sounds of sizzling fat, and the yelps of hounds kicked away from the fire. As you stand in it and listen to your guide you can see the cooks and the servants, the men-at-arms lounging in from the guardroom, ready to slice a peace of meat from the roasting carcase with a dagger. Then from above would come a great shout from a wide opening in the rock: 'Hurry up there, you scum, St Clair's hungry!'

For Roslin Castle has perhaps the earliest speaking-tube and service lift in the world. The hall was above, so what easier to those relentless architects than to bore down through the rock to the kitchen, and make a hole big enough for an ox to be hauled through?

Outside is the most venerable-looking tree on earth. This yew is said to have been planted at the beginning of the fourteenth century. It looks like the ancestor of all yew-trees. It casts an almost black shade over the mouth of the dungeons. Its sinister arms wave in every direction. Its trunk, furrowed by centuries, is supported by a buttress of wood. I am sure that if I searched for the White Lady I would discover her some night under this tree.

There is also a tremendous Scotch thistle higher than a man. Bits of this mighty thorn grow and blossom in every part of the world.

'I'm always sending shoots out to people who have been here,' said my guide.

A short walk from the castle is Roslin Chapel, the most extraordinary Protestant church in Scotland.

It is the most ornate piece of Gothic in the British Isles. It is the choir of a great church which William St Clair founded in 1446, but never completed. Every liberty which men of abundant imagination could take with the chastity of Gothic has been taken with a sort of competitive enthusiasm. One can imagine them scheming and plotting to work in an extra saint or a redundant spiral. There is not an unsculptured inch in the building. The effect is fine, but distressing. They could not let the stone rest. They refused to allow beauty of line to speak for itself. It is the strangest – most alien – thing I have seen on Scottish soil. The nearest extravagance of the kind is probably the church of Belem, near Lisbon.

The caretaker asked if I were a Freemason. When I said 'No' he was disappointed. Apparently only a Mason can understand Roslin Chapel. I wish some Mason would go there and explain it to me!

Beneath the chapel lie the St Clairs, buried in full armour. Roslin Chapel stands over them, in fantastic flamboyancy, a choir without a nave, as though it had exhausted the invention of its makers.

2

The Palace of Linlithgow, like Kenilworth, in Warwickshire, is the roofless shell of its former self, but enough of it remains for a man to prowl round in the silence, hearing in imagination the creak of harness, the skirl of pipes, and the uneasy footfall of sad kings and even less happy queens.

In the great dining-hall, with its tremendous fireplace and its gallery, it is possible to reconstruct the banquets held between successive tragedies – the brief moments of music and laughter stolen from fate – and to see those pale, heavy-lidded Stuarts, melancholy, sensuous, piling up an inheritance of intrigue which was to flower in a woman; and all the time sure of nothing in life but failure, until in the decency of time the red hat of Henry, Cardinal Duke of York, came down to extinguish for ever the worn-out flame of their ambition.

It is strange how the tears of women work their way into the stone of buildings. As I sit in these roofless apartments of this old royal palace of Scotland, refurnishing them, hanging tapestries on the walls, strewing rushes and sweet herbs on the floors, I see kings, it is true, but more vivid are their queens. There is a little turret at the end of a long spiral stair that overlooks a lake that lies 150 feet above sea-level, and here it was that Margaret, the Queen of James IV, 'all lonely sat and wept the weary hour', waiting day after day for the return of her husband from Flodden – one of the blackest tragedies in Scotland's history.

No national tragedy in England is remembered with quite the same sorrow with which Scotsmen, even today, remember Flodden Field; and, I think, no Scotsman can stand in 'Margaret's Bower' and look over the loch to Bonnytoun Hill without a twinge of emotion.

What a change of feeling comes over a man when he crosses the Border and looks back on old battles with the eyes of another nation. In England no one remembers much about Flodden, except, perhaps, that the Earl of Surrey upheld English valour against the bravest foe and the most chivalrous, if impetuous, king which England ever encountered in the field; but, in Scotland, Flodden is still a pain at the heart. Songs and a lament of pipes have handed the pain down to the Scottish nation century after century. I cannot hear the 'Flowers o' the Forest' on pipes without wishing to hide myself from the gaze of men. Chopin's 'Marche Funebre' and the Dead March in Saul are just musical compositions in comparison. This lament is a living sorrow; it is as if all the tears of all the women of Scotland who mourned at that time had been preserved for ever in some indestructible urn.

When I first came to Scotland I borrowed a gramophone and played this lament, and also the song, again and again until people in hotels believed that I was mad. I recommend this to other earnest travellers. There is more in them than in guide-books. And how amazing is the song. No wonder Scott wrote in his note to it in *Minstrelsy of the Scottish Border*: 'It required the most positive evidence to convince the editor that the song was of modern date.' Let any ear tuned to the sound of an ancient ballad listen to it:

I've heard them lilting, at the ewe-milking,
 Lasses a' lilting, before the dawn of day;
But now they are moaning on ilka green loaning;
 The flowers of the forest are a' wede awae.

At buchts, in the morning, nae blithe lads are scorning;
 Lasses are lonely, and dowie, and wae;
Nae daffing, nae gabbing, but sighing and sabbing;
 Ilk ane lifts her leglen, and hies her awae.

We'll hear nae mair lilting, at the ewe-milking;
 Women and bairns are heartless and wae:
Sighing and moaning on ilka green loaning —
 The flowers of the forest are a' wede awae.

It is surely one of the greatest curiosities in Scottish literature that this magnificent song should have been written by a lady who died in the nineteenth century! She was the daughter of Sir Gilbert Elliot of Minto, Lord Justice Clerk of Scotland. The story is that her father made a bet with her that she could not compose a ballad on Flodden. Accordingly she took the broken fragments of an old song and composed a masterpiece which for tenderness and beauty stands among the finest ballads in the language. Here again is surely proof that the Celt has a genius for the interpretation of sorrow.

James IV, twelve Scottish earls, thirteen lords, five eldest sons of peers, fifty chief knights, and 10,000 men fell at Flodden. It often happens when the king, or a great hero, is cut down in a calamitous battle that popular legend persists in the theory that he left the field in disguise and is still alive. The legend that Lord Kitchener was not drowned in the *Hampshire* is an excellent instance of this. It was so at Flodden; and rather strangely in face of such definite evidence of James's death.

'The Scots,' says Sir Walter Scott, 'were much disposed to dispute the fact that James IV had fallen on Flodden Field. Some said that he had retired from the Kingdom, and made a pilgrimage to Jerusalem. Others pretended that, in the twilight, when the field was nigh ended, four tall horsemen came into the field, having each a bunch of straw on the point of their spears, as a token for them to know each other by. They said these men mounted the king on a dun hackney and that he was seen to cross the Tweed with them at nightfall. Nobody pretended to say what they did with him, but it was believed that he was murdered in Howe Castle; and I recollect that about forty years since there was a report that, in cleaning the draw-well of that ruinous fortress, the workmen found a skeleton wrapt in a bull's hide and having a belt of iron round the waist. There was, however, no truth in this rumour. It was the absence of this belt of iron which the Scots founded upon to prove that the body of James could not have fallen into the hands of the English, since they either had not that token to show or did not produce it. But it is not unlikely that they would lay aside such a cumbrous article of penance on a day of battle; or the English, when they may have despoiled his person, may have thrown it aside as of no value. The body which the English affirm to have been that of James was found on the field by Lord Dacre, and carried by him to Berwick, and presented to Surrey. Both of these lords knew James's person too well to be mistaken. The body was also acknowledged by his two favourite attendants, Sir William Scott and Sir James Forman, who wept at beholding it.'

As I stood in Margaret's Bower, remembering this legend, I wondered how many Scotsmen know that the sword, dagger, and ring taken from James IV after Flodden are to be seen today in a case in the College of Arms, London. And how many know that the head of this unhappy king was buried, without a tablet or other memorial, in the churchyard of St Michael, Wood Street (now demolished), just off Cheapside, London? John Stow saw the body of the dead king and tells the queer story in his *Survey of London*:

'After the battle the body of the said king, being found, was enclosed in lead, and conveyed from thence to London, and so to the monastery of Shene (Richmond), in Surrey, where it remained for a time; but since a

dissolution of that house, in the reign of Edward VI,
Henry Grey, Duke of Suffolk, being lodged and keeping
house there, I have been shown the said body, so lapped
in lead, close to the head and body, thrown into a waste
room, among the old timber, lead, and other rubble.
Since the which time workmen there, for their foolish
pleasure, hewed off his head; and Launcelot Young,
master glazier to Her Majesty (Queen Elizabeth), feeling
a sweet savour to come from thence, and seeing the same
dried from all moisture, and yet the form remaining with
the hair of the head and beard red, brought it to London,
to his house in Wood Street, where for a time he kept it
for the sweetness, but in the end caused the sexton of that
church to bury it amongst other bones taken out of their
charnel.'

So the proud, impetuous head which refused advice at
Flodden lay at the last among tradesmen in Cheapside. . . .

In another part of the palace is the room in which Mary,
Queen of Scots, was born. Here is more sorrow. It is a
roofless chamber, and through the tracery of the window I
can see the great fountain in the courtyard below and the
Gothic gateway under which, like a river in spate, the sad
story of Scotland flowed century after century.

I am sure it was a wild December night when the girl
who should have been a boy came into the world, with
death stalking the Border and the scots flying from Solway
Moss. Tragedy walked side by side with her from the first
moment of her life. And the messenger rode north with the
unwelcome news to Falkland, where her father, James V,
had dragged his broken heart. It was one of Scotland's
many wild nights. The English were over the Border. The
reivers were out in the dark. The very grass smelt of blood.
Eyes were fixed to the bowslits of peel towers from Berwick
to Ayr, horsemen came through the night, cattle before
them, death behind them, and in the wind that always

howls through the soggy heather someone with the 'second sight' must have recognized the spirit of evil.

When they told the King that his child was a lass he said: 'The devil take it,' and died in a few days of a broken heart, they say certainly of failure, at the age of thirty. In this room in Linlithgow the widowed Queen, holding at her breast the most luckless child in history, lay 'in great fear through divers factions among the principal noblemen . . . contending among themselves for the government of the realm and the keeping of the Princess's person'.

So the dark forces of jealousy and ambition which were to lead her in time to Fotheringay gathered round five-days-old Mary Stuart.

A man came into the room as I was making these notes. He was red-haired. I thought that he was a Scotsman, but he was English. He thought that I was sketching. I found subsequently that he was an artist, so I must forgive his attempt to look over my notebook without seeming to do so. We began talking about Mary.

'She had to die,' he said; 'but it was a dirty business – first the Casket Letters and then the faked evidence at Fotheringay.'

'I wonder what would have happened had she and Elizabeth ever met.'

'Don't forget Cecil, Lord Burghley.'

'Did she ever love Bothwell? Did she enjoy the luxury of being swept off her feet?'

'Who can say? She was a refined girl and he was the worst type of sheik.'

'I cannot imagine why no one loved her with sufficient intelligence to send a knife home in Bothwell.'

'Nor I. Then, if only one could have stopped her from seeking refuge in England. Surely anyone who knew Elizabeth must have known that Mary was done for as far as Elizabeth was concerned when at the age of sixteen she went to a tournament in France with heralds crying, "Make way for the Queen of England".'

'Have you ever read Sir James Melville's memoirs, in which it is clear how jealous Elizabeth was, how she asked questions about the colour of her skin and her hair, and how, when poor Melville admitted that Mary played the lute and virginals, he was summoned the next day to hear Elizabeth perform and was forced to confess that she was the better player?'

'Elizabeth must have been a dangerous old cat, but she gathered the right men round her, while Mary always attracted the wrong ones.'

So we talked in this room, coming at length to the inevitable topic when two men remember Mary.

'She must have been amazingly beautiful.'

'Yes, even washing out Chatelard and Brantôme as courtiers, her beauty is beyond question. Even John Knox could not avoid it. She must have been a raving beauty when she came over from France at the age of eighteen.'

'Someone said a fire cometh out from her that hath consumed many.'

'I believe,' said my red-haired friend, 'that today she would have been the first girl in Edinburgh to shingle her hair!'

'And how easily her night club complex could have been satisfied today. Sometimes she seems like a modern among the medievals.'

Alone again in Linlithgow I thought of her in that brief playtime at Holyrood. They say that you could see the burgundy red in her throat as she swallowed. I imagine that crowds would gather before Holyrood at night to watch the lit windows and to hear the scraping of foreign fiddles. Many a wild Highlander at that time in Edinburgh with his chieftain must have heard stories about her, how she bathed her body in wine, how you could see her riding her horse full tilt for the gates with her court far behind scattered like a hunting field over the 'Royal Mile'; how sometimes on dark nights you might meet her stealing through the streets, hiding her beauty beneath a manly cloak. . . .

Perhaps a curtain would be pulled aside and this Highlander would see her for a second against the candlelight, with pearls shining in her hair. And he would ride his shaggy pony north through wild gorges, thinking of this queen, taking with him something of her beauty, her strangeness, her remoteness from anything Scotland had ever known, home to a lonely stone hut in the heart of the hills.

So she became a legend at the age of eighteen. . . .

I leave Linlithgow and this room. This palace is ghostly; and in the dampness of its stones are, it seems, the tears of sad queens.

3

The Forth Bridge flings its three double steel cantilevers across the water to the Kingdom of Fife. It is the most familiar bridge in the world. It is seen on posters, framed in railway carriages and in all kinds of books. To see the Forth Bridge is rather like meeting a popular actress, but with this difference: it exceeds expectations. It is a memorable sight. It is more impressive than its pictures. Its proportions are so tremendous that you do not realize how vast they are until a train crosses over, skied above you in an intricate tracery of girders. Then you are astonished. It is even higher than it appeared without the train, and therefore longer and in every way more stupendous. The sound of trains crossing the Forth Bridge is a queer, fascinating and peculiar sound: something between a roar and a rumble, and with a hint of drums.

As I waited for the iniquitous ferry which crosses the Forth where a traffic bridge should be, I watched a small boy on the edge of the tide trying to capture a loathsome fish like a small octopus. Each time he approached it the horrid gelatinous mass heaved itself up on suckers and backfired a dark, inky fluid into the water. I would not have been surprised to have seen this creature in an aquarium, but it was, to the eyes of a landsman, a queer fish to find under the Forth Bridge.

However, the ferry arrived before the contest had been settled, and in half an hour or so I was spinning along a wide but deserted road. And it led to an excellent wide but deserted place: the once world-famous naval base of Rosyth. I had heard that the German cruiser *Moltke* had been dredged up in the far north from Scapa Flow and towed to Rosyth to be broken up as scrap metal. I felt that it would give me satisfaction to see this. Could I have known during the war that the day would come when I should place a foot upon the prostrate *Moltke* what a mighty difference it would have made to my general outlook at that time! I determined to try my luck.

Now, ten years ago I would have been shot as a spy for trying to get into Rosyth; and with something of the fear of those days over me I approached the dock gates and timidly spoke my heart to a man in uniform:

'Come in, sir! Just sign your name in the book.'

What a difference ten short years can make! I signed the book and went in to one of the most remarkable sights in the British Isles.

Rosyth was desolate. The largest and best equipped naval base in the world was a city of the dead. It is the only dockyard in Great Britain in which every ship in the Fleet can anchor at any state of the tide. Millions went to the making of it, wide roads, straight as knives, lead to it, and all empty of traffic. Rosyth was 'axed' by Admiralty economies in 1925. Its army of cranes was silent. Its enormous workshops were locked. The docks to which the great ironclads came limping from conflict or accident, as to a hospital, were deserted. The offices which so recently held naval secrets, guarded by armed sentries and all the astuteness of the Secret Service, gazed innocently with blank windows over wide squares on which the grass grew.

Just a faint stir of returning life was visible, but so vast is this place and so recent its frantic activities that stray fatigue-parties, marching with rain shining on their black oilskins, only accentuated the utter loneliness and inactivity which peace and reduced armaments have brought to it.

Here is a city built to minister to the Grand Fleet in northern waters, and now that northern waters no longer have the same attraction for a Grand Fleet the city is deserted, and its inhabitants might never have existed.

I walked for a mile or so in pouring rain. Reserve destroyers were being drafted to Rosyth. They lay somnolently in pale grey rows, manned by skeleton crews who presided over them with 'spit and polish'. They were packed tight as motor-cars in a popular garage, and how, if ever, they would be able to gain their natural hunting-grounds again without first scratching each other's paint was a mystery of navigation too deep for my ignorant eyes.

And the only sound in this dead mystery of the Great War was the noise of men breaking up a German battlecruiser lately fished up from seventy feet of water in Scapa Flow. All round our slim, trim destroyers lay at anchor, with hooded guns, taking a nap, an occasional Cockney brooding on their decks in cynical solitude. The wireless masts of this flotilla peeped over the edge of the gigantic dry dock in which the *Moltke*, Germany's 23,000-ton battlecruiser, lay upside down, rusty, disembowelled, and too utterly defeated to rouse any feeling of triumph in even the most bitter and vindictive soul.

I was aware of a strange emotion. I had just come from Linlithgow and had thought of Flodden. Here before my eyes was evidence of a national disaster as great as Flodden, without the glory of Flodden, it is true, but with all Flodden's tragedy of failure. This shapeless, shameful thing before me was once part of the great German Fleet, whose end in Scottish waters will be told as long as the history of nations has interest for humanity. It was almost like standing on a battlefield before the slain had been removed, or, more truly, like watching a spade open up the earth to reveal some awful thing that once had been a man. The *Moltke* was horrible.

When the Germans scuttled their fleet in Scapa in 1919 this ship turned turtle and sank in seventy feet of water. A workman who was leaning against a shed on the dockside gave me a description of her end:

'You see, as she sank upside down her masts stuck in the mud at the bottom of the sea. The weight of 23,000 tons made the steel bend like matchwood, and, you see, as she settled down her steel funnels crumpled and her bridge was crushed, and in time the weight even displaced her gun turrets. But we pumped compressed air into her and she lifted, still upside down, and we towed her, still upside down, into the Firth of Forth. She's a mess, isn't she? I wonder what the old Kaiser would say if he could take a walk round her.'

I went 'aboard' by a gang-plank and walked on the rusty slope of the monster hull. The largest mussels I have ever seen have almost eaten their way into the metal. The whole ship was scarred with marine growths. You could take a pick and knock off buckets of shellfish. The muzzles of her guns were stopped with mussels and seaweed. Fish and trailing weeds had found their way through open scuttles into the most remote mysteries of the cruiser: into cabins, storerooms, chart-rooms, and torpedo shafts.

The German Fleet had been beneath the waves for only nine years, and yet the *Moltke* could not have seemed a more antique wreck had she gone down with the Armada. When she came up, dripping with seaweed, fish still swimming round the 70,000 horse-power turbines, crabs and lobsters firmly established in ammunition lifts, she must indeed have been an almost incredible sight.

'Divers told me,' said a man on the hull, 'that they had never seen such tough seaweed before. Some of the stems were as thick as your wrist. They had to slash it away with clasp-knives.'

The crowning humiliation was a little tin hut, like a cab shelter, erected in the centre of the hull, where workmen took refuge from the rain and chatted between shifts.

I peered down into the inconceivable tangle of rusty machinery, everything upside down, steel ladders leading nowhere, gun stations with the roof where the floor should be, a crazy nightmare of defeat and disaster. What still lies in the horrid mystery of the ship? I put this question to a man who had explored its oozy depths.

'Oh, we found a cat o' nine tails in the engine-room,' he said, 'and some toys which the crew had been making before they sank the ship. Here's a souvenir for you. . . .'

He gave me a five-pfennig piece, black with salt water.

'And what will happen to the scrap metal?'

'Cinema girders and things.'

'Ambition's debt is paid.'

'Yes,' said the man doubtfully, 'and ashtrays and all sorts of things.'

So I went away through the rain, chilled by a sight which this age, let us hope, will never see again, the very symbol of defeat in war. On the dockside a Cockney sailor was moodily examining his late opponent.

'Blinkin' awful, ain't it?' he said. 'The end of a perfect day – I *don't* think.'

4

When the benevolence of the late Andrew Carnegie descended on the world in a shower of organs and free libraries the old town of Dunfermline emerged, slightly dazed, from the peace of centuries to grapple with public swimming-baths, libraries, public parks, colleges of hygiene, and generally to learn the responsibility of having given birth to a millionaire with the strong homing instinct of the Scot.

The experience of Dunfermline is unique. There can be no other spot like it in the world. Here is a great and ancient town, the Winchester of Scotland, which played its part as the capital city before Edinburgh emerged from the mists of history. Robert the Bruce lies under a brass in Dunfermline Abbey. All its inspiration was in the past. It sat in the 'Kingdom' of Fife at its spinning-loom, rather like the dear old lady, in the Lyceum drama, whose son is lost in foreign parts.

One day, however, he knocks at the cottage door, often on the eve of an eviction order, and, lo! the desert blossoms and the old lady finds herself smothered in expensive affection. It is one of the prettiest stories in the world. *And this has happened to a whole town!*

In spite of the desolation of Rosyth, with which it has had financial adventures, Dunfermline must be one of the richest towns in the British Isles. It was the inevitable target for Andrew Carnegie. One has only to look at those small eyes, hard as steel, and that tight mouth, which even the beard could not hide, to guess at the remarkable depths of sentimentalism which existed there – outside business hours! I can imagine him tearing a trade union limb from limb, and then going home to design a new crèche for Dunfermline.

Every millionaire is a dual personality. Dunfermline today, teeming with benefactions, and with the town elders planning with a trust fund of £750,000 how to bring 'more of sweetness and light' into the 'monotonous lives of the toiling masses' (these are Carnegie's own words), represents the other side of the millionaire, the good little boy side – the almost pathetic little boy side – so well hidden (in business hours) behind a steel mouth and steel eyes.

The cottage, No. 4, Moodie Street, in which Carnegie was born has naturally participated in the local glory, and has become swollen to the proportions of a museum and memorial hall, only the little upstairs room in which he was born and the adjoining attic having expensively retained their original poverty.

When I went there the place was packed. It is one of the famous sights of Scotland. Thousands go there every year to marvel at the achievement of the man born in the garret above. The sightseers behave as if they are walking – as perhaps they are! – through a fairy tale. The rapidity with which half a million – mated with the other half – breeds seems to hush them. There is, indeed, something awesome about it! The achievements of great wealth – such as that probably untrue story of the late Lord Leverhulme disliking a view in Stornoway and removing a hill – all partake of the fantastic.

Carnegie, in common with all men who have made millions, thought that everybody else could do it if he would only get up early enough and give up smoking, so that the numbers of earnest young Scotsmen examining the rectorial robes of many universities and the pictures of steelworks had come there, I suppose, to get strength.

My first feeling was one of overwhelming sympathy for Carnegie. One room is full of caskets, illuminated addresses and scrolls in monkish script returning thanks for the 'munificent' gift of a free library. There apparently arrives a stage in gratitude when town councils have to decide when a gift ceases to be 'generous' and becomes 'munificent'. Every time a Carnegie library went up in a village the millionaire had to receive one of these expressions of gratitude. The collection is, I imagine, a record. They are things which even a millionaire could not very well sell, and with the exception of the canoes and the wild beasts which a generous Empire gives now and then to the Prince of Wales I can conceive of no more embarrassing possession. Still they remain in Dunfermline in this rather surprised-looking cottage, a monument to the gratitude of the British Isles.

One of the finest things which Carnegie did for his native town was to give Pittencrieff as a public park. In this lovely glen birds are tamer than I have seen them in any town.

Children are encouraged to make pets of them, and of the squirrels which come and shake their tails almost under your feet.

'Ye know the reason why he gave us the glen?' asked a man with whom I was discussing the dollars of Dunfermline. 'Ye see, when the late Mr Carnegie was a wee lad he wasna pairmitted to enter the park. It was a private property. And he never forgot it! When the time came he gave it to Dunfermline so that no wee child should ever feel locked oot of it as he was. . . . Aye, it was a graund thocht. . . .'

And the other side of Dunfermline? An old grey town with hilly streets and a ripe air of experience; grey ruins; Norman arches; an old abbey whose nave has the finest Norman pillars in Scotland.

Under a memorial brass lies the body of Robert the Bruce. In 1818 they opened the tomb and discovered the great patriot wrapped in a shroud interwoven with threads of gold. Those who looked at his body saw that the ribs were sawn through. Thus the old story was proved true that Bruce's heart was taken from his body after death at his own request and borne on a crusade. . . .

Bruce and Andrew Carnegie link up over the misty centuries in the 'auld grey toon' of Dunfermline. One beat the English at Bannockburn; the other beat everybody at Pittsburg, both using the same metal. One the King of Steel; the other the Steel King!

5

I paused on a hill and looked down on the plain of Stirling. It was early evening and the mists were rising. The rock on which the Castle stands was blue-black against the grey of the fields, the mightiest thing in the wide plain, vast as a galleon on a quiet sea, fretting the sky with the line of its ramparts.

It may have been my mood, it may have been the light

that evening, or it may have been something of both, but I went on with the feeling that I was approaching Camelot. Durham is a great city to approach; so is York, whose twin towers beckon you on from Beverley, but Stirling in the evening, with a blown-out storm in the sky and the air drenched with the melancholy of autumn, is like a chapter of Malory. Your heart goes out to it; something of the good manners of an age of swords seems to meet you halfway and lead you on to the grey battlements.

Once in Stirling these expectations are not realized. Where would they be? Stirling has streets like other towns, suburbs, and neat houses, shops of all kinds which prove to you, in spite of all appearances to the contrary, that Stirling does indeed belong very much to the world.

No town with a cinema and motor-omnibuses in its streets has any right to look from a distance so like a weary knight resting on a hill!

Stirling is the twin brother of Edinburgh. I am sure that every writer on Scotland has already called this town the 'sister' of Edinburgh; but I cannot feminize these grizzled old sinners who sit up on their hills like robber barons with swords across their knees. The family resemblance is, however, absurd. Stirling has not grown so great in the world as his brother. Events have not shaped him in the same way. In one thing, however, they are equal: in battle, in the friendship of kings and queens, in experience, and in the rich memories of the past.

Edinburgh is like an old soldier who has entered public life; Stirling is like an old soldier living in a house full of the trophies of his youth, fingering a sword, shaking his head over a battle-axe, sighing mysteriously over a glove, and, though acutely conscious of the present (the railway sees to that!), liable at any moment to withdraw himself into more exciting reverie.

The twin rocks on which the twin castles of Edinburgh and Stirling rise spring from the plain at the same angle. When you see Stirling for the first time, especially in the evening, you feel that you are seeing a vision of Edinburgh as he was in his youth.

And the rock of Stirling, when you stand and look up at it from the flat lands where tournaments were held, or from those meadows still scarred with the ghosts of ancient gardens, is even grander than that of Edinburgh. There must be moments throughout the year, in early morning perhaps, when Scotland can show no prouder sight than Stirling rising from the plain. The view from the ramparts of Stirling Castle can hold its own with any view in this world. A man who travels much sees hundreds of views which impress him, but few which he can never forget. The incredible panorama of Scotland which lies below Stirling Castle is unforgettable.

I stood there on one of those sunny afternoons which bring summer back to autumn, and I watched the Forth making its silver loops through the green plain, twisting and turning, bending back on its course, as if reluctant to leave so fair a land and lose its identity in the sea. So fantastic are the windings of the Links of Forth that six miles by land are twenty by water! I believe it is a fact that the Forth in this part of Scotland is the only navigable river in Europe on which a sailing ship would in the space of a few miles require wind from every point of the compass. The smoothness of the Carse of Stirling is as lovely as the Vale of Avalon from Glastonbury Tor.

The Wallace Monument lifts its head from trees; away to the north-east, across Ballangeich, rise the Ochils; under the soft red and yellow of autumn woods hides the Bridge of Allan and the road that runs to Sheriffmuir. But look to the edge of the distant horizon! Etched in pale blue – the lovely blue of distance – lying piled against the sky almost like clouds, are the mighty Grampians, whose very name is a gallop of wild horses.

And you look at them and recite their titles – Ben Lomond, Ben Venue, Ben Ledi, Ben Vorlich – remote giants guarding the Highlands of Scotland, unmatchable, unconquerable.

I do not know where the Highlands officially begin, but I feel on Stirling ramparts that I am looking towards a frontier; a new country seems to lie beyond the horizon. There is something definite about it; and Stirling stands like an outpost in the plain watching the far hills: the eye of the Scottish Lowlands.

'D'ye ken the seven battlefields?' said a voice.

I turned to meet the humorous eyes of a little guide with a strong general resemblance to Sir Harry Lauder. He pointed out the seven sites with a stick, including that of Bannockburn. He described the actions with that singular air of imparting a rare confidence which is one of the Scotsman's most amusing narrative tricks, and, brushing aside my assurance that I was imbibing knowledge by myself with, 'Hae ye seen the room where James murdered the Douglas? No? Och, ye've no' seen a thing!' took charge of me with the grim determination to educate me.

We had a successful tour, descending into dungeons, tramping up stairs and down, coming at length to the palace with its grotesque symbolic figures in stone sculptured by a Frenchman. He confided in me, after glancing round, presumably to see that no women were present, which figure was Love and which was Lust. Presbyterian winds and rains since the Reformation have done their best to obliterate them, but have succeeded only in rather tactlessly confusing them.

As he sits on Stirling ramparts, a man, if reckless, may permit his imagination a little rein. . . .

The year is 1566.

There are several remarkable children in England. Walter Raleigh is a lad of fourteen, Philip Sydney is twelve, and Francis Bacon, now five, is self-propelled. In Stratford-on-Avon, in the green heart of England, where the drums of the morris dancers go thudding over Clopton Bridge in May-time, Mrs John Shakespeare, whose maiden name was – so beautifully – Arden, feels with her first finger one of the miracles of the world: the teeth of her infant, Will. He is two.

In the adult world Her Majesty the Queen, aged thirty-three, has light-heartedly placed her virginity at the service, but not at the disposal, of English foreign policy; which is a policy of neutrality exalted to the realms of genius. She may be heard, playing – such exquisite humour – the virginals to princely, puzzled, but still strangely hopeful suitors from Catholic States. Over Europe shakes and rumbles the important thunder of Protestantism. Stolid but hostile crowds surge round Spanish altars in Holland, and the Duke of Alva, buckling on his armour, parades an expeditionary force. The storm sways out over the Atlantic. English Protestants are whipped naked through the hot streets of Mexico. Many a Spanish galleon, cruising round the coasts of El Dorado, is urged onward through the seas by men who forget their bleeding hands as they remember Bideford in Devon or the smell of Bristol docks. And, without warning, John Hawkins, who has no idea how important he is to be, appears in improbable creeks and bays of the New World with a cargo of negro slaves under the hatches of a ship called, without the slightest irony, the *Jesus*.

White towns, standing among palm-trees with their feet at the edge of the sea, smoke gently, sending up black clouds into the clear air. Flies buzz above untidy figures that sprawl huddled in the white glare of a deserted *plaza*. On the skyline rolls an English galleon homeward bound with silver candlesticks strapped to her masthead; and the captain pledges his second in command in Spanish wine quaffed from a silver chalice. Spain replies with an extra turn to the rack and another twist to the thumb-screw; and more faggots. In France the Huguenots are fattening innocently for the eve of a not too distant saint's day. The crews who will man the Great Armada have already been born in Spain. The Pope looks out westward from Rome towards the revolt of Christendom, ready to launch a Bull, which falls on the new world like a damp squib, and ever ready to give audience to dusty envoys who post to the Vatican from the lands of Antichrist. In this busy and virile year Suileman the Magnificent, Caliph of all Islam, dies, quite young, and with no knowledge of Lepanto, after a triumphant life, during which it was unpleasant for Catholic or Protestant to spend a holiday in Algiers.

It is the December of this exciting year. Forty gentlemen of England, with the Earl of Bedford at their head, ride towards Scotland through the rain and mud bearing, at great personal inconvenience, a gold font that weighs two stones. They are riding to the christening at Stirling of Prince James, the six months old son of Mary, Queen of Scots. It is really a most amusing situation. They have plenty of time to dwell on it as they plough north with muddy girths, clattering like a cavalry squadron through sleepy towns and over wild moor and wilder hill. Beford smiles to himself as he remembers the message he bears from Elizabeth to her 'dear cousin'. He is to tell her gracious majesty of Scotland that the gold font 'had been the right size when it was made, but if too small by this time it would do for the next occasion'. What a dry humour. (She had cried out when the news of the birth came to her: 'The Queen of Scots is mother of a fair son, but I am but a barren stock!' A strange lament for a virgin queen! However . . .) In the same breath in which she gave Bedford her message she instructed him and his suite to pay no honour to the fool Darnley. He must be addressed by the English as 'Henry Stuart', not as 'your majesty'.

The horsemen cross the Border. It is rather like going back to the opening indecision of the Reformation. Here Catholics are, it appears, still tolerated. Although Presbyterianism has embarked on its long series of covenants with the Deity, people can still attend Mass in comparative safety.

The gentlemen of England cannot know that beneath the thin crust of indecision Scotland's mind is made up, or rather has been made up for her by a man remarkably like Moses, who, having made a middle class, is determined to lead it to a Promised Land that flows with the Swiss milk of Calvinism. It is strange to the English, who have left a country where the Crown represents the English nation, to find themselves in a country where the Crown represents France and Rome. It is not quite comfortable. So, after lodging the night in Edinburgh at Kirk o' Field – now but two months from its immortality – they set out on the following day for the Castle of Stirling bearing with them the Protestant font for the Catholic christening. (By my faith – I mean, by my halidom! – a most amusing mission, all things considered!)

Stirling is full of foreign fashions and loud with the tongues of France and Italy. Europe has gathered round the cradle. Ambassadors from France, Savoy, and Piedmont have conveyed the congratulations of their several courts. Cardinal Laurea, the Papal Nuncio, dispatched by the Vatican in a moment that lacked local advice, has been tactfully intercepted at Paris, where his Eminence is probably only too happy to remain. Every house in Stirling lodges members of the courtly suites. Foreign swords lean against homely Scottish firesides; barns are full of foreign horses. Crowds follow each extravagant cavalcade as it breaks into a walk up the steep path to the Castle, and, above, December clouds, blowing inland from the sea, sweep on over the Carse of Stirling in chill mist.

In the Palace of Stirling, before the eyes of Europe – or, anyhow, the only eyes in Europe that matter – Bedford, with the gentlemen of England at his back, delivers the jocular message from his mistress to the Queen of Scots. He sees a woman of twenty-four who has been playing hide and seek with happiness since she was eighteen. The game is becoming rather unfair. She is not the merry widow of report. Unusually thick eyelids give to her face a deliberate, considering expression, as if she is trying to think of something solemn in order to refrain from unseemly laughter. Deep, deep eyes. Her ears are larger than most women's, but she does not mind. She draws back her hair from them and hangs a pearl in each. Her upper lip is full, a gay and tender lip, even a naughty and provoking lip, but the lower is compressed and firm – a contradictory lip. Her beauty is of strength, not of weakness. Courage and gentleness are written not only in her deliberate eyes but also in her high, smooth forehead, in her high cheekbones, in the generous space between her eyes and her ears. As she gives to Bedford a smile from those clever eyes of hers under arched, thin brows, shrugging her sloping shoulders in a French way, not an Englisman sees her but wonders how on earth the loon Darnley won her. She is brilliant and made for brilliance. She is happy too! See how she smiles! Stirling is a palace of smiles! The French Ambassador, however, watches her with more knowledge than most. He found her in private weeping as if her heart would break.

Somewhere in Stirling Castle the unspeakable Darnley is sulking. He will take no part in the triumph. His suit of cloth of gold has been delayed by the tailor. (Bothwell's blue suit, however, has arrived!) Darnley knows that Bedford and his men have had orders to humiliate him. He glooms alone, playing with the idea of running away and becoming a pirate; but that, in this year 1566, is one of the overcrowded professions. The man who, filled with terror on the road to Dunbar after Riccio's murder, whipped up the horse on which his wife, six months with child, was riding, crying, 'Come on, in God's name, if that one dies we can have others!' would have made a great pirate! And, as he sits alone, his son's christening comes to him in odd snatches of sound: a fanfare of trumpets, the clamour of distant voices, and the tread of feet. Does he walk to the window – to read his fate, perhaps, in the blown mist that eddies downward to the plain – he sees nothing but the greyness blowing softly past, the edge of a cloud in which the wind now tears a hole, framing for one instant an acre of distant woodland or a link of the Forth like a silver worm in the grass. Even as he frets the smallpox is almost on him; and in Edinburgh in some dark cellar is already a barrel of gunpowder.

And now to this bleak rock in Scotland comes a thin, unfamiliar echo of the Tuileries. It is rather pitiful. But who among the rough, watchful men can see the pathos of it; can see in the wilful extravagance of it how a woman's mind is groping backward into a happier world? She is doing honour to the darling of her heart, the child from under her heart; the heir to the crowns of England and Scotland: her son. And she is doing it in her usual pretty French accent. Festivities and elegancies trip their way over the chill face of Stirling rock. Wanderers at night gazing up see the Castle, lit at every window, burning against the stars. Clansmen on the edge of the Highlands, looking down from their mountains on clear nights, see Old Stirling all ablaze and remember almost forgotten things. And night after night the people of Stirling listen to the foreign noises – the hautboys, the jigging of fiddles, and the high squealing of flutes. On the seventeenth the prince is baptized.

The barons of Scotland in two files form a lane from the door of his nursery to the door of the Chapel Royal, each one holding a pricket of wax. There is a chanting of Latin. In the open doorway of the chapel stands the Archbishop of St Andrews, mitred and holding his great gold crozier, behind him a hedge of pastoral staves and a gleam of gold crucifixes. The censers swing in and out, puffing thin spurts of incense into the cold air. There is a rich gleam of vestments beyond the dark arch: their lordships of Dunkeld, Ross, and Dunblane; and among them the shaven head of the Prior of Whithorn. So they wait.

Slowly between the line of baronial prickets moves Mary's last royal pageant. His Excellency the French Ambassador, De Croc, bears the infant prince. With him is the Countess of Argyll, who represents the Queen of England. There is the Earl of Athol. The Earl of Eglinton bears the salt vat. Lord Ross bears the basin and the laver. Of twelve Scottish earls in Stirling this day only two – Athol and Eglinton – will enter a Catholic church for their Queen. Only three barons of all the chivalry of Scotland have the resolution to stand in the church with their Prince.

The Archbishop and the Bishops meet them at the door and go before them to the altar.

Round the open door Murray, Bothwell, and other staunch Protestants watch, but do not realize that they are watching the last meeting in Scotland between Crown and Mitre. The Earl of Bedford, at the door, also, like a good Englishman, sees, not realizing that he is seeing, the baptism of England's first Stuart king. John Knox is there too, watching and waiting, bleak and indignant in the incense.

They consecrate the child in the Catholic Faith and give him the names of Charles James, taking him to the gold font, which is indeed too small for him. But they baptize him in this Protestant font; thus James VI and I takes his first prophetic taste of England.

Someone is crying. (There are sufficient secret tears in Stirling this week to baptize a hundred princes.) Someone has noticed against the gates of the Castle a poor man begging for alms and holding on his knee a monstrosity – a child with a gigantic head. The idiot thing falls from side to side; and the man peers through the gate towards the christening of the prince. That is why someone is crying. It is, perhaps, an evil omen. John Knox sees it too; but he does not cry. He makes a mental note of it. . . .

The forty gentlemen of England, with the Earl of Bedford at their head, ride down the slope of Stirling on the road to Edinburgh and home. They have heard and seen much. Their mistress will be entertained. Bedford has a chain of diamonds which the Queen of Scots gave to him. So they ride, taking it easily, talking of their stay in Stirling, remembering little elegancies: the way she dropped her heavy lids, the way she worked at being merry, the whiteness of her throat, the firm beauty of her bust, the soft voice she has, the quick parrying wit of hers, the yellow-auburn hair with darker shadows that makes pearls look almost warm. And what a pity that the cub Darnley should have gone to earth. . . .

The thing, however, on which they dwell most as they jingle away through Border bogland is the villainous affront of the French knave Bastien. Only the Queen's presence saved him from an English dagger. It happened at the masque which Master George Buchanan had written in order to liven up one of the banquets. The stage-manager was this French hog, Bastien. As the great doors of the banqueting hall were flung wide a table loaded with food ran into the hall of its own accord. Everyone laughed to see the ingenious trick. And, as the table came, there ran, surrounding it, nymphs with flying hair and other maskers furred and painted to resemble satyrs. These had cloven feet and long, shaggy tails. They danced grotesquely round the table to the great amusement of the Queen and all her guests. But – incredible to remember – when these satyrs passed the English courtiers they lifted their tails and wagged them! The forty gentlemen of England, with the Earl of Bedford at their head, boil with uncontrollable rage at the memory. But for the Queen, and Bedford, there would have been bloodshed in Stirling.

These gentlemen of England could not foresee a time when a man of a later age would come across this incident in a history-book and wonder what all the fuss was about. Why should such a stupid gesture bring out the most sensitive dagger? Oh, men of England! in the Castle of Stirling in the year 1566 was expressed in dumb show the most deadly insult the medieval world could fling at the nation. The Catholic Middle Ages believed that Englishmen are born with tails! The legend began with a story that the men of Dorset, at the instigation of their friend Satan, attacked St Augustine and his holy monks and drove them away with the tails of skate, or ray-fish, attached to their gowns. The Divine vengeance decreed that ever after the English should bear tails. This is the legend that runs through the Latin and French chronicles of the early Middle Ages. The synonym for an Englishman all over Europe was *tailard*. If you wanted to see an English dagger you said that word. It was enough! So sensitive to this insult was the Englishman of that time that he could hardly have watched a cow flicking flies away with its tail and not felt the blood rush to his head. And on Stirling rock tails were actually wagged, taken up in French hands and positively wagged, under the very noses of forty gentlemen of England!

They ride southward, those forty horsemen, through wintry days. They arrive home in England. Shakespeare is still two. Bacon still five. A young man called Francis Drake is about to go to sea with Hawkins. Blindly, fatefully, the right men fall into their places so naturally beside Elizabeth. And on a lonely rock overlooking the Carse of Stirling another Queen is deserted of all but the wrong men. She looks out beyond the windows into mists torn by the fingers of the wind into queer rents like wounds. The old pain in her side grows worse. The thin echo of the Tuileries is quite lost in the mocking silence of the hard Scotch rock. The mist draws queer, horrible shapes in the air. She turns from the window. The Queen is alone. The Queen is weeping.

CHAPTER FOUR

Tells how I go on through rain to Lochleven, where there are more memories of a Queen, how I find St Andrews playing golf in its sleep, how I cross the Tay to Dundee and go on to Perth, where I meet a Calvinistic packman drinking rum and beer

I

NEAR Stirling on the slopes of the Ochil Hills is a place called Dollar. It is amusing to discover it side by side with Stirling, and also within a few miles of the authentic dollars of Dunfermline! Scotsmen, who are reputed to like indiscriminately sterling or dollars, must find their hearts warm in such a district. Above the village, against a steep hill and near a gorge, is a glen; and in the glen is a ruin which was once a castle belonging to the Argyll family. I was told in Dollar that in ancient times the castle was called Castle Gloom, beside the waters of Griff, or Grief, in the Glen of Care, in the village of Dollar, or Dolour, surely the most miserable address on earth! It sounds like Bunyan.

It was a wet day. The clouds hung so low over the hills that it seemed possible to stand on a chair and touch them with a stick. The thin rain came slanting down in successive windy sheets, wild gusts flung themselves round corners and appeared to be cast upward into the air again by the violence of the wind. The whole countryside seemed prostrate in grief. There are days like this in Scotland when earth and sky abandon themselves to sorrow. Against the background of a weeping earth and a tearful sky the cheerful good nature of the people is flung in brilliant relief. Fires never look brighter in inn parlours, never comes with more seductive softness that voice asking:

'Will ye take an egg to your tea?'

I like this phrase. Not will you have an egg? or do you

want an egg? or would you like an egg? or can you eat an egg? but – 'Will you take an egg to your tea?' There is something old and courtly about it. I always feel as though I should go into the kitchen and offer my arm to the egg.

Another phrase: 'A knock *came* to the door.' Never there was a knock at the door or on the door. English knocks just knock, but Scottish knocks arrive. They are so much more dramatic. You visualize that knock afar off, a thing that is not yet a knock but is already fraught with all the ominousness of a knock, approaching with the inevitability of a Greek tragedy until it stops outside in an almost terrifying pause before it delivers itself on the door. There must be a shivering moment in all Scottish fairy tales:

'An' then – are ye listenin'? – an' then – a knock *came* to the door, AND . . .'

2

In the fading light of late afternoon I came to a loch, silver-white under a grey sky. It was whipped into waves at the edges and pricked all over with falling rain. A man, standing in a little boat and wearing a glassy oilskin, cast a methodical fly on the water, whipping the loch neatly down the wind. Against the sheet of quicksilver I could see the minute black dots of his cast riding the ripples. It was a perfect day for him: rain and wind and cloud.

Out in the loch was a dreary island, just a cluster of dripping trees with a slow mist wandering through them like an old witch gathering poison berries. I took a boat and put off for the island. The trees grouped themselves as if to hide some secret, and in the island I saw what they try to hide – the shell of Lochleven Castle.

There is a square peel tower, a courtyard, a wall, the scars of vanished buildings, green moss, shrubs, and a hedge of trees against which the dark, oily waters turn themselves gently with soft, lake sounds. It is right to go straight from Stirling to Lochleven, because that is what Mary, Queen of

Scots, did herself. This is one of many places in Scotland seen best on a wet day. . . .

We left the Queen of Scots looking through a mist down to the Carse o' Stirling, Prince Jamie in his cradle, Darnley in the sulks, and Bothwell in a grand blue suit. That was six months ago. (What a lot can happen to a woman in six months!) It is now June 1567. Two months previously the explosion to Kirk o' Field, which awakened Edinburgh, startled courts as far away as Rome. In the flash of the gunpowder, England, France, and the Holy See received a pin-sharp picture of Scotland which shook even the hardened nerves of the sixteenth century. The Queen's consort murdered. The Queen implicated. The Earl of Bothwell more than implicated. Talk of love between them. No one minded murder in the sixteenth century; it was a good old Scottish custom, and elsewhere it was recognized a political expedient: one cheap assassination saved many an expensive war if plans were laid well and truly. No one regretted the end of the miserable Darnley, a poor, drunken coward; but what stirred the conscience of the age was the news that the Queen of Scotland was ready to bring her husband's murderer not to the gallows but to bed. Even Elizabeth, who was not Mary's best friend, became human and wrote to her 'dear cousin' the kind of letters that one woman writes to another in a moment of unguarded sincerity, imploring her to see justice done. But no: Mary, Queen of Scots, was fated to drink the cup of sorrow to the very dregs.

Has any woman lived more violently, yet more mysteriously, for we shall never really understand her heart, than Mary for the six months before Carberry Hill? We see her in situations which link Holyrood to Hollywood. There is the amazing evening in Edinburgh when, surrounded by armed men, the lords of Scotland sign Bothwell's document naming himself the Queen's suitor. There is the amazing hold-up outside Edinburgh, a flash of steel caps and swords but no fighting, and Bothwell riding off to his Castle of Dunbar with the Queen. What can we make of it? Was she his victim or did she fly to his brutality as to a stronghold? There is the silent ten-day honeymoon in the castle beside the North Sea. There is the amazing marriage on a summer morning in the Council Hall of Holyrood; then, for the first time in the history of Mary's misfortunes, is heard a new note: the angry murmur of common people couched in the blunt vernacular. As if the drama had not been exhausted, we see Mary in flight, riding through the night to her strong man disguised as a boy! They lock themselves up in Dunbar and prepare to face the storm together. She has no clothes with her but the doublet and hose of a page. They borrow garments, and in these she rides out with Bothwell to meet her nobles at Carberry Hill, a queen in the gown of a burgher's wife. There is no battle. Bothwell offers to fight any man of equal rank in the opposing army. Events hang fire.

Mary will not hear of Bothwell's combat. Why? Surely because she loved him? She learns that the nobles will make no terms for his safety. They are resolved on his death. All her heart is set on securing his escape. 'Whereon,' as an eyewitness has written, 'she caused the duke to depart with great pain and anguish, and with many long kisses they took farewell, and at last he asked her if she would keep the faith she had given him and she answered that she would. Thereupon she gave him her hand and he with a small company galloped off to Dunbar.'

She had the heart of a lion. From five in the morning until eight at night she had sat foodless and in the heat of a June sun whipped by terrible emotions – and who knows what secret foreknowledge of disaster? Yet when the lords came to escort her into Edinburgh she taunted them and threatened them. One thing only touched her to tears. She was riding behind a fence of lances with a banner waving above showing Darnley's body lying cold under a tree. Above the dust and the clatter of the cavalcade she heard the coarse cry of a man-at-arms: 'Burn the whore!' And then Kirkaldy of Grange spurred his horse into the ranks and brought silence with the flat of his sword. But she had heard the voice of her people.

There is a terrible glimpse of her at a window in the provost's house, her hair about her shoulders, crying and appealing to the crowds to save her. She would not eat, she could not sleep, and there was no woman with her. Next day a company of hackbuteers clatter down to Holyrood, and she, in the midst of them, thinks that she is to be queen again. Late that night they warn her that she must ride out on a journey. In the dawn, half dead with fatigue, she is brought to the lakeside at Lochleven, where a gloomy island rises in the mists of morning. Mary's long captivity has begun.

There are three scenes in Mary's life known to everyone: Riccio's murder, the execution at Fotheringay, and the escape from Lochleven.

This old ruin in the lake is the scene of that adventure which, of all her adventures, is most like the romances she loved to read in French. Her humiliation is complete as the captive of the Douglases and under the surveillance of old Lady Douglas, once her father's mistress. Fears crowd round her waking and sleeping. There is the thought that she bears Bothwell's child. There is the ghastly fear of burning. An old Highland woman with the second sight had prophesied that she should have five husbands and be burned alive during the lifetime of the fifth. This fear never leaves her. Added to this is ignorance of the world beyond her prison. One day she hears cannon and sees bonfires. The Laird of Lochleven enters and asks if she will not make merry because her child James has been crowned King of Scots.

Her magnificent courage revives in time. Ink and paper are forbidden, but she manages to get messages out of Lochleven written on pocket-handkerchiefs in water and soot from the chimney. The time comes when bands of mysterious horsemen ride along the banks of the loch; and at this time young Willie Douglas, a lad of sixteen, writes his name in the pages of romance. He was a dependent of the laird. Who knows what pure, wild fires were lit in him by the eyes of Mary? On the night of May 2nd, 1568, Willie Douglas manages to secure the keys of the Castle. Mary receives a pearl ear-ring as a sign that all is ready. The evening is alive with her adventure. Old Lady Douglas, looking through a window, sees a party of horsemen in Kinross. She is bent on sending a messenger to the mainland to discover their business. Mary hears her with beating heart and traps her from her resolve into an argument about the Earl of Moray. Later, the laird, looking through the window, sees Willie Douglas tampering with the boat chains. The boy is making it impossible for any of the boats to be launched in pursuit! The laird asks him what he is doing and calls him a fool. Once again Mary's heart beats fast, and, feigning an attack of faintness, she draws the laird from the window. So the appalling suspense wears on.

It is after supper. The courtyard is full of servants. Mary, wearing the kirtle and cloak of a peasant woman, crosses boldly, passes through the door, which Willie Douglas locks after her, and enters the boat. She flings herself under the steerman's seat. Douglas pushes off from the island and begins to row to the mainland. When the boat is in the middle of the loch the Queen can lie still no longer and seizing an oar she helps her rescuer to speed towards the little band of horsemen on shore. Willie flings the Castle keys into the loch, and no sooner has the boat touched land than Mary, Queen of Scots, leaps ashore with tears of joy falling down her cheeks, free at last after eleven months in prison! Among the waiting horses is one with a side-saddle. In a few moments the cavalcade is mounted, but Mary refuses to move until she has seen Willie Douglas in the saddle. That night they cross the Firth of Forth. . . .

Eleven days later Mary sees her forces routed at

Langside. Once more the smell of burning faggots surrounds her. She flies in panic. She rides for sixty miles. Across the Solway she sees England. A small fishing-smack takes her towards nineteen years of sorrow.

3

Never shall I forget my first night in St Andrews. A dangerous small boy was swinging a new driver at an invisible ball on the hotel mat. Three men, leaning on the visitors' book, were arguing about a certain mashie. A girl in the lounge was shrilly defending her conduct on the home green. At the next table to me in the dining-room sat a man in plus fours who cheered his solitude by practising approach shots with his soup-spoon. When the spoon, fresh from a bunker of oxtail, was no longer playable, he did a little gentle putting with a bread pill and a fork.

I sat there thinking of Newmarket. Both these towns are lost to the world in a magnificent obsession. All Newmarket runs to the windows at the click of bloodstock on the road; all Newmarket lives with prints of Diomed winning the Derby in 1780; as far as Newmarket is concerned Shakespeare and Dante lived in vain; but let any man challenge Mr Ruff or appear to scorn Nat Gould!

To a St Andrews' man the sight of the stars at night is a hint that the time has come to uproot daisies from a green. When he sees a shooting star I am sure he cries, 'What a drive!'

In Newmarket and in its golfing parallel a man feels as he felt the first time he stayed in a monastery. He is back in the age of faith! His load of worldly knowledge lies heavy on his shoulders, and all he can do is helplessly to watch other people performing their offices. There is something almost religious in this single-mindedness. After a life spent in planting tea in Ceylon or commanding cavalry in India, how sweet to take an enlarged liver to a mental monastery where faith burns with an almost savage heat, and each day brings a new point to argue.

There has been nothing quite like Newmarket and St Andrews since the Dissolution!

The town is a delight; an old grey town of ancient houses and monastic ruins; full of men in plus fours and women with golf bags on their tweed shoulders; of undergraduates in splendid scarlet gowns; of happy meetings in cakeshops; of wayside gossip; of fine windows full of silk nightdresses, Fair Isle jumpers, brogues, golf clubs, golf bags, and, strange to say, one or two bookshops, presumably for the use of the Oxford of Scotland.

All the time the North Sea unwraps itself restlessly on the curve of the lovely bay, beyond which lies that sacred strand, the golf links, backed by the stern bulk of the M.C.C. of golf – the 'Royal and Ancient'.

In the early morning St Andrews, having dreamt of getting over the burn in two, awakens to thoughts of golf. Men go to factories behind small shops and turn out clubs destined to react to various handicaps all over the world; but specially in America. St Andrews affects the American golfer much as Stratford-on-Avon affects the American college girl. It also attracts many a reckless 'birthplace fan' who has never in his life swung a club. Such men – a well-known type – go quickly round the world collecting useless experiences, apparently as an aid to after-dinner conversation. They arrive breathless in St Andrews, but smiling all over their faces.

'Guess I cain't go home,' they declare winningly, 'without saying I've hit a ball over this course of yours! Now, see here, can a guy hire a club in this town for half an hour? Gee, that's fine! Say, now – what kinder club do I want?'

I would much like to see this sacrilege in progress. One of the most Batemanesque sights of the year must be that of St Andrews weakly ministering to the ambition of such phenomena.

I was invited to the 'Royal and Ancient'. Its atmosphere

is as solemn and masculine as that of the M.C.C. Its air of supreme authority is equalled only by the Jockey Club – and the Law Courts in the Strand!

There is a 'silence' room. (I suppose no club is in greater need of this retreat.) In this room an enormous safe is let into the wall. Inside, in an illuminated glass case which suggests the Crown Jewels in the Tower, lies the Regalia of Golf.

Foremost among the treasures is the silver club given in 1754, by certain 'noblemen and gentlemen being admirers of the ancient and healthful exercise of the Golf', who each contributed five shillings to the first St Andrews' trophy. Then comes the gold medal given in 1837 by William IV, who endowed the club with the title of 'Royal and Ancient'. Golf is spelt on this medal 'golph', the error, presumably, of some uncivilized London goldsmith!

Members may be observed gazing reverently at the Crown Jewels of Golf, tiptoeing up in silence and sighing a little. There is also a museum containing clubs of antique shape and golf balls made of leather stuffed with feathers.

The windows of the club provide an unsurpassed view of players setting out over the Old Course – how critically we watch them take their first drive – and of the fine, green sweep of the links, bounded by sand-dunes and the white horses of St Andrews Bay.

This 'setting out' is among the most solemn events of the day. The caddies sit cynically in, and around, a glass pavilion in which the result of the daily ballot is set up for all men to see at what time 'the B. of London' – for such is Dr Ingram at St Andrews – will go forth with 'Wilkins', who may be a lord or only major.

The balloted sit waiting in the club telling one another stories about the 'Elysian Fields', smoking, watching, waiting until the time comes for them to rise like men called on to prove themselves. Then as they go out there is a stir among the corralled caddies, a whisper of interest among spectators who hang round the links all day, then soft turf under their feet and the tee under the ball.

But I am told the best golf at St Andrews is often played by the ratepayers, who are the hereditary owners of the links. They have been practising their strokes since the sixteenth century. Every ratepayer in St Andrews has the freedom of the links, and at certain times in the day and year the chimney-sweep takes precedence over the most urgent visiting millionaire. Golf at St Andrews is a sport in its most democratic form. The famous links faithfully reproduce the spirit of a game whose first championship match was played by a king and a tradesman in partnership against two nobles.

I am sure that the man who snored in the next bedroom was the man in plus fours who played golf with his soup-spoon. His snore sounded exactly like: 'Fore!'

4

I bought a book called *St Andrews Ghost Stories*, published locally and written by Mr W. T. Linskill, Dean of Guild. I read it in bed by the friendly light of an electric table lamp.

I had no idea that St Andrews was so fearful a spot. There is a phantom coach which runs locally on certain nights. The horses make a queer ticking sound on the road, and no one has ever seen the face of the shrouded figure of the driver. There is 'The Screaming Skull of Greyfriars', 'The Smothered Piper of the West Cliffs', 'The Beautiful White Lady of the Haunted Tower', and many another perfect bedside story.

What interested me as much as the ghosts was the rich aroma between the lines. The author's convivial cheerfulness, like that of the would-be philosopher, insisted on 'breaking through' the gloom.

The real ghosts in these stories, to me at least, were undergraduate days in Cambridge, days in London when peers were interested in the Gaiety chorus, and days in those Continental spas frequented by Edward VII. This is a typical opening to one of Mr Linskill's blood-curdlers:

'We were sitting over a cosy fire after dinner. It was snowing hard outside, and very cold. Our pipes were alight, and our grog on the table, when Allan Beauchamp suddenly remarked:

' "It's a deuced curious thing for a man to be always followed about the place by a confounded grinning skull."

' "Eh! What?" I said. "Who the deuce is being followed about by a skull? It's rubbish, and quite impossible." '

I like the word 'grog'.

In one story he mentions a 'cheery golfing Johnny'; in another a military friend of the author says, 'Zounds, sir,' in a moment of emotion.

This author, I thought, is no anaemic, psychic investigator. There is nothing clammy about him. In the morning a St Andrews man said:

'You don't know old Linskill? Go and meet him at once. He founded the Cambridge University Golf Club. He is seventy-four and looks fifty. He knows more about St Andrews than the rest of us put together. . . .'

I found the ghost-hunter looking remarkably like a possibly violent retired major-general. My first feeling was one of pity for the ghost who attempts to haunt him. An enormous voice, a baggy suit of plus fours, a pipe, a drooping grey moustache, a pair of eyes which have not altered since he was thirty. Here were seventy-four years carried with the gallantry of fifty. He looked as though his life had agreed with him like a good dinner. He talked exactly like the 'military friends' in his ghost stories:

'Well, sir, and what the deuce can I do for you?'

'I hoped that you might talk, sir.'

'Be seated, sir. Cigar? Well – smoke what the deuce you like!'

Meeting Mr Linskill is rather like exchanging salutes before coming on guard in a fencing school.

'Yes; I took golf to Cambridge when I was an undergraduate. Founded the Cambridge University Golf Club. Initiated the inter-'Varsity match! Played in two of 'em! Dashed long time ago! Deuced difficult game to start in Cambridge; in fact, the most deuced difficult thing I ever did in my life! When undergraduates appeared in public carrying golf clubs the whole town turned out to laugh. It took some pluck to play golf in those days. *However . . .*'

Mr Linskill has a trick of clearing his voice and booming the word 'however', which has the effect of a wet rag wiped over a blackboard, clearing it for the next topic.

'Golf today,' he said, 'is a ladies' game compared with the golf I remember at St Andrews half a century ago. I remember playing with hand-hammered gutta-percha balls. Damned annoying things when they broke! The rule in those days was that you put the new ball on the place where the largest fragment of the old one fell!

'I was taught by "Young Tom" Morris. By gad, sir, in those days the daisies were so thick at St Andrews that we never played a white ball! I remember how the caddie used to say: "Red or yellow ball, sir!" And, by Jove – the moonlight games! How dashed well I remember playing when the moon was full, with 'fore caddies to tell us where the ball had gone, and a fellow following behind with a wheelbarrow full of refreshments! Those were the days, my boy! *However . . .*'

Mr Linskill has one of the best memories I have ever encountered. He has spent seventy-four years in perfecting the art of narrative. One of his most dramatic stories is how on the whim of the moment he got out of a train on a wild Sunday night in 1879. That train was the one blown from the Tay Bridge. Every passenger in it was drowned like a rat in a trap:

'I was coming up from Edinburgh with a friend. We were going to Dundee. But just as the train was leaving St

Andrews on that awful journey we got out. . . . By Jove, that night! The wind! The dashed chimney-pots were playing in the streets like children! *However . . .*'

Mr Linskill tapped his pipe on the hearth, sighed vigorously, and, looking steadily at me, or through me, said:

'Jove! Kate Vaughan was a good-looking girl! And dear Nellie Farren. Just names to you young men, eh? Perhaps not that! But, by gad, they were fine girls!'

And he talked so vividly of London fifty years ago that I could smell the powder of green-rooms and hear the pop of champagne corks, and the clippity-clop of cab horses in the Strand. He remembers the last dying breath of the Georgian Age – for such it was as recently as 1878 – when men still rode on horseback to business and footmen in plush breeches opened every other door west of Temple Bar.

'Tell me about your ghosts!'

'I've never seen one. Tried deuced hard all my life. Not a hope! I spent a night in the Haunted Tower when I was a young man – with a bottle of whisky. Even then I couldn't see anything! I've sat with various mediums, including the famous Home. Nothing doing! Once I attended a séance, and was put in an armchair as an "unbeliever". A strange thing happened. They were all sitting round a table. Suddenly every one slowly looked up to the roof! They all took their hands off the table! It was funny to see them all lying back staring up at the roof. Then, very slowly, they lowered their heads and put their fingers on the table. "Did you see that?" they said to me. "Did you see the table float up to the ceiling, remain there a second, and float down as lightly as a feather?" "I was watching the table the whole time," I replied, "and it never moved an inch from its place!" Now, if that was not hypnotism, what was it? Indian rope trick over again, eh?'

He told me the extraordinary story of Brother Plater, a monk who murdered the Prior of Montrose. He haunted a local billiard-marker. The ghost became on most friendly terms with the billiard-marker, standing beside him in the saloon and chatting away to him during the course of his duties. Eventually he asked the billiard-marker to dig in a certain spot and give his bones Christian burial. The bones were found. The late Marquis of Bute became interested in his ghost. Quite a number of people became interested.

'I told them they must be mad,' said Mr Linskill. 'However ... they wrapped Plater's bones in the robe of an Augustinian friar, and buried them as the ghost directed. The billiard-marker went to Australia to get away from the ghost. . . .'

A clock struck twelve. Unwillingly I prepared to go.

'Let me tell you about the Bewitched Ermentrude. . . .'

He did. Then I said goodbye and walked through moonlit St Andrews to my hotel. Mr Linskill is a great possession for any town, and a still greater one for any publisher who could get a book out of him. Seventy-four years have never sat more lightly on a man, and, in spite of his youthfulness, he is refreshingly of an older and a happier age: the age of squires and 'Johnnies', horses and fine manners, and men who really did, when worked up, say 'Zounds, sir!'

5

Halfway between St Andrews and Newport the motorist who knows a Norman church when he sees one jams on his brakes as though he had suddenly met a great cow on the road. Leuchars Church! The sight of that astonishing apse, like a Norman knight in chainmail sitting a warhorse among gravestones, just takes the breath out of a body!

The Norman pillars of Stirling are good, the nave of Dunfermline is grand, the Margaret Chapel in Edinburgh is a little gem, but this unique apse which time has bequeathed to a village church in Fife is the most beautiful relic of the period I have seen in Scotland. There are, of course, much finer Norman churches in England, but I know of nothing quite like this apse. It is a Norman curiosity. I have not had such a thrill since I saw Cormac's Chapel on the Rock of Cashel in county Tipperary and the miniature Norman church at Tickencote in Rutland.

When you stand outside, for the exterior of this apse is its strong point, you see the east end octagonal tower and lantern of a church which has been standing for nearly eight centuries untouched by marauding English or vandal Calvinists. The apse is arcaded with blind arches and pilasters. When you look at these arches you can trace on the stone the marks of Norman axes as clearly as they are to be seen on the pillars of the crypt in Canterbury Cathedral.

Attached to this perfect poem in stone, a thing as authentic as the Domesday Book or the Battle of Hastings, is an ugly stone box which serves as the body of the modern church. I have received so many shocks in ancient churches in Scotland that I was almost afraid to go inside. I was quite prepared to find that the only worthwhile part of this church had been boarded up or otherwise insulted and humiliated. The Reformation in England vented its fury on martyrs but showed some respect for Catholic architecture; in Scotland they did not do so much burning, but they got their own back on stone; which is most regrettable because a new martyr rejoices heaven, but a beautiful thing in ruins is a crime against God and man. However, I went inside. It was not so bad. There was the usual townhall atmosphere of a Presbyterian church, the usual varnished pews, the usual chilly windows, but the people of Leuchars have not banished that lovely apse as a relic of Popery: they have permitted it to become the east end of their church. They have a treasure. It is good to know that they appreciate it.

I went on cheered, and singing at the top of my voice, for it is not often that you meet a Norman knight in chainmail sitting a warhorse among gravestones. . . .

The Newport-Dundee ferry was packed. I was sandwiched between a van horse of uncertain temper and a young woman with freckles and hair like a prairie fire whose small two-seater tried, with clumsy affection, to sit on my offside mudguards. All round us were carts, vans, and cars on their way to Dundee.

Ferries are an unfortunate feature of motoring in Scotland. Some of them, notably Queensferry over the Forth and, I am told, the Kyle of Lochalsh ferry to Skye, design their charges on the ancient assumption that all motorists are wealthy. It costs ten shillings to cross the Forth, a business of a few minutes, and fifteen shillings to make an even shorter voyage to Kyleakin. These charges naturally infuriate the Scot, who combines an almost quixotic generosity with a great sense of value for money. Possibly, if London were a little nearer to Edinburgh, there would have been a traffic bridge over the Forth long ago. The Tay, too, deserves something more than a railway bridge.

The Dundee ferry is, however, reasonable – three shillings for a Rolls-Royce coupé and three shillings and sixpence for a Ford four-seater. Cars are assessed on their seating accommodation!

Dundee lifted its chimneys in a cloud of smoke. It looked to me as if Sheffield had gone to the seaside. But even as I looked the wild wind that whipped the Tay into white flecks blew the smoke towards the Highlands; and, clear against the hills, I saw the third largest city in Scotland.

There was nothing very 'bonnie' about Dundee from the ferry, except its amazing situation. What a place for a city! Its wharves and docks lie against a two-and-a-quarter-mile wide river, and within sight, almost within sound, of the sea. It is like Liverpool, the Tay its Mersey, and where the river widens is the blue-green line of the ocean.

Dundee was that morning busy with its marmalade, its jute mills, its cakes, its linen. There was a deep Manchester rumble over the stone setts as the jute wagons went by. It is a city that has mysteriously effaced its past. It has a long and exciting history. William Wallace was a grammar-school boy there. In the old days England took it, and Scotland won it back almost as frequently as Berwick. Even if one did not know these things, such names as Nethergate and Seagate are as good as a pedigree stamped and sealed by the College of Heralds; but, look where you will, Dundee has replaced the ancient by the modern.

One of the main exports is, of course, journalists. I imagine that Dundee, with Aberdeen as a close runner-up, has let loose on the forces of error more grim champions in the form of earnest and unbelieving young men than any other city on earth. Blue pencils over the Border!

Dundee has Calcutta in its pocket. There are men now in Calcutta thinking only of retiring on Dundee. To understand the wealth of this city you must go and look at the houses of Broughty Ferry, Carnoustie, and Newport. No city in the world could have been kinder to its rich ones.

But, like all industrial cities subject to the ebb and flow of prosperity, it is a place of fearful inequality; riches and poverty are side by side; opulence and squalor hand in hand. There are hilly streets in Dundee where the children play barefoot in the gutter. It is always washing day there. I heard the Irish brogue, and saw Pat smoking his pipe at the cabin door:

'Out of work?' I asked one man.

'I am.'

The place looked neat and clean. He explained that his wife worked in the mill, while he was nurse, cook, and housemaid! He looked extraordinarily incompetent. This unnatural domestic life is, I believe, a characteristic of Dundee when the shipyards are idle, as it is of Londonderry, which has work for women in the shirt factories, but little, or none, for men.

I asked him how it felt to be dependent on a wife. He appeared unconscious of any humiliation. He said it was a good day's work to look after two children, and he would rather do a day's work than wash one baby! But his wife knew how things were. She gave him beer money, and sometimes took him to the pictures!

Dundee should be a thoughtful town. Right in the heart of it is one of the most gloomy and impressive cemeteries in Great Britain. It is called the Howff. Here sleep three centuries of dead Dundonians, mouldering under an army corps of headstones. It is the perfect retreat in moments of sadness. Here you could just gloat over your misfortune and enjoy to the full the art of being miserable. All round the Howff, on the other side of a wall, the busy city goes about its work, unconscious, I think, of that city of the dead. No city could have wiped out evidence of its history more thoroughly; yet, strangely enough, no city could live in more intimate contact with the dead men and women who made that history. . . .

The first among Dundee's treasures is the great hill of Dundee Law. Edinburgh and Stirling both have high places from which their citizens may take a broad view of life; but Dundee snuggles against a perfect tower of rock from which a man can look down the very chimneys of the city.

Here is another great view in Scotland, different from anything I have seen, and, in its way, as magnificent. Dundee lies below – street piled on street, chimney above chimney, the broad Tay crossed by the astonishing two-and-a-quarter-mile bridge. To the left the docks and the open sea; right ahead, over hills and remote in distance, the golden sands and the roofs of St Andrews. On a sunny day, with the wind blowing over Dundee Law, your blood tingles and you want to shout.

But turn round and look inland. There is that promise that gleamed so far off at Stirling; there are the Highlands of Scotland! The Grampians, still remote and still mysterious, blue and cloud-tipped, lie against the sky.

This is the vision that Dundee men carry with them to

the ends of the earth. No wonder that they always go back there some day.

7

On the country road not far from Dundee is the inn, not pretty like an English inn, nor squalid like an Irish drinkshop, but just useful and practical. An old man with the face of an apostle sat on a wooden bench. He was drinking beer. In profile his spirituality was startling: a long, fine nose, a splendid chin half concealed by a straggling white beard: the face of a saint. To see him full-face was to feel that you had witnessed a moral landslide. No longer was he such a heavenly old man; he was merely an acute one. The lid of one eye was not working, thus giving him a permanent wink, but all the vitality of the unfortunate eye appeared concentrated in its wide-open fellow, which shone and sparkled and had a penetrating life of its own, equal to that of any two normal eyes. On the floor beside the old man was a great pack covered with black oilcloth and with a leather strap for the shoulders. He was a Scottish packman, a relic of a dying race.

His clothes were remarkable. They represented a variety of human experience. He wore a sinful old hat which defies analysis. His green, tartan overcoat might, in an incredible youth, have been worn by the Marquis of Aberdeen; his trousers, too, had a distinct air of good breeding, but his boots had known all their life only the long road and the constant ache of miles.

When he opened his aged coat he exposed his strangest garment: a Highland evening dress waistcoat. It lurked beneath his rags with an air of complete shame. One of the original buttons gleamed with a defiant pride, suggesting, perhaps, evenings spent in the society of fair and noble women in castles among the hills; but the rest of the garment, no longer proud, no longer defiant, but stained, torn, and humiliated beyond belief, had, after putting up a great fight for its identity, surrendered to inevitable debauchery.

I looked at the old man and his Eye looked at me. I wanted to talk to him. I helped him with his pack, and he dug into a weird assortment, all very neat, of pins and needles, tape, buttons on cards, hooks and eyes, ribbon, combs, brushes, and every kind of small annoyance.

When I asked him to have a drink the Eye gleamed with intense intelligence, and he asked me to buy him 'a rum and a schooner'. A 'schooner', I discovered, is an intermediate measure of beer, a little less than a pint, I think. He drank the rum neat, and chased it swiftly with the 'schooner'. All the time the Eye watched me, but he said little except that the weather was fine, life expensive, and the pack heavy for a man of seventy-five.

When I asked him to have another rum and 'schooner', the Eye told me that he accepted my acquaintance. Before this he had, I felt, been patronizing me. He was a strange old man. He talked in a slow, cultured voice. I felt when he was talking that you could dress him up, put a ribbon across his chest and palm him off anywhere as a distinguished diplomat. His dead eye and his abnormally live eye suggested somehow extreme secrecy and excessive cunning side by side.

I asked him where he went to school. He said that sixty-five years ago he had gone to 'a penny school'. Like all Scotsmen, he had burned with a desire for knowledge. He was until lately a great reader.

'What did you read?'

The Eye moved round thoughtfully:

'Theology.'

I watched him, in profile, toss down his rum. He was exactly like a saint!

During a relapse into thought I discovered the Eye fixed with a double register of wistful regret on his empty glasses. He was mellowing slightly. The Eye came round on me, and . . . yes; he would, indeed, appreciate another rum and 'schooner'! I was now becoming tired of him.

But with this rum and 'schooner' a queer thing happened which held me fascinated. The somnolent eyelid began to move slightly. Once it flickered and shut down again. Once it almost opened. I watched it anxiously, as one awaits the sunrise. After moments of trying indecision the lid moved up, and I found myself looking into two perfectly good, strong, brilliant blue eyes.

This transformation seemed to penetrate his whole personality. He was now entirely a saint. I looked at him in genuine admiration. Front and side view were equally perfect; and he lost his diffidence, and, giving the table a bang with his hand, he lifted up that amazing admonishing forefinger (which John Knox has handed to every Scotsman who drinks three rums and 'schooners') and said, with tremendous conviction, that:

'The wor-r-ld and all that in it is stands on the brink o' hell fire!'

I asked him why, and in return he told me the story of his life.

It was all very muddled. It seemed that in his turbulent youth he had knocked down a policeman in Edinburgh – or, rather, the policeman fell just as he was thinking of knocking him down – and they put him in jail. Here he picked oakum. He said this was most unpleasant.

He went into business. He never made much money. A few vague women's names drifted through this portion of his life. There was, if I remember rightly, another innocent conflict with authority, due entirely to high spirits, and this changed his whole life. He converted himself in prison. He sat in a cell the evening before a murderer was hanged thinking all the things that John Knox had embedded in his subconscious. He thought of hell fire. He thought of God. He received an inmost conviction that his soul was immortal, and that the only way to save it was by prayer and a good life. He also wanted to make a clean break with his old life. He wanted fresh air and green trees:

'So I tramp aboot on ma daily work thinkin' ha-r-rud aboot the eter-r-nal verities!'

'Are you happy?'

'Happy? Aye, man, I'm happy.'

He looked at me with the expression of an early Christian martyr.

I gave the old man and his pack a lift to Perth. He took his place in the car with the air of an ambassador stepping into his state coach. His manners were perfect. We talked all the way about life and the silly things people chase in life, and he sat firmly on the rock of his Calvinism, and laid down the law according to his belief. I stole a glance at him when he was worked up; he was extraordinarily like John Knox.

I dropped him at a common lodging-house. He said good night to me gracefully, and bade me take heed of the things he had told me.

I was disappointed to see the Eye again; its companion had retired once more. So the gloom of the lodging-house swallowed him and the big pack, which he hitched from his old shoulders as he went in at the door.

8

Perth, like Gloucester, where matches are made – this is no pun – is full of small, pretty girls. They spend the day, I am told, in dyeing the garments of Great Britain; but they appear to have nothing to do in the evening but to walk arm in arm up and down High Street until at some mysterious hour of the night they remember their homes and vanish.

I was told that I would not like Perth; but I never pay attention to such prophecies. I found Perth full of atmosphere. I was astonished to learn that Dr Macfarlane, in his famous *Tour*, considered Perth to be pervaded by 'the cheerful air of a provincial town in England'. This is, to me, incomprehensible. The air is cheerful enough, but it is as Scottish as a plate of cockaleekie or a warm bannock.

The winds of the Highlands blow into Perth day and night. And the voice of 'Pairth' is the voice of Scotland! Here you meet memories of the clans for the first time. As soon as the stranger begins talking about Perth he is told how the Clan Chattan and the Clan Quhele fought thirty champions a side on the North Inch. Perth like an English provincial town? You might as well put a Highlander in gaiters and call him a Devonshire yokel!

Never for one minute can you feel unconscious of the wildness which lies beyond the gates of Perth: the roads go north to Pitlochry and Drumtochter, to Blairgowrie, and to the Spittal of Glenshee; and at night, as you walk through grey stone streets, modern but still, in their sky-line and their grim bulk, recalling a more ancient Perth, you smell a wind that comes sweet over miles of desolate heather.

The River Tay, which the legions of Agricola hailed as the Tiber, gives a rare beauty to Perth as it runs swiftly beneath its bridges.

All cities which have played a great part in history retain, no matter how time alters them, an air of assurance and solidity, and this Perth possesses to an unusual degree. It is interesting to prowl round in search of Old Perth. You find, for instance, that the site of the still mysterious Gowrie Conspiracy is today the fine modern County Building. Andrew Lang wrote: 'An old Scottish lady four generations ago used to say, "It is a great comfort to think that at the Day of Judgment we shall know the whole truth about the Gowrie Conspiracy at last."'

I suppose this story is as well known to Scotsmen as the Gunpowder Plot to Englishmen, but to English ears the Gowrie Conspiracy is just a name – perhaps not even that – so I will give the bare bones of it.

Early on Tuesday morning, August 5, 1600, King James VI was going out to hunt the stag from Falkland Palace dressed in a new suit of English green cloth, velvet-topped boots, and socks decorated with five ounces of silver. As he

mounted his horse, the Master of Ruthven, brother of the
Earl of Gowrie, rode up and told him a strange story. He
had met a man with a pot full of gold. This man had been
detained in Gowrie House. Would the King like to come
and see him? James loved a golden guinea as much as he
loathed a witch or a Jesuit plot. The idea, perhaps, was that
this man was a Jesuit agent with smuggled gold to be used
for seditious purposes. Anyhow, James had he lived today
would have been one of Edgar Wallace's most devoted
readers because he could never resist a mystery! He, of
course, agreed to ride to Gowrie House in Perth when the
stag had been killed; which happened before luncheon-time.

The Earl of Gowrie with a company met the King on the
outskirts of Perth and escorted him to Gowrie House. After
a delayed and apparently scratch luncheon, His Majesty
was taken secretly by the Master of Ruthven up to a turret.
The King was surprised to observe that a door was locked
behind him as they went up. Now, while the King was
absent his nobles went out into the garden to eat cherries.
Some strolled into the road. A report was spread that the
King had ridden off alone. There was much running to and
fro as his suite contemplated saddling and riding after him.
While they were wondering where to find the King
someone heard James's voice and, glancing up in the
direction of it, saw the King looking out of the turret
window, hatless, his face red, and a hand gripping his face
and mouth. He cried: 'I am murdered. Treason! My Lord
of Mar, help, help!'

Most of the lords ran up the main stairway and were
stopped by the locked door. One took a narrow doorway
which led to a spiral stairway to the turret. He rushed into
the room and saw the King wrestling with the Master of
Ruthven, and behind the King stood an armed man. James
cried to his rescuer: 'Strike him low, because he wears a
secret mail doublet.' In the fight that followed Ruthven was
slain. The mysterious armed man vanished. The confusion

and the fighting continued and the young Earl of Gowrie also was killed.

James said afterwards that Ruthven, observing great secrecy, took him to the turret, where, instead of the man with the pot of gold, stood a man with a dagger at his girdle. Ruthven, said the King, put on his hat, drew the man's dagger, and held the point to the King's breast 'avowing now that the King behoved to be at his will, and used as he list; swearing many bloody oaths that if the King cried one word, or opened a window to look out, that dagger should go to his heart'.

To indicate the many ramifications of the Gowrie Plot, the mystery of the man in the turret, the various manuscripts and narratives bearing on it, would be to write a book – which Andrew Lang has already done. Even so, the plot is as deep a mystery as ever it was. Did the King devise it himself to slay Ruthven and Gowrie? Did these two lords intend to capture James and ride off with him? Was the Queen, Anne of Denmark, implicated? She was fair and frivolous and the lords were young and handsome. Was there a man in the turret? If so, who was he? Here is a mystery in Scottish history fit to stand for ever beside its companion, the Casket letters. . . .

Nothing could look less mysterious today than the site of Gowrie House; but that is the way with Perth. Like Dundee, it has turned its historic places to useful ends. Somewhere beneath Perth, I believe, sleep a king and queen. James I and his queen were buried in a Carthusian monastery on a site between the Hospital and King Street. If we could X-ray that ground perhaps we should find them there sleeping still with the glory and the woes of old Scotland still about them.

Perth deserves the gratitude of every man interested in architecture. This city has broken with the old-time Calvinism and has restored its splendid church of St John to something resembling its former glory. This excellent resurrection is Perth's War Memorial. I do not know what the sterner Presbyterians of the last generation would have said to all this. The services of the Church of Scotland are now held in one of the finest cathedrals in the country.

St John's – like many another Scottish church – until recently housed three separate congregations! Now that the barriers are down it is possible to see for the first time for centuries its real beauty and the true proportions.

If Perth works hard at its factories, its railways, its cattle markets, it also plays hard. The city is the 'birthplace of cricket' in Scotland. A local antiquary told me an interesting story about this.

'During the Napoleonic wars,' he said, 'Perth housed thousands of French prisoners. They were guarded with great care, and several regiments of militia and one regiment of English cavalry were sent from the south. The Hussars played cricket on the South Inch – watched, of course, by the boyhood of Perth. So the game took root here, and has been played ever since. By the way, you may not know that during the first fifty years of its existence the Perth Cricket Club beat the famous I Zingari by thirteen runs. . . .'

Perth, too, has made golf history. The game of golf dates its popularity from the invention of gunpowder. It was put down by law in the early days because Scotsmen practised golf instead of archery, with the result that the English longbow worked havoc among the ill-trained Scots archers. When gunpowder made bows and arrows obsolete, there was no longer any reason to prohibit golf, and the early golf clubs were made by the 'bowyers', who found their trade in bows declining. These clubs were made in Perth.

In old days Perth rivalled St Andrews as a golfing centre, and among its famous golfers was Bob Andrews, who could drive a ball off the face of a gold watch without damaging it!

I climbed Kinnoul Hill before breakfast. The morning was cold with the chill of early autumn, but the sun shone in a cloudless sky. When I left the road to strike up over grass to the summit my footsteps were printed black behind me in the thick dewfall. . . .

I have written of the views from high places in Edinburgh, Stirling, and Dundee. What can I say of the country that spreads itself below Kinnoul Hill in the still hush of an autumn morning? It must be one of the grandest sights in all Scotland.

Perth and its clustered streets lie below – a 'fair city' on the banks of the Tay; and you follow the silver ribbon of water through the green Carse of Gowrie, watch it twisting through the fields, disappearing for a little while into woodland, then going on, widening mile after mile seaward between the shores of Forfar and Fife.

You have the impression that you are in a stationary airship. You are actually 729 feet above the plain. All the land lies crystal clear below you to the horizon, where the mountains lift their heads in a faint blue haze: nearer now, no longer vague peaks and ridges riding the sky as they seemed from the ramparts of Stirling Castle. There is a view indicator on the summit of Kinnoul Hill – a large disc covered by glass and protected by wire-netting – on which black arrows point over fifty miles of space to the distant peaks of the Grampians. The dew had fallen on it, covering the glass with drops of water, so that I had to take a stick and push a handkerchief under the wire to clean the glass before I could find my way over the rising and falling barrier of blueness that closed the tremendous view.

There can be no grander introduction to the Highlands of Scotland than to stand on Kinnoul Hill in the early morning and read the titles of the Grampians as you follow the flight of the black arrows – Ben-y-Gloe, Beinn Dearg, Cairn Toul, Ben Macdhui – and can that remote monster lurking in the misty distance be Ben Nevis?

On the way down I heard a school-bell ringing. Small boys with marvellous Scots faces were trying not to be early and not to be late. Their boots were polished as if for some competition. One of them came up to me. He was a typical young Scot, red, freckled, and blunt.

'Have ye a cigarette car-r-ud?'

I went through my pockets while he waited in a condition of suspended hope. I found him some.

'Who cleans your boots?'

'Masel'.'

'Do you like school?'

'I like it fine.'

'What are you going to be when you grow up?'

'I havena decided,' he replied with great gravity, 'but I'm minded to be a farmer.'

What a refreshing lad! No engines in his soul!

He went whistling down the road, kicking the dew about with his polished boots until he met a friend, and from the look of the meeting I think that, like a true Scot, he was trading my cigarette cards for something he wanted more!

CHAPTER FIVE

In which I climb into the Highlands over the Devil's Elbow, attend the Braemar Gathering, see Balmoral, also the Town which exists by Royal command, ending with a long glide into Aberdeen by the light of the full moon

I

THE big hotel in Perth, which calls itself an inn, is patronized by commercial travellers and by American ladies who wish to experience the harmless romance of sleeping in Bonnie Prince Charlie's room. This is the least inspiring of the series. The date 1699 on the grate glowers across at a wash-basin with hot and cold water 'laid on'.

Every morning the population of this inn changes. The motor-cars of commerce gather in the morning and the guests of the night before disappear to spread civilization – which is the multiplication of unnecessary things – over the length and breadth of Scotland. In the evening, from north and south, come more motor-cars with more ambassadors of production.

I met in Perth a man who sells hats to the women of Skye, another who takes china to the Shetland Islands, a third to whose activity the people of the Outer Hebrides owe their washtubs. Perth is the frontier town of the Highlands. Here the commercial traveller going north writes out the orders of Dundee, Stirling, Glasgow, and Edinburgh with the hope that these will justify the temporary hiatus in his affairs represented by the long mountain road to Aberdeen.

During the interesting social reconstruction of these times the actor, the journalist, and the commercial traveller – hitherto the prodigal sons of professionalism – have been accepted into the bosom of society. Practically the only people who remain outside are press photographers and burglars. I am not, however, too sure about burglars. In days not so distant the commercial traveller was a man with soiled cuffs who was always on his way with a Gladstone bag to catch a train. The problem of the Victorian hotel-keeper was how to segregate him from the travelling gentry. Accordingly, he constructed a gloomy place known as a 'commercial room', where in little mahogany and glass cells, which prevented cribbing from the man on right or left, the weary vagabonds might file their orders in an atmosphere of monkish seclusion. They were seen helping themselves round the country by a system of mysterious handclasps and assembling in the evening with ill-concealed bitterness to forget their sorrows in a bar. The only envy which the commercial traveller awakened in the minds of more leisurely wanderers was the vague, but unsubstanti-ated, suspicion that he was the Lothario of the linen cupboard.

Now, however, in this age of commercial knighthood salesmanship is no longer casual labour. The commercial traveller is a gentleman. If he sells nasal douches he is probably a doctor of literature; if he sells Bibles he is probably a rowing blue; if he sells silk stockings he is perhaps a doctor of divinity! He arrives in a smart two-seater motor-car. He never chucks the chambermaid under the chin as in days of old, but, it is to be presumed, takes out a picture of his wife, which he places on the dressing-table before descending to the mundane facts of his profession.

As he steers his car into every nook and corner of a countryside, the modern commercial traveller becomes a snapper-up of local customs, dialects, traditions, and history. He was always a more or less keen student of psychology. As his work brings him into direct personal touch with so many people, contact with him is not only pleasurable but profitable. The motor-car has restored to him the proud position of the commercial traveller of antiquity whose galleys from Tyre and Sidon combined the functions of commerce with those of the historian, the journalist, the geologist, and the geographer.

'So you're off to the Highlands tomorrow,' said a traveller. 'What do you expect to find there?'

'Why do you ask?'

'I just wondered. Americans go there to wear badly-fitting kilts and skean dhus made in London. Trippers go there – heaven knows what trippers go anywhere for! Most people go there to drivel about Bonnie Prince Charlie and the clans. You, as a writer, will, of course, do that.

'Few people who go there know that the Highlands are a tragedy. They share with Ireland the awful tragedy of the Gael. The 1745 Rebellion finished the Highlands, and it couldn't be helped, because they were an anachronism in modern life. New wine had to get into the old bottles somehow, and of course – bang! What else could happen? Could the feudal system work in England? The clan system was much older. It had to go as soon as the Highlands established definite contact with the modern world. Behind all the romance and sentiment of the Highlands is the awful spectre of depopulation. The Highlanders, like the Irish, have to clear out in order to live. A fifth of the total area of Scotland is a deer forest. The old Highland chiefs have, of course, gone and the new chiefs shut up inns and mountain paths in the interests of deer-slaying. It's all wrong! Some day, perhaps, we shall see a serious attempt to establish Highland industries and to stem the tide of emigration. But don't let this stop you from enjoying the grandest scenery in the British Isles and – what Scotsman will deny it? – in the whole of Europe! And if you do meet Bonnie Prince Charlie don't shed too many tears! It had to happen, and, as things have turned out, it is probably a good thing that it did happen. . . .'

2

I set out on a clear morning towards Blairgowrie with a mind as eager as that of any tourist. The commercial traveller had told me nothing which I did not already know, but I was glad to have it in his own words.

In days before the Highland clans migrated to the London Telephone Directory – and this point in their 'tragedy' must not be overlooked! – they constituted the last colony of uncontaminated Celts. They were the only Celts in the British Isles who never knew the proud foot of a conqueror. No Roman satrap attempted to line them up with the Empire, no Norman count tried to bring them into the feudal system. They were isolated in a prehistoric atmosphere which they retained until modern times when, as my friend of Perth might have put it, Bonnie Prince Charlie's defeat broke down the barrier between the new world and the last stronghold of the old.

In Ireland the Celt suffered a different fate. True, he escaped the Romans in order to enjoy a brief era of culture devoted to the export of saints; but the time came when he went down before the chainmail of the Norman. Not so the Highlander. His bare knees flash through history at frequent intervals, the skirl of his pipes is heard in the front of various battles, but no matter how far he may stray he is always observed returning to the fastness of his mountains and the birthplace of his clan. It is truly astonishing that a tribal system as old as man existed and flourished in the Highlands into modern times. The political events which caused the Borders to sheathe a sword that had been flashing for centuries had no effect on the Highlands. These men remained wild and warlike when the rest of Scotland had been tamed.

Most Englishmen, who know little about the history of Scotland and nothing at all about that of Ireland, do not realize that, with the exception of the North and South Poles, the Highlands of Scotland were the last portion of the earth's surface to be explored. This sounds inconceivable, but it is true! America was already an old country when the Highlands were discovered. Until the Rebellion of 1745 opened them to travellers they were a land of mystery. Burt, in 1726, wrote: 'The Highlands are but little known even to the inhabitants of the low country of Scotland, for they have ever dreaded the difficulties and dangers of travelling among the mountains; and when some extraordinary occasion has obliged any of them to make such a progress he has generally speaking made his testament before he set out, as though he were entering on a long and dreaded sea voyage, wherein it was very doubtful if he should ever return. But to the people of England, except some few and those chiefly the soldiers, the Highlands are hardly known at all; for there has been less that I know of written upon the subject than of the Indies, and even that little which has been said conveys no idea of what a traveller almost continually sees and meets with in passing among the mountains.' (This omission has, however, been speedily amended, as anyone will agree who receives book catalogues on Scotland!)

But how amazing to think that as recently as 200 years ago there existed within 500 miles of London an enormous tract of country inhabited by tribes whose way of life was that of Brian Boru! Here in the Highlands were until modern times many 'miniature courts' – to use Macaulay's words – 'in each of which a petty prince attented by guards, by armour bearers, by musicians, by a hereditary orator, by a hereditary poet laureate, kept a rude state, dispensed a rude justice, waged wars and concluded treaties.'

I have been reading with profit and some amusement the adventures of Sir James Carr who toured through Scotland in 1807 and wrote a book called *Caledonian Sketches*. He tells a story which proves that the miniature courts described by Macaulay were flourishing in the reign of Queen Anne! And what could prove more vividly the absolute isolation of the Highlands than Carr's story of the Highland chieftain who had never heard of the queen?

'Many of the chiefs, in distant periods,' he writes, 'were regarded with superstitious veneration, and were as absolute as any Princes of the East, and frequently displayed a power

not a little terrible to those who called it into action. It is
related, that soon after the accession of Queen Ann, when
Prince George of Denmark, her husband, was Lord High
Admiral of England some Scots gentlemen represented to
him that Scotland could furnish the navy with as good
timber for masts, and other naval uses, as Sweden or
Norway, and at more reasonable prices; upon which two
surveyors were despatched to ascertain the truth of the
representation. At Edinburgh they procured a letter of
introduction to a great chieftain in a remote part of the
Highlands to forward their commission. Upon their arrival
at his house they announced their object, and produced the
warrant and instructions from his Royal Highness. After
deliberately perusing them, the chieftain observed that he
knew nothing of such a person. The surveyors informed him
that he was the husband of Queen Ann; upon which he
replied, "*I also know nothing of her*; but there came hither,
some time ago, such as you, from Ireland, as spies upon the
country, and we hear that they made their jests upon us
among the Irish. Now you shall have one hour to give a
better account of yourselves than you have yet given; and, if
you fail, I will have you hanged upon that tree" – pointing
to one adjoining; a menace which his attendants seemed
perfectly disposed to execute. In this dilemma the chieftain
left them, without having seen the letter of introduction
from their friend at Edinburgh, which the surveyors thought
would not be noticed after the treatment which the royal
mandate had experienced. However, after they had paced
up and down the garden for some time, seeing death at
every turn before them, they conceived they might as well
produce the letter of introduction, which after some
difficulty, as the hour was on the point of expiration, they
discovered, and presented to the haughty Laird, who, after
perusing it, observed: "Why did you not give me this at
first? If you had not produced it I would have hanged you
both immediately." Upon this he courteously led them into

his house, gave them refreshment, and granted them permission to make a survey of his woods next morning.'

This happened in the reign of Queen Anne! It is the sort of thing that might have happened to Ulysses! This explains, to some extent, the attraction which the Highland clans hold for the modern world. They are a genuine link with the Golden Age. There is a primitive splendour about them. Looking back at them from the safety of our own time and with a critical faculty unbiased by a lifted herd of cattle or the working out of a blood feud, we seem to see the Highlanders as the lineal descendants of the Homeric heroes. What could be more Homeric than the Macneill who, as Kenneth Macleod states in his notes to the *Songs of the Hebrides*, used to send a trumpeter to his castle tower every evening after dinner to make the following proclamation: 'Ye kings, princes and potentates of all the earth, be it known unto you that Macneill of Barra has dined – the rest of the world may dine now!'

How absurdly – magnificently – Highland that is! How many times have you heard a Highlander at the height of a heated discussion – and perhaps heated a little with his native wine – suddenly lose patience with words, call on his clan and invoke his regality with the cry: 'My name's Campbell and I don't care who knows it and – ye can go to hell!'

Surely it is exactly the same challenge that Macneill of Barra flung from his battlements to a world that had never heard of him!

Everyone who numbers a real Highlander among his friends knows that he inherits a number of qualities which mark him off from ordinary men. He is quick to take offence and he is a fighter. He is as punctilious in matters of honour as an Italian nobleman. Personal loyalty is a tradition with him. So is whisky. He loves to arrange, often on the flimsiest pretext, occasions for convivial celebration, a relic perhaps of old times when men, separated by mountain and flood, would meet together and pledge themselves in strong drink. He is supposed to be dour and mean. As a matter of fact contact with the world softens him and often induces the generosity, or the meanness, of an extremist. He is, like all Celts, a preordained exile, and exile is necessary for him unless he is to stagnate. There is something in the environment of the Highlands and also of Ireland which saps the initiative and fosters the natural laziness of the Celt, so that if you want to see the Highlander and the Irishman at their best you must seek them in London or New York.

The Saxon, settled on fat lands for centuries, has no race memory of emigration. He is dumb in his love of England and has to be subjected to the tropics before he finds his voice; even then there is no heart-breaking pathos in it: his cry is not that of a parted lover so much as that of a lost child. The Highlander, on the other hand, is a vocal patriot, and in this he is assisted by his sense of poetry. Mountain burns and the sound of old battles are always in his soul. One of the finest things about him is his pride of race. The Highlander is a born aristocrat. The enormous gulf between baron and serf which existed in England for centuries was unknown in the Highlands, where the meanest clansman bore the name of his chief. The Highlander goes through life with a fine superiority complex: his name is itself a crest for all men to see.

It was Sir Walter Scott who introduced him to polite society. Before that time the courteous Highland gentleman, filled to overflowing with the sturdy virtues of the Golden Age, was by his contemporaries regarded as a low-down cattle lifter and assassin. All lowlanders regard all mountaineers as thieves and bandits. But when Walter Scott turned the light of romance upon him all the meanness left him and he stood before the world in the grandeur of his rugged virtue. Here, it was discovered, stood Nature's last perfect gentleman. Even the death of the clan system against the bayonets at Culloden became a noble and heroic thing. The clans were dead. Long live the clans! The tartan, driven from the hills by cruel Acts of Parliament, began to return again, not to the hills, but to the drawing-rooms. And then a shape rears itself in the mists of Deeside. Balmoral is ready to be born.

3

Where was I? Upon the road to Blairgowrie! It was a brilliant day of sun with plenty of high white cloud. There was no mistaking the road. I had said goodbye to the Lowlands. I was going on towards hills like clouds and clouds like hills. The wind came down over miles, cold and sweet from the top of Lochnagar. I came at length to Blairgowrie. It belongs as clearly to the Highlands as Biskra belongs to the Sahara. Blairgowrie! The name sounds like the rattling of casements on a wild night!

It is a small town of puritanical appearance. The stone houses group themselves up and down hilly streets in reserved attitudes. You look at the place and think how bleak it must be in the winter. Farmers stand at the crossroads talking to the village policeman, a fisherman girded for the fray walks on towards a bridge, a girl carrying a gun in a leather case strides past in speckled tweed. Blairgowrie, which – it is difficult to believe – grows raspberries in season for the jam makers, turns its autumnal thoughts to grouse and fish. And I left it with the knowledge that I had crossed the frontier. . . .

The road runs on between mountains. Rowanberries are reddening, the mountain ash flings out sprays of leaves soon to be the colour of blood, but now just thinly veined with pink. Vast clouds sail overhead sending their shadows racing over the moorlands, and every mile leads into a deeper desolation. Beyond low stone walls polled Angus cattle coated in black satin stand and gaze in the fields, but, as the valley narrows to a grim gorge, these are left behind and their place is taken by horned sheep, nimble as mountain goats. There is now no sound but the bleating of sheep and the rush of water down in the valley and the bright tinkle of some small burn falling from the hills.

The road rises towards Glenshee. Clouds cover the sun. There is a quick shower of rain; but on the other side of the valley the sun is shining. The road through Glenshee leads on into a land that is wild with the spirit of the Grampians. I am among the giants. On the left hand loom Ben-y-Gloe and Beinn Dearg; ahead, on the left, are Ben Macdhui, Cairn Toul, and Cairn Gorm. The valley on the right is dominated by the immense presence of Lochnagar. As I go on the foothills hide him, the mists swirl over him; but now and then I catch a glimpse of him standing with his bald head in the sky. There is only the bleating of sheep, the sound of water, the sough of the wind, the slow, drooping flight of crows, and the shadow of a cloud no bigger than a man's hand sweeping over the ravines and gullies of the mountains. Sunlight follows rain and I dive on into a glen of rainbows. Never have I seen so many rainbows. They arch themselves, as if trying to bridge the glen, they come in frail splendour over the heads of hills and fall, vibrating with brief life, into the distant fields. I see one that ends in a white house! It pours itself out over the chimneys in a broad band of purple, yellow, and blue, like watered silk. Do they know, I wonder, that the golden crock lies there somewhere beneath the floor?

A rainbow mightier than the rest almost brings me to death at the Devil's Elbow – a hair-raising hairpin of a bend – and now the road shoots up skywards, rising as sharply as 1 in 8 and 1 in 12, and I reach the summit of the highest road in Great Britain; and here I draw a breath and stop, 2,199 feet above sea-level.

I sit on a stone wall watching the clouds steam over the dark head of Lochnagar. Far off on the horizon, to the left, I count the peaks of the Cairn Gorms in whose awful clefts the snow lies all year long. A wild sense of exhilaration comes to me. I feel a violent desire to run, to sing, or – what a queer thought? – I feel that had I a sword I could give a good account of myself up here among these savage peaks. Mountains affect men in various ways. As I look again the barbarian in me sinks in a sea of humility. The slow clouds, the dark rock, the distant earth are like some landscape from the very beginning of time. The first man might have gazed on such a sight, cowering in the fear that the cloud that steams over Lochnagar might part and reveal God. . . .

I dip down into the Clunie Valley. Here is gentleness. The fields and the woodlands are smiling in the last sunlight of afternoon. Beside the river that flows through this lovely glen I see the sight that hangs in every lodging-house in Bloomsbury. A group of Highland cattle standing at the edge of water turn their shaggy heads my way, gazing at me through matted locks, short-legged and vastly horned in glum and bedraggled hairiness. They might have been placed there by a publicity agent for Scotland! Behind them a pine wood as thick as the bristles on a brush runs up the steep side of a hill, and behind the hill is a parent mountain lifting towards the sky a head hazy with a crown of purple.

So I come to the sound of running water, and with the late sunlight flashing between the long, slender pine-trees, into Braemar, which positively hums with life. Are men preparing to unfurl another standard on the braes? In a way, yes! Tomorrow is the day of the Braemar Gathering.

'Aye, yer room's kept for ye! Will ye be takin' dinner?'

'No; I'll take eggs to my tea!'

And above the purple of the heather, away up beyond the last pine-tree, the first star burns and the calm hush of a September evening comes down over Deeside.

4

I watched a round moon lift itself above the pines and swing clear of the hill. Dark belts of woodland were dusted with a gold haze; the Dee moved on over its brown pebbles like a stream of molten bronze. High up, in unlikely places on the hills, shone little sparks of light: the windows of cottage and farmhouse. Dogs barked far away, and the dogs of Braemar answered with uneasy whinings and sudden baying, as though conscious that something not of this earth was abroad on the beams of the moon.

It was a magic night, with something borrowed from the wild hills in it. Moonlight in England is so safe. When I was a boy I slept out with the moon in my face beside the Avon in Warwickshire, and even the unbridled imagination of youth could conjure nothing from the moonlight more terrifying than Peaseblossom or Mustardseed. But in Ireland and in the mountains of Scotland the moonlight has a sharper edge to it. It suggests not the amusing playful fairies of the Saxon but the witch and the warlock of the Celt. If you did see a fairy by Scotch moonlight it would be on its way to steal a baby.

Owls called in the wood. Once, twice a fish leapt from the river, a splendid sight, a little half circle of glimmering gold and then a soft splash and an oily eddy where it broke the surface of the water. I sat in the peace of this night listening to the strange half sounds, the queer rustlings and sudden scurrying, the hint of wings. From down the road came loud, deliberate footsteps and a voice said:

'Hae ye a licht?'

I produced matches. An enormous Scotsman approached carrying a bulky sack. The match illuminated a tangle of auburn beard and two acute, challenging eyes. A cloud of abnormally strong tobacco went up in the moonlight.

'Aye-he!' sighed the red man contentedly, handing me the box, 'it's a graund nicht!'

He puffed a moment and showed no inclination to depart.

'A fine dee the mor-r-n, I'm thinkin'.'

'Are you taking part in the games to-morrow?'

'Aye, tossin' the caber.'

I looked at his tremendous fists and arms.

'Och, it's just a knack,' he said modestly; 'if ye've the way o' it its no' at a' deeficult. Ye're frae England?'

'Yes.'

'Aye-he!'

He drew at his pipe reflectively.

'Fraw London, nae doot?'

'Yes.'

'Aye-he! Aye, it's a graund nicht. See yon fush jump? Yer first veesit tae Sco'land maybe?'

'Yes.'

'Aye-he!'

I felt that it was now my turn.

'Where did the Earl of Mar raise the standard in 1715?'

He smoked a while as if considering the advisability of informing me, then he pointed with his pipe.

'Ye ken the Invercauld Arms?'

'I'm staying there.'

'Och weel, ye're sleepin' on the verra spot. . . . Aye, the Ear-r-l o' Mar, he was the man; and he unfur-r-led the flag for James on September the sixth.'

He sent out clouds of nasty incense.

'Are there any stories still told about it?'

Another reflective pause.

'Weel, no, I canna say that! There isna much recollected aboot it the noo! But . . .'

Here he puffed.

'I recollect when I was a wee bairn. . . .'

More puffs.

'An auld, auld maun frae Kirkmichael who was sae fu' o' it that he couldna open his mouth wi'out a story. And . . .'

Puff.

'I hae har-r-d him say . . .'

Puff.

'That . . .'

Puff.

'When the Ear-r-l o' Mar unfur-r-led the staandard the brass ball frae the top o' it fell doon on the groond and the clans were awfu' consairned, and some didna wish tae go on wi' the Rebellion. Mony a man would hae tur-r-ned back then and there tae gang hame. Why? 'Twas an omen o' bad luck, and bad luck it brought them – as ye can read for yersel' in the history buiks.'

He explored his memory reluctantly and told me that he thought the standard which was unfurled for the son of James II was blue in colour, on one side the arms of Scotland in gold and on the other the thistle. He wished me good night and clumped deliberately down the road. . . .

5

'Queen Anne is dead!'

Why should this obvious statement have survived as a kind of catch phrase until modern times? A music-hall comedian will sometimes bring down the houses with it. If he said, 'King Charles is dead' or 'Queen Elizabeth is dead', there would be no response; but the equally stupid 'Queen Anne is dead' never fails in its reaction on the English mind. As I was sitting on this wall at Braemar it came to me that perhaps this phrase is the last reverberation of the political storm let loose on England and Scotland when Queen Anne – inconveniently dying after her doctor had assured the Whigs and Tories that she was good 'for six years and a half' – divided the country between the claims of her brother James (the Old Pretender) and the Act of Settlement which gave the crown to the Protestant Elector of Hanover, George I. It was a time of wild rumours and secret meetings behind locked doors. The pathetic little Stuart court at Saint-Germain received many a courier from Scotland; the vulgar little court at Herrenhausen in Hanover watched the health of Anne as the stock market watches a dying millionaire. 'Surely,' writes James to Anne, 'you will prefer your own half-brother to the Duke of Hanover, the remotest relation we have.' Surely, said the court of Herrenhausen, it would be a good idea if George took his seat in the House of

Lords, to which Anne – who had Queen Eizabeth's hatred of her successor – replied that 'to bring over a Hanoverian would be like placing a coffin before her eyes'. High ran the Stuart hopes at this. It was rumoured in the coffee-houses of London that James had come disguised to St James's and had been closeted with the queen, his half-sister. But little good it did him. On a Sunday morning in August 1714 it was announced for the first time that 'Queen Anne is dead!' The Jacobite Tories wavered; the Protestant Whigs acted, and in a few hours a courier was riding to the coast with dispatces for Hanover beginning 'Most Gracious Sovereign'. He returned with others headed 'Georgius Rex'. At Bar-le-Duc a melancholy young Stuart, who at the unlucky age of thirteen had been proclaimed at the gates of Saint-Germain King of England, Scotland, and Ireland, aimed the first of his long series of proclamations at the world, pointing out, like a pained genealogist, that over fifty claimants stood nearer in lineal succession to the throne of England and Scotland than 'this usurper ignorant of our laws, language, and Constitution.'

It is probably a good thing – almost certainly a good thing – that James in 1715 and Bonnie Prince Charlie in 1745 were dogged by bad luck and bad generalship. 'England would perforce have been governed by Irish and Scottish adventurers,' writes G. M. Trevelyan in his *History of England*, 'who knew nothing of her needs, and by a Prince whose later life became as ignoble as his youth had been gallant and brave. We might soon have been engaged in a new cycle of civil wars, fatal to civilization and industry at home, and to commerce and the empire overseas. Precise speculations are idle, but the consequences of a *coup d'état* by wild Highlanders in London must in any case have been both tragic and absurd.' In spite of this cold statement every man must be, at heart, a Jacobite! The brain may reject it but the heart warms to it. It is impossible in these days of religious indifference to enter into the feelings which moved men in those times. Looking back on them it is difficult to believe that anyone – Protestant or Catholic – could have supported the unpleasant little German princeling against the son of James II and Mary of Modena. One was a prince of the blood royal and the other looked and behaved, as they said in the Highlands, like a 'wee wee German lairdie'. 'Unable to speak English,' says G. M. Trevelyan, 'with blowsy foreign women for his mistresses, with a grim domestic tragedy in the German background, he had no redeeming touch of wit, generosity, or nobleness of soul. . . . That Jacobitism failed to overthrow even such a king as this was due to the admirably obstinate refusal of the exiled Stuarts to be Protestants and play Charles II's game over again.'

Had the first Hanoverians possessed any spark of heroism the two Jacobite rebellions would not have appealed to us today, to English and Scots alike, as pages which seem to have slipped into the eighteenth century from the pen of Malory.

So the mists blow aside to show us on the Braes of Mar a gathering of wild clansmen and their impetuous chief letting out on the winds of the Highlands the blue banner made by his lady for 'the King over the water'. Pendants of white ribbon fluttered from it. On one was: 'For our wronged King and oppressed country'; on the other: 'For our lives and liberties.' They marched from Braemar into Perth proclaiming 'James VIII, King of England, Scotland, France, and Ireland'; and while the news was flying round the Highlands there came a ship from France announcing the death of the old king, Louis XIV. How many times did Scotland build up her hopes on France only to find them shattered? Mary, James, and Charles Edward – surely the Stuarts are the Micawbers of history! – believed that something would turn up in the nick of time from France; and all of them were disappointed. And the clans, hearing that the great armada of arms, ammunition, stores, officers, engineers, and reinforcements, had gone down, so to speak, at the king's bedside, grumbled and muttered among themselves and were all for going home and calling the rebellion off before it had started. While the clansmen stood irresolutely, the chiefs sent an urgent message asking the Chevalier to come over and place himself at the head of his troops; and the Earl of Mar sat down and wrote two letters, one of them a stilted proclamation signed 'Lieutenant-General of His Majesty's Forces', ordering John Forbes, the Baillie of Kildrummy, to put his men under arms and march on Braemar, and the second one a private letter to the same man which is much more interesting:

'Jock,' he wrote, 'ye was in the right not to come with the 100 men ye sent up tonight, when *I expect four times that number*. It is a pretty thing when all the Highlands of Scotland are rising upon their King and country's account, as I have accounts from them since they were with me, and the Gentlemen of our neighbouring Lowlands expecting us down to join them that any men should be found refractory. Is not the thing we are now about that which they have been wishing these twenty years? And now when it is come and the King and country's cause is at stake will they for ever sit and see it perish? I have used gentle means too long, and so I shall be obliged to put other orders I have in execution. . . . Let my own tenants in Kildrummy know that if they come not forth with their best arms that I will send a party immediately to burn what they shall miss taking from them. You are to tell the Gentlemen that I'll expect them in their best accoutrements, on horseback; and no excuse to be accepted of.'

So the Fiery Cross goes out over the mountains in those fateful autumn days and the tartan columns march south-ward in the weakening sunlight, to hover indecisively here and there and to move on with one eye on the Hanoverians

and the other on the seacoast. There is a flash of claymores
and a terrible mix-up at Sheriffmuir:

> Ther's some say that we wan,
>   Some say that they wan,
> Some say that nane wan at a', man!
>   But one thing I'm sure,
>   That at Sheriffmuir
> A battle there was which I saw, man.
>   And we ran ... and they ran ...
>   And they ran ... and we ran ...

On a stormy night at the end of December a French
privateer, armed with eight guns, slips unexpectedly into
Peterhead, and a number of sea captains come ashore,
among them a silent, pale, sad young man of twenty-seven.
The King has come over the water; James VIII is in
Scotland! But where – oh, where – is the army he was to
bring; where the chests of bullion?

His cause is already lost. His discouraged clansmen have
been allowed to grow cold with more than the snow which
now falls and blocks the road to Perth. But James, flinging
off his mariner's disguise, rides as king into Scotland, issuing
long and excellent proclamations, permitting his cold hand
to be kissed, and chilling men with his reserve as surely as
his son, Charles, was to inflame them in thirty years' time
with his enthusiasm. And into the majestic proclamations
posted up in the winter snow of Scottish towns creeps a little
wistfulness from Saint-Germain. 'It will be no new thing,' he
says in one, 'if I am unfortunate; my whole life, even from
my cradle, has shown a constant series of misfortunes.'
Terribly human; terribly appealing; but not the right note
for a wronged king! And how quickly Bonnie Prince Charlie
would have struck out those words!

James was a much finer character than his son. His life in
exile was that of an exceptional man. Biographers have not
done him justice. It is, strangely enough, only in this
Rebellion that he shows up as a rather futile person. He
wastes time in Perth making unnecessary preparations for

his Coronation which he fixes for January 23rd. How easily his son would have solved the difficulty of the Coronation oath which obliged him to maintain the Protestant religion. James, however, refused to compromise.

January drags itself out with blinding snowstorms in which squadrons of Georgian dragoons pass ever on the lookout for a glimpse of tartan. Columns march and counter-march through the icy defiles. There are campfires all over Scotland but no musketry. One morning the clans retreat northward from Perth, and as they go over the white roads, ploughing north through the drifts, 'James VIII' sheds tears and tells the Earl of Mar and his gentlemen that instead of having brought him to a crown they have brought him to his grave. (This, as Prince Eugene of Savoy said when he was told the story, was 'not the way to conquer kingdoms'.) And all the time, as the clansmen march nearer their homes, they become conscious of the army that marches on their heels. The Duke of Argyll has split his forces into two divisions and is advancing on Aberdeen. But the cause is lost; and they know it for sure at Montrose.

It is eight o'clock at night. The clans are ready to move off. The Chevalier's horse is brought to his lodgings. The mounted guard which attends him sits waiting. But a pale, unhappy young man slips out on foot over snow to the lodging of the Earl of Mar. Cloaked men join him. They go quickly by a footpath to the water-side. A boat is waiting. They row out over the dark sea to where the *Maria Theresa* of St Malo is ready to sail. The sails fill, and the ship glides off. The shores of Scotland fade astern in the winter night. The 'Fifteen' is over!

Probably it would not have cheered the unhappy young man that night to be told that in five years' time he would have a son called Charles.

It is time to go to bed. Braemar is already asleep. I walk back in moonlight to that hotel where in 1715 the Earl of Mar did something brave but reckless with a blue flag.

The clans begin to gather in Braemar days before the games begin. There is the Clan Mayfair, the Clan Belgravia, the Clan Edinburgh, the Clan New York, the Clan Chicago, the Clan Washington, with various septs and dependents wearing their national horn-rims and monocles. They gather in long touring cars. They fill the hotels for miles around with bright chatter of grouse and salmon. Here and there among them is a genuine laird whose knees are voted by the beautiful girls of the Clan Chicago, 'just too cute for woids'.

But Braemar takes its games with the dour solemnity of the Scotsman in *Punch*. It apparently sees nothing funny or pathetic about them. They do not appeal to Braemar as the sentimental obsequies of a dead age. Braemar is not annoyed by the kind and patronizing smile which plays round the mouth of modern society. So why worry about it? It is really stupid to fall into the Gaelic trap and to dream of a poetry revived, a literature revived, and the Highlands brave once more with tartan worn by Scotsmen, because it is perfectly clear that all this has gone beyond the point of artificial respiration. It would be a good thing to treat Gaelic as we treat Latin. Even Ireland is finding it a little trying to go shopping in Gaelic. If you must have a bee in your bonnet, however, there is none with a more charming buzz than that of the synthetic Gael, as in Ireland they call those who wear the kilt and refuse to speak English even to their wives. I am always fighting a strong touch of synthetic Gaelicism in myself. Dr Johnson, a most unlikely victim, caught it in Scotland! I would like nothing better on earth than to isolate myself on an island of the Hebrides and, in the intervals of writing long Ossianic poems, to found a clan of tartan-wearing youths trained from their earliest years to tear Income-tax collectors limb from limb. However . . .

The Braemar Gathering is about to begin. The hills fling back the sound of the pipes. Old men who yesterday were seen plodding round in coats and trousers are suddenly transfigured. Majesty and nobility have descended on them. They do not walk: they stride. There are men in Duff tartan with sprigs of holly in their glengarries, there are Balmoral men in Stuart tartan, there are Farquharsons with fir sprigs in their bonnets. You can go all over the world but you will never see the male more splendidly arrayed. The swing of the kilt is a declaration of independence: it is the symbol of aristocracy.

'I wonder,' I heard an Englishwoman say, 'why the Scotch don't wear the kilt more. It's so becoming, don't you think, Henry?'

I suppose, like nine out of ten English people, she did not know that for forty-five years a Highlander in a kilt was liable to be shot at sight. The destruction of the clan system and the stamping out of the national dress was part of the appalling cruelty with which the Whig Government followed up Butcher Cumberland's victory over Charles Edward at Culloden. In 1746 an Act for the 'Abolition and Proscription of the Highland Dress' forbade Scotsmen 'on any pretext whatsoever' to 'wear or put on the clothes called Highland clothes' under a penalty of six months' imprisonment for the first offence and seven years' transportation to 'plantations beyond the seas' for a second offence. Those who were suspected of an attempt to evade the law were hauled before the authorities and forced to take the following horrible oath:

'I swear as I shall answer to God at the great day of judgment, I have not, and shall not have, in my possession any gun, sword, or arms whatsoever, and never use tartan, plaid, or any part of the Highland garb, and if I do so may I be accursed in my undertakings, family, and property; may I never see my wife, nor children, nor father, mother, or relations; may I be killed in battle as a fugitive coward, and lie without Christian burial in a foreign land, far from the graves of my forefathers and kindred; may all this come upon me if I break this oath.'

How the Highlands accepted this cruel order was well expressed in Gaelic by a bard, Fair Duncan of the Songs, who wrote: 'Though compelled to accept the breeches as our dress, hateful to us is the fashion by which our legs are now constrained: heretofore we moved boldly and erect with our belted plaids. Alas! we are now disgraced. Since we have appeared in this detested garb, we can scarce recognize each other at feast or fair. I have seen the day I would answer the man with contempt who should tell me that I ever should wear so unmanly a costume – so foreign to my kindred. Now our heads are thatched with dingy hats and our backs with clumsy cassocks. Our smartness and our picturesque appearance are now gone. Alas! how unfit is the dress for ascending our mountains, and coming down from the heights. We blush in it when in the presence of the fair. We are like slaves, disarmed and humbled, without dirks, guns, swords, crossbelts, or pistols, and are scorned by the Saxons. Our indignation is great.'

The Duke of Cumberland's brutalities founded our modern attitude to the Highlands as surely as Nero's extermination of the Christians created the saints. After nearly half a century of suppression the Highlander was seen through a revulsion of feeling as a high-minded martyr; and it was only necessary for the wizard of Abbotsford to fling a sentimental plaid over his wronged person for the whole country to flock north in belated sympathy. The vile Act was repealed in 1782; but so well had it done its job that many tartans had been lost and even the ancient manner of wearing the old Highland costume had in many regions been forgotten. The little sticks which once were to be found in every Highland cottage marking the number and colour of the threads to a tartan 'set' had been broken up or lost. But the tartan came back to the heather to some extent. Many a treasured kilt carefully hidden since the '45 must have been pressed into shape again and worn by a son or a grandson. Sir John Carr in 1809 saw this revival and has left a rather amusing note on it: 'Feminine delicacy has been sufficiently accustomed,' he writes, 'even in the south, to contemplate the kilt, or short petticoat, of the Highlander without a shock, and I am therfore heartily glad that he is restored to his semi-nakedness, by which he is enabled to spring over his mountains with perfect ease and is no longer restrained within the rigid bounds of southern breeches.'

If the eye carries away from Braemar the undying memory of the kilt, what of the ear? From early morning until late evening the pipes come sobbing or shouting over the hills, now in an ecstasy of sorrow, now in a scream of triumph. The piper in a city street is a misfortune, but pipers marching with the wind over a hill send blood to the head and make fingers itch for a sword. The bagpipe is the voice of the claymore. It sings the song of the sword: the sword drooping from dying fingers, the sword flashing in battle, the sword whistling in triumph, the sword sheathed in failure. Why should I try to pin down the splendour of pipes when Neil Munro has already done so in his work *John Splendid*?

'On a sudden there rose away before us towards the mouth of the glen the sound of a bagpipe. It came on the tranquil air with no break in its uproar, and after a preparatory tuning it broke into an air called "Cogadh no Sith" — an ancient braggart pibroch made by one Macruimen of the Isle of Skye — a tune that was commonly used by the Campbells as a night retreat or tattoo.

'My heart filled with the strain. It gave me not only the simple illusion that I saw again the regimentals of my native country — many a friend and comrade among them in the shelter of the Castle of Inverlochy — but it roused in me a spirit, very antique, very religious and moving too, as the music of his own land must in every honest Gael.

' "Cruachan for ever!" I said lightly to McIver, though my heart was full.

'He was as much touched by that homely lilt as myself.
' "The old days, the old styles!" said he. "God! how
that pibroch stings me to the core!" And as the tune came
more clearly in the second part, or Crunluadh as we call
it, and the player maybe came round a bend of the road,
my comrade stopped in his place and added with what in
another I might have thought a sob: "I've trudged the
world; I have learned many bravadoes, so that my heart
never stirred much to the mere trick of an instrument but
one, and the piob mhor conquers me. What is it, Colin,
that's in us, rich and poor, yon rude cane-reeds speak so
friendly and human to?"
' " 'Tis the Gaelic," I said, cheered myself by the air.
"Never the roar of the drone or a sob of the chanter's
but's in the Gaelic tongue." '

That is what the pipes mean to a Gael. They are not so
much something in the air as something deep in the heart.
The Englishman does not usually understand the pipes. He
may be thrilled by them as he would be thrilled by a sudden
charge of cavalry, but they cannot bring tears to his eyes.
The honest English opinion of bagpipes has never been
better or more frankly, expressed than by old Sir John Carr
when he heard them over a century ago in Scotland. It is
interesting to contrast his heartfelt remarks with those of Mr
Neil Munro:

'I was promised a rich treat, as the competition of the
Scottish pipers was at hand. That no part of this musical
banquet might pass untasted I was invited to a rehearsal
in the ancient Assembly Room, before the judges, and
informed that it was a great favour to be admitted. I shall
never forget it! As soon as the prize-judges were seated,
the folding doors opened. A Highland piper entered, in
full tartan array, and began to press from the bag of his
pipes, which were decorated with long pieces of ribband,
sounds so loud and horrible that, to my imagination, they

were comparable only to those of the eternally tormented. In this manner he strutted up and down with the most stately march, and occasionally enraptured his audience who expressed the influence of his instrument by loud and reiterated plaudits. For my part, so wretched is this instrument to my ears that I could not discover any difference in regard to expression between "The Gathering of the Macdonalds" and "Abercrombie's Lament", each sound being to me equally depressive, discordant, and horrible. Whether in derision or not I do not pretend to say, but Dr Johnson is reported to have appeared very fond of the bagpipe, and used often to stand for some time with his ear close to the great drone. I believe it might have been three hours that common politeness compelled me to endure the distraction of this preliminary trial of skill; and I left the room with nearly the same sensations with which I would have quitted a belfry on a royal birthday.... The bagpipe is among the very few remaining barbarisms in Scotland.'

Of the three things which confound Englishmen in Scotland – Burns, the bagpipe, and haggis – the last is by far the easiest to understand, especially when accompanied by whisky.

Lassies in kilts dance flings, their silver medals shining on velvet jackets thick as buttons on a 'pearlie's' coat, ancient men with white beards and faces the colour of old mahogany fling off their tunics and stand braced against the weight of the caber, brawny young Highlanders twirl round rapidly like dancing dervishes and put the weight (exposing trews, by the way, and setting many an Englishwoman's mind at rest, for this problem is always in debate across the Border!). Pipers strut here and there emitting the sounds which poor Sir John Carr so detested, or, standing still and beating time with a buckled shoe, send out over the hillsides of Braemar the wild and solemn elegy of the pibroch.

But all this stops suddenly. The news comes that the royal procession has started from Balmoral. The Mayfair and

Belgravia clans sit their shooting-sticks with renewed expect-
ation. There is a great parade of tartan over the hill, the
flash of claymores, and a preliminary squeal of pipes. Then
the royal carriages come softly over the grass, there is much
Royal Stuart tartan, much bowing, and royalty is led to a
rustic arbour to take the salute of the clans. This is the great
moment of the Braemar Gathering. The clansmen come on
the field with drums beating, banners waving, and with a
skirl of the war pibrochs. Many of them are veteran stalkers
who have spent their lives in the hills round Braemar. First
come the Balmoral men in Stuart tartan carrying Lochaber
axes, then the Duffs with their ancient pikes, then the
Farquharsons, each man bearing a flashing claymore. As
they come to the saluting base the chieftains lift their sword-
hilts to their lips, then down in military salute.

'Eyes left!'

And what an array of tanned faces is turned to royalty!
Young and old are in the march past, but it is the old that
one notices because they look like patriarchs who have
walked from some antique saga. It is difficult to realize that
if the King invited you to stalk the deer at Balmoral you
might draw as a gillie one of those leonine old men.

If you slightly close your eyes you can visualize a rougher,
wilder gathering on the Braes o' Mar, and you know what
that furious infantry was like which flung away their
muskets after the first volley and leapt sword in hand on the
bayonets at Culloden. And the lesson of the Braemar
Gathering? Is there one? If so it is that something heroic
and noble went out of life when the last colony of Celts gave
way before the modern world . . .

Until darkness falls the clansmen stand at cottage doors
brave in the tartan, which comes out once a year. They
watch the traffic of the Highland Derby speeding home
along the mountain roads. The drone of the bagpipe comes
out of the dusk. Braemar, it seems, is unwilling to let the old
times go. Night falls; and tomorrow the pagan gods will
walk the earth as ordinary men in trousers.

If you would see a perfect picture post card stretch of
Scotland take the road from Braemar to Ballater any
afternoon when the sun is shining. Every yard of this road is
a coloured post card. All the graciousness, all the gentleness,
all the sweetness and the prettiness which is denied the
majestic mountain pass from Perth has taken root in the
valley of the Dee. Here on fine days the Highlands wear a
perpetual smile. It is true that there are wild places, but you
are never quite deceived by them: you know that every
pine-tree near Balmoral has a valet, and that no matter how
cold the wind, how cruel the mountainside, how bleak the
rolling moor, there is a hot bath at the end of every day.

These are the Highlands which have been so often
pushed through your letter-box in London with the
inscription: 'Birds terribly scarce this year', or 'Want rain
badly' (this, of course, from a fisherman); and in spite of the
fact that they do not thrill as the hard, naked hills can thrill,
there is a charm about Deeside which is the charm of an
armchair after a storm.

I went on beside the Dee, for this road is like a
promenade beside the river, and I saw that characteristic
sight, a fisherman up to his thighs in the stream wielding a
great salmon-rod, in the background an experienced and
slightly cynical gillie holding an as yet unnecessary gaff.
Over the trees on the right of the road fluttered the Royal
Standard from a turret of Balmoral. This baronial castle of
white Crathie granite lies at the foot of Craig Gowan beside
a bend of the Dee, and it is haunted by the ghost of an
elderly lady in black who admires the scenery from a little
trap drawn by a shaggy Highland pony. The Highlands will
never forget Queen Victoria. I talked to an old man in
Braemar who referred to her always with a spiritual
genuflexion as 'her late gracious majesty'.

And among the delights of this road from Braemar are
the little pine woods beyond the boundary wall. They are
dappled with sunlight and carpeted with the softest fern. I

explored more than one, and found myself in a green heaven of bird song through which trickled a thin tinkle of invisible water. In little clearings among the pungent pine-trees were blue harebells and yellow buttercups; in the darkest part of the wood were alluring toadstools painted pink and scarlet. Through the tall stems of the pines I could see the great mountains on the opposite bank of the river towering to the clouds in a haze of mauve and purple. There is in Scottish landscape, even in lyrical woodlands, something which is most dramatic and definite. A wood is much the same the world over. I know woods in Italy which might be in Sussex. But the Scotchness of these little brakes beside the road along Deeside is such that I feel that the pine-trees rule them. It's when they sigh. If a man were taken up blindfolded and shot from the other end of the world to open his eyes on Deeside, he would say at once: 'I am in Scotland!'

Ballater. . . .

Here is a little town which has apparently not discovered the peril of living on princes' favours. In fact, Ballater rejoices in the act, and there must be great competition to squeeze into the small main street one more 'By Appointment to His Majesty the King'. Every shop, it seems, bears the Royal Arms over the door.

The railway gives up at Ballater, with a sigh of relief. This is the railhead station for Balmoral. All the notabilities of the Victorian Era, and a good many of the Edwardian and the Georgian, have stepped down on its platform. The station officials have developed such an eye for personalities that nothing so recommends itself on this station as a statesman-like bearing. A Gladstone collar would create a panic! Guards of honour have often been posted outside the ticket office. Distinguished parcels are, throughout the autumn, carried tenderly from luggage vans.

Worship for members of the Royal Family is probably carried to greater lengths at Ballater than anywhere else in a loyal kingdom. Even the Prince Consort is still revered in

Ballater, and no one in this town has ever been heard to utter a word against the Albert Memorial. To do so would be disloyal.

It is a glorious spot. The fishing hotel, complete with loyal lithographs and the slightly indignant heads of dead stags, is built beside the Dee, so that you could fish from the bedroom windows if you were a lazy millionaire. They look out over the old bridge to wooded hills, and night and day there is the sound in Ballater of the shallow Dee moving gently over its amber stones.

I bought petrol in Ballater, and the man who worked the pump – obviously a man who in early life could rub down a horse and pull a tail – wore a royal tie-pin. That is typical of Ballater.

8

I slipped out towards Aberdeen on a white ribbon of moonlight. Craigendarroch was immense, lying back over Ballater; and I sped on to Cambus o' May, where fir woods climb steep mountains on either side the Dee. . . . Dinnet and a wide moor all ghostly grey under the moon. . . . Aboyne with a fine green heart to it. . . . Kincardine O'Neil, near Lumphanan, where Macbeth died. . . . Banchory and a slight detour to the Bridge of Feugh, where the water foamed and boiled over the moonlit stones, roaring steadily under ancient arches.

> Folks come frae far to thrang the Brig
> When kelpie spates wid dance a jig,
> To see the Feugh gang roarin' by
> And watch the salmon loupin' high. . . .

And what a night for kelpies it was with the moon glimmering over mountain and through wood; and so on along the road to Durris and journey's end.

CHAPTER SIX

I describe a mystery of Aberdeen never before explored, I see the fishing fleet come in with the dawn, eavesdrop at a wedding, and encounter a man in a kilt

I

IN Aberdeen is the most mysterious building in Scotland. It is a solid and impressive affair constructed, like the rest of Aberdeen, in grey granite, which after a rainstorm 'sparkles as if powdered with diamonds'. (I raise my hat to every writer on Scotland and return thanks for that phrase.)

The visitor, who can enter only with an introduction signed by the Lord Provost and countersigned by the Principal of the University and the Chief Constable, finds himself ascending a massive flight of stairs at the top of which is a swing door guarded by a tremendous commissionaire. He examines the credentials and then asks in the sharp voice of an ex-sergeant-major:

'Home or export?'

'Home,' you say.

'Tak' the lift tae the fir-r-st floor-r and tur-r-r-n tae the richt!'

On this floor granite gives way to the marble of long corridors. You turn to the right, and, passing doors, some marked 'Private', others named 'Professor MacDougal', 'Professor Epstein', 'Professor Frank P. Hicking', 'Professor Cheng', approach a room which resembles an American newspaper office or the sorting-room of a G.P.O. A hundred men sit at little desks all round the room. The centre is occupied by a horseshoe table at which sit men writing busily. Now and then one of the men at the small desks rises and approaching the bookcases, with which the room is lined, consults a volume, and returns thoughtfully to his work.

All the time there is much coming and going of office-boys in neat uniforms. They enter with empty wickerwork baskets, and approaching the man who sits at the head of the horseshoe table depart with their baskets filled with neatly folded slips of typescript. These they take to a carpeted ante-room. Here an official superior even to the man at the horseshoe table eagerly scans the typescript, some of which he destroys; the rest he stamps with a rubber imprint and, flinging it back into the baskets, says briefly:

'Sorting-room!'

The boys dart out with their baskets through another door. It is all very efficient, as silent as the British Museum reading-room, as deliberate as the Bank of England, until – and this to the visitor is always disconcerting – the great room suddenly rings with a yell of uncontrollable laughter! But no one shows any surprise! The men at the horseshoe table continue to write; the men at the little desks writhe slightly and proceed with their tasks. But in a corner of the room one occupant of a small desk rocks with wild mirth! He flings down his pen, jumps up, and cries:

'I've got it! What do you think of this?'

'Oh, go away!' shouts a companion to whom he has gone for encouragement.

'But listen . . .'

'*Will* you go away? I don't want to hear your filthy old chestnut!'

An awful pallor passes over the face of the man who laughed.

'It's not a chestnut,' he says gravely, but with a heart-catching uncertainty in his voice. 'It's a new one.'

'Well, don't bother me! Go and ask the professor.'

He crosses the room with dignity and goes up to the man at the horseshoe table.

'Sir,' he says deferentially, 'an Englishman, an Irishman, and an Aberdonian were having a drink of whisky . . .'

'Indeed,' remarks the professor blandly, looking over his spectacles. 'How remarkable.'

This seems to chill the young man, who gulps slightly and continues:

'Of whisky, you see, sir . . .'

'Continue.'

The young man falters.

'You haven't heard . . .'

'Proceed, my dear sir. It is never possible to deliver judgment on so familiar a beginning.'

'Well, sir, you see, as they were having a drink of whisky three flies fell, one into each glass.'

The professor's eyes become steely hard behind his glasses, but the young man, now committed, blunders on.

'The Englishman took a spoon and lifted his fly out, the Irishman dipped his finger in the whisky and took his fly out, and the Aberdonian . . .'

'*Wrung it out!*' shouts the professor in a voice of thunder. Heads look up all over the room and work ceases.

'Mr Johnson!' cried the professor, livid with passion, I am ashamed of you! That story was cabled back from Toronto last Thursday week. Come to me in my office tomorrow at twelve!'

The young man slinks back to his desk and buries his head in his arms. No one pays any attention to him. His companions now and then give way to laughter; there is a sudden clicking of a typewriter and a slip thrown into a basket. Sometimes a man approaches the professor and whispers. Sometimes the professor smiles broadly and pats his colleague on the back; sometimes he shakes his head doubtfully; sometimes he whispers: 'Go outside and try it!' and the man so instructed runs for his hat and leaves the building.

There is a lift. On the fourth floor a room runs the length of the building. Over the door is the notice:

EXPORT

NO ADMISSION EXCEPT ON BUSINESS

A travelling band runs round this room, laden with full

wickerwork baskets. To each one has been fixed a label: 'Siam', 'Malay States', 'Kenya Colony', 'Mexico', 'Japan', 'India', 'Canada', 'United States of America' – the whole world is represented in this room. As the baskets move over the band they are snatched by men standing under labels which correspond with those on the baskets. They empty the contents out, pack them neatly in strong boxes, on them slap a label already addressed to distant parts of the earth, and shoot them into a lift which carries them to the postal department.

'So you are interested in Aberdeen Publicity,' says an alert man of middle age. This is Professor X (his name is never mentioned), the head of the department. 'Our production goes up by leaps and bounds. We are this year 500,000 new anecdotes ahead of last year. Now that Turkey has reorganized the alphabet we are finding an enormous field over there. Stories about Aberdeen are, in fact, used in the schools. Excuse me . . .'

An official holds out a strip of paper.

'Look at that, sir.'

'Good heavens! The old one about the weighing machine penny! Where did you find it?'

'Australian box, sir.'

'Terrible! Send it back to the Sorting Department and instruct them to have it translated into Chinese. It was sent round Australia six months ago.'

The official departs.

'That man is authorized to dip into the foreign jokes to test their freshness. There is always a chance that an old one may slip in by mistake.'

'What do you do with the old ones?'

'Come this way!'

He opens a door and you enter a room full of men working at top speed.

'This is the translation department. An Aberdeen joke is officially old in four weeks; in five weeks it is stale, in six weeks it is bad, in seven weeks it is dead – officially speaking, that is – actually an Aberdeen joke never dies: it is immortal. But when a joke has been launched it is immediately translated into every foreign language; and even then we are frequently beaten unless we employ the cable, which is a most expensive way of propagating a reputation for meanness. However . . .'

As you go towards the lift the professor pauses and asks:

'You have noticed, no doubt, that one of the characteristics of the city is that as soon as you arrive a fellow guest in the hotel seeks an opportunity of asking: "Have you heard this one?" '

'I have indeed!'

'Do you know how that is done? Well, I will show you one of our secrets. Many an Aberdonian is in ignorance of the thing you are now to see.'

We enter on the official side of a long counter. On the door is painted 'Out-Patients' Department'. The public side of the counter is divided into a series of small cabinets, so that the man in one cannot see the man on his left or right.

'This is carried out in the greatest secrecy,' says the professor. 'The source of a good story must always be mysterious. A good story should drop like manna from above. Now watch . . .'

The doors from the street open. Men enter the cabinets and rap on the counter as if demanding a railway ticket.

'*Got a good new one?*' they whisper anxiously.

A clerk picks up an envelope and swiftly passes it across. '*Anything new about Jews and Aberdonians?*'

'Certainly, sir.'

So it goes on.

'The Out-Patients' Department is open all night,' explained the professor. 'We should lose a lot of publicity if we were not – people going on the night trains, you know.'

'What an amazing sight.'

'Yes, it is! Now if you dash round to your hotel at once you will just be in time to hear the stories which you saw handed over the counter. Well, I must say goodbye. By the way, this hasn't been put out yet: A Jew in Aberdeen for the first time noticed that there were few taxicabs, so . . .'

I said at the beginning that in Aberdeen is the most mysterious building in Scotland. I am sure it exists!

2

Aberdeen, or to give it the right subtitle, the City of Bon-Accord, is obviously one of the corner-stones of modern Scotland. Lacking Aberdeen, Scotland would not be so securely balanced. This is a city which, to mix metaphor, nails down the map of Scotland on the north-east with the hard metal of the Scottish character. It is rather curious to discover this vivid and stimulating community in a part of Scotland where you might have expected a kind of haphazard Galway.

The Aberdonian is, to my eyes, the most distinct of all the city types of Scotland, but that is perhaps because I know him better than any other, having in my youth suffered agonies from his relentless passion for accuracy. English journalism is red with the hair of Aberdonians. Newspaper proprietors feel safer when these hard-heads are about, because they reduce to the lowest minimum the risk of libel actions. The dreadful blue pencils of Aberdonians travel cautiously over the world's news, cutting out the cackle and getting down to the bare bones of reality. A pencil in such hands ceases to be a pencil: it becomes a surgical implement. But the finest training for a young writer full of that mental flatulence which he mistakes for the divine afflatus is a year of hell under an ex-schoolmaster of Aberdeen. I hit up against the Aberdeen mentality when, as a young journalist from the provinces, I took the post of junior sub-editor on one of the big London dailies. One night a reporter wrote a short article stating that the fig-tree in St Paul's Churchyard had given birth to seven figs. In the course of a long night's work I sub-edited this and put a headline on it and forgot it. Three days later I was carpeted by the Aberdonian night editor.

'Did you do this?' he asked, flinging a clipping at me.

'I did.'

'Don't you know,' he cried, hitting his desk at every word, 'that-the-fir-r-st-requirement-in-your-profession-is-accuracy? Read that!'

He tossed over a letter from one of the meddling idiots who read newspapers in the hope of tracking down minor errors – probably Aberdonians! – to the effect that the writer had been to St Paul's Churchyard and had counted not seven but eight figs. He leant across his desk, his red hair tousled and his eyes blazing with anger.

'St Paul's is five minutes' walk from this office! Did ye not think of running down to count the figs?'

'No, sir. Besides, the story came in at eleven at night and it was pitch dark.'

'Could ye not have borrowed an electric torch?'

'I never thought about it.'

'Well, ye'll not go far in your profession! I have just come from St Paul's and' – here he paused and let the awful words sink in to me – 'there *are* eight figs on the tree! Now be more careful in future. . . .'

After a year of this I knew every book of reference backwards. I used to read *Who's Who, Crockford*, and *Lloyd's Register* for amusement, and in the process of being brought down to hard 'fac's' I conceived a tremendous admiration and respect for the Aberdonian mentality. It is capable of producing the most efficient subordinates on earth. In various walks of life the Aberdonians bring to bear their sharp sense of fact and their microscopic capacity for painstaking detail. Their brains are like iced encyclopaedias.

Aberdeen is their logical habitat. They made Aberdeen and Aberdeen made them. Here is a city, built of the hardest known stone, in a part of the world which must be unfit for human habitation for several months of the year. Its people have to their credit centuries of struggle, not only against the forces of nature but against the disadvantage of their material position. Struggle and ambition are in the air of Aberdeen, so that this city seems to me like the world's greatest monument to that god who helps those who help themselves.

There is probably no other city which to the stranger seems to embody more definitely the grim, plodding determination of the Scot. A large part of the rock-like splendour of the Scottish character is due firstly to a complete absence of any social inferiority complex – a trait not noticeable in the English character – and secondly to a resolve to rise by sheer hard work and merit above the misfortunes of birth. It is not surprising that Aberdeen looks like a heavy anchor to reality; less surprising that in this city they say, 'Tak' awa' Aberdeen and twal' mile roun' and – where are ye?' ('Ye', of course, refers to the universe.)

I am more conscious of education in Aberdeen than in any other place I know, with the exception of Oxford and Cambridge, which is not a fair comparison but a remarkable one. Grey Marischal College is one of the most impressive buildings in the British Isles. I was told to see it after a shower of rain, but I saw it, more marvellously, I think, in the light of a full moon. It is, with the exception of the Escurial in Spain, the largest granite building in the world, but its beauty, its balance, its stern nobility exceeds that of any Gothic building made of this stone.

This is a portion of that university which the Highlands regard as the pathway to fame. There are 250 bursaries. In little crofters' cottages all over the Highlands these bursaries seem as desirable a prey as a herd of cattle in older times. Every year young men descend on them with full brains but empty pockets, determined to profit by them to the uttermost farthing. Over a door in Marischal College are written the words which Bernard Shaw carved over the mantelpiece in his old flat in Adelphi Terrace:

Thai haif said – Quhat
Say thay
Lat hame say

They were first uttered by the founder of the college, George Keith, fifth Earl Marischal, as a defiant answer to those who questioned his right to Church lands given at the Reformation.

Aberdeen impresses the stranger as a city of granite palaces inhabited by people as definite as their building material. Even their prejudices are of the same hard character. The beauty of Aberdeen is the beauty of uniformity and solidity. Nothing so time-defying has been built since the Temple of Karnak. And it is obvious that in a few years when certain ancient streets disappear that Aberdeen will be, after Edinburgh, the most architecturally impressive city in all Scotland.

Wigan in Lancashire and Aberdeen are two places known throughout the kingdom by virtue of a joke. When I was in Wigan the town clerk pleaded with me to do what I could to discount this joke. Aberdeen, however, with its superlative sense of business, enjoys stories against Aberdeen as much as Jews enjoy stories against their race. This, contrary to popular belief, is the only resemblance between the two peoples. The real Aberdeen joke is, of course, the free publicity given to the city by those who spread it!

3

It is early morning. The sun is rising. The sound of Aberdeen at this time is a bright jingle as dray horses plod steadily over the stone roads. I go through the half light to one of Aberdeen's most fascinating sights – the morning auction in the Fish Market.

At the bottom of Market Street I am pulled up by an unexpected beauty. The rising sun, struggling through a veil of clouds in thin streamers of lemon-yellow and flamingo-pink, flings a bridgehead in dark silhouette against the sky. I have no doubt that in ordinary lights this is a very ordinary bridge, merely a path of steel girders linking quay to quay.

But in the early morning its round turrets, like a Border keep, stand mirrored in the still water of a dock looking for all the world like some ancient fortress of romance dreaming above its moat.

The Fish Market is something that no visitor to Aberdeen should miss. Every fish market is fascinating. That man is not normal who will not linger beside a fisherman in the hope of prying into his basket. How much more exciting, then, are these markets on whose floors are laid out the stranger mysteries of deeper waters?

This fish market is the largest in the country. It is a broad, covered way built right round the Albert Basin. The trawler fleet lies – 'berthed' is, I suppose, the right word, but 'parked' is much more expressive – at the quayside, thick as motor-cars at the Derby. They steam gently with the effort of their incoming. Their decks are foul with fishscales and slippery with crushed ice. Salt is on their smokestacks, and their high fo'c'sles are wet still with North Sea spray. The grimy faces of engineers peer up from hatchways; down companionways clatter the crews in enormous thigh boots. Vivid, arresting, and even, as are all things connected with the sea, exciting as this fleet is, it simply fades before the spectacle of its cargo.

Imagine a million bare babies being soundly smacked, and you have the sound of Aberdeen Fish Market as a million fish are slapped down on the concrete! The sound of this slapping continues perhaps for an hour until each ship has landed her catch. Then come men who sort out the fish according to their kind, and other men who take each limp pyramid and dress it by the right in neat, fearfully defunct, rows. The sight of so much death before breakfast might be considered a saddening experience. The same number of sheep or oxen lying prone would turn any man towards vegetarianism; but death, which is, no doubt, as real to a fish as to a mammal, is to us the normal condition of a fish. Only goldfish are pathetic in death, and then probably because their end may seem to reflect on us.

I walk, it seems for miles, past dead fish. Imagine the Strand from Temple Bar to Charing Cross carpeted with haddock, plaice, soles, whiting, hake, cod, skate, ling, and lobsters, and you have a hazy idea of the thing that happens in Aberdeen every morning of the year. I am told that things might be better with the trawler trade; but I cannot believe it. This daily harvest of the sea is an amazing spectacle. It is difficult for a landsman to believe that it can go on day after day the year round.

I walk with a faint feeling of generalship. It is like inspecting several army corps. The poor fish lie in rows with an N.C.O. at regular intervals set at a slightly different angle to indicate the count. There are gigantic skate with tails like sting ray, there are colossal hailbut taken from deep waters, there are cod like young sharks. Some of the fish has come from the Faroe Islands.

'How much is there in the market?'

'Och, it's no' a guid catch the dee!' replies a market official. 'It isna more than four hundred tons.'

'Four hundred tons? Forty ten-ton railway truck loads! A train of forty trucks not a good catch?'

'Na, na, man; it isna guid at a'! Ye should see seven hundred tons laid oot, and then ye might say ye had seen something. . . .'

When the fish is paraded there happens the most mysterious commercial transaction I have ever witnessed. The auctioneers appear with little books. They walk up to each battalion. A crowd of buyers follows. There is no shouting, no gesticulation; they might, in fact, be performing a burial service in some unknown tongue. I defy a stranger to discover unaided what passes between auctioneer and buyer in Aberdeen Fish Market. A man may be able to buy a Rembrandt at Christies for £100,000, but I am willing to bet him that he would find it impossible to buy one haddock by auction in Aberdeen! It is not an auction: it is a secret society.

The formula, whatever it is, could not be more effective.

In less time than it takes to perform a leisurely walk round the victims each dump has been sold. Fish begins to melt as swiftly as snow in sun. Large areas of asphalt become visible. Soon there is not a fish to be seen.

'Where does it all go?'

'London mostly.'

'When does it arrive?'

'Tons of it will be eaten for breakfast tomorrow morning.'

That is Aberdeen's most spectacular hour.

4

The hotel is large. Its cosmopolitan life centres in the lounge, which from seven p.m. until past midnight is filled with visitors and the local 'bloods'. A debauched-looking walnut piano stands among the gilded chairs like a wise old man among fools. When midnight strikes, empty whisky glasses rest on its jaundiced keys and pose with an air of dead gaiety on its lid.

Outside is the rigorous Aberdeen night: a dance club, several cinemas, and long, stone streets of shuttered shops full of young people passing and re-passing, often smiling, seldom meeting, prettily playful, vaguely virtuous.

The hotel lounge wears, however, an expression of potential wickedness. Two commercial travellers, whose wives and whose firms would at this moment not approve of them, sit drinking with two young women who are obviously not natives of the town. But they are pretty. Even the fatherly old man in the corner thinks so, as he pretends not to look over his newspaper at the pink and *diamanté* garter above a careless, silk knee. Young men drawn by business from all parts of England and Scotland lie relaxed in chairs with the air of men who would like to paint the town red if they could only find the paint.

The clock strikes twelve. A harassed-looking page-boy takes an order for more whisky, gathers empty glasses from the dissipated piano, and wearily disappears. The visitors eventually regain their reason and go to bed, leaving behind them a pall of foul tobacco smoke, crumpled newspapers, empty glasses, an apparently dead man in a chair, and a strong impression that there is no place like home.

It is two o'clock in the afternoon of the following day. The lounge, which at midnight looked like a lifelong roué, seems to have been dipped in the Well of Youth. The sun shines through the windows. The gold chairs stand round the walls, prim as footmen. Even the alcoholic piano has in some marvellous manner regained its innocence. The wide, pseudo-Adams grate is swept and garnished, and in the open space of the cleared floor stands a writing-table, on it a fair sheet of virgin blotting-paper, pens, ink, and a Bible. A wedding will take place at two-thirty p.m.

This may appear strange to English people, who, being the most romantic people on earth, cling to the belief – quite contrary to all theological teaching – that marriages having been made in heaven should naturally be solemnized in a church. Even the registry office goes against the grain in England. In Scotland a marriage can be solemnized anywhere. The declaration of a man and woman that they take one another for husband and wife is a legal marriage. Hundreds of marriages are held in the hotel lounges of Scotland. Marriages still take place in the rustic atmosphere of Gretna Green. . . .

The guests arrive under a shower of confetti provided by girls assembled on the pavement. Departing Rotarians receive mouthfuls as they leave the hotel. The head porter, master of the wedding ceremonies, stands with a clothes-brush ready to receive each sprinkled guest. A Jew who asks about trains to Edinburgh is referred to the boots. A page-boy sweeps up the confetti as it blows into the hotel.

'Aye,' says the head porter, 'it's an awfu' daft custom. And rain's coming. It'll stick to the steps like coloured porridge. . . .'

A car drives up. Out steps the minister. Will they throw

confetti? They will not! He walks, stern and immune, wearing a frock coat and a silk hat, and carrying a Bible like a shield over his heart. The transformed lounge fills with men and women, the men in morning or lounge suits, each wearing a pink carnation; the women in their bonniest afternoon gowns. The minister, entering gravely, stands behind the table, fiddles with ink and pens, and then discovers that his coat-tails are too near the fire. Several young men move the table forward to the exact spot occupied at midnight by the gay commercial travellers and the girl with the *diamanté* garters.

The head porter becomes officious. He runs to the lift-boy.

'*Bring doon the bridegroom!*' he orders with the voice of an executioner. 'Room number thir-r-ty-two!'

The bridegroom comes down in the lift with the best man, both raw and sheepish. They stand before the table, facing the minister.

'*Bring doon the bride!*' orders the head porter. 'Room number fufteen!'

Up shoots the lift on its glad errand.

'It's an awfu' anxious business,' explains the head porter. 'They mustna see each ither until they meet at the wedding. It's awfu' bad luck. . . .'

He turns quickly to the descending lift, and opens the door to the little white bride. Then a most astounding thing happens! As the bride and her bridesmaids enter the hotel lounge, thin and sweet sounds the Wedding March from 'Lohengrin'. The incredible piano is taking part in the ceremony! Those keys, so lately alcoholic – that keyboard which every night welcomes its row of empty glasses is now greeting the bride! The sound of its cracked voice transforms the lounge and gives it a soul at last.

Bride and bridegroom stand together, nervously. Once more the amazing piano lifts its antique voice:

> *O God of Bethel! By whose hand*
> *Thy people still are fed;*

Who through this weary pilgrimage,
Hast all our fathers led. . . .

The service proceeds. It is impossible to reconcile this touching, sincere, reverent scene with the other moods of the lounge! All manner of unlikely people tiptoe up and try to peep behind the screen. Bad old men who were drinking whisky until two a.m. stand hushed and somehow pathetic in their interest. People in a hurry stop and say, 'Oh, a wedding!' smile, and go by quietly. The dull corridors are full of a warm humanity. Even the cooks down in the kitchens must feel that the hotel is more than an ordinary hotel. The impertubable women in the reception office are faintly flushed as with a reflected glory – a remarkable sight.

But, presiding over the forecourt of the temple, immense and autocratic, is the head porter with his whispered: 'Damn that boy! Tell Bob to keep quiet wi' that broom?'

The bridegroom, fumbling a moment in the pockets of his brand-new striped trousers, produces a ring. Women all round the room try hard not to cry. The bride holds forward her left hand. He clumsily slips the ring on her finger. His ears are red. The minister proclaims them man and wife. They bend their heads. He lifts his hands and blesses them. They are married. They edge just an inch nearer to each other. She slips her hand through his sleeve and there is just the slightest caress.

'Got him!' says a cynical young man in plus fours outside in the hall. No one heeds him, least of all the bad old lizards who peer through at the wonderful thing that has happened in their lounge. They are strangely still and reverent, rather like wicked spies regarding the Promised Land.

Once again the battered hero of the lounge uplifts his husky voice, and, with a few notes absent in the treble, plays the wedding party into the wedding breakfast, where a white pagoda of a cake lifts its snowy storeys high above the flowers. . . .

It is seven o'clock. The bride and bridegroom have

departed; but not so the guests. In the hall where Rotarians assemble another and a more agile piano plays a reel. There is a regular rhythm on the floor, feet stamping, bang, bang, bang, and then a wild shrill 'Hooch!' and peals of laughter. . . .

In the lounge . . . but the lounge has reverted to type! It has become profane once more. It is full of cigar smoke. The lizards are back. An Aberdonian is making a joke about Aberdeen. The waiter drifts in preceded by a tray of dry Martinis. A *diamanté* garter shines above a silk knee.

And someone has left an empty glass on the misunderstood piano.

5

While the wedding, so faithfully described in the foregoing pages, was in progress I encountered a kilted Scotsman. He passed through the hotel. Everybody turned to look at him, and everybody waved to him. He was a typical Jock. Had you painted him black and put him in Zulu warpaint he would still have been broad Scots. He was small, sturdy, middle-aged, and smooth of face. He wore hexagonal glasses and smoked a six-inch briar pipe. His glengarry was worn at a jaunty angle, and, as he walked, the almost ankle-length Inverness cape which he wore exposed a bit of a MacLeod tartan kilt. Someone whistled:

Just a wee deoch an doruis;

someone else:

Stop yer ticklin', Jock;

someone else:

Roamin' in the gloamin'.

To all of which the little man in the kilt smiled cheerfully and waved a hand.

'How are you, Sir Harry?'

'An' hoo's yersel',' replied the little man.

The superior person will perhaps sniff if I suggest that no

man since Sir Walter Scott has warmed the world's heart to
Scotland more surely than Sir Harry Lauder. Is there a part
of the world which, thanks to him, does not know the
meaning of at least one Gaelic phrase – 'deoch an doruis' –
or such Scots words as 'gloaming' and 'glen' and 'lassie', or
such extravagancies as a 'braw, bricht, moonlicht night'?
Millions of people who have never seen, and never will see,
Scotland have experienced affection for the country whose
homelier characteristics are so deliciously exaggerated in
this man. Lauder's genius is a thing apart. Observe that
sudden extra tenseness which comes to an audience when
he is announced; see him come on the stage, a grotesque
little 'Highlander' with a deformed yellow walking-stick;
watch him advance right to the footlights and, in the
apparently effortless certainty of his genius, grip his audience so tightly to him that his slightest inflexion becomes full
of meaning, the hardly perceptible movement of a muscle
significant. Rarely does he say anything witty. An audience,
however, is willing to welcome anything he may care to say,
no matter how commonplace, with a constant ripple of
laughter. His personal magnetism is irresistible.

How masterly is his trick suddenly of breaking off in the
middle of a song to treat his audience to a brief confidential
talk. The Scots expression and the Doric are the ideal
medium for quiet little heart-to-heart chats; and when
Harry Lauder talks between songs it is never possible to
believe that he thought it all out deliberately beforehand.

He will sing a rollicking song like 'Roamin' in the
Gloamin' ' or 'Stop yer Ticklin', Jock', and when he has
carried his audience with him, and they are ready to go on
in that mood indefinitely, he will switch over into pathos.
He is too clever to do it abruptly; but watch how he will
concentrate his effect on one good laugh quickly followed
with another, funny but with a serious side to it; and then,
suddenly, startlingly, and with a simplicity and a sincerity
impossible to question, he is telling some story of the war.
There is not a sound in the theatre. The little Scotsman

stands in the full flare of the footlights speaking words which come straight from his heart. Every word rings true. In two minutes he has carried hundreds of men and women of different types and mentalities to the opposite pole of emotion. There is real feeling in the theatre now; an emotion which few great actors can command. Something essentially honest, good, pure, and simple in the little Scotsman is speaking to those same qualities in his fellow-men. Then he switches back to laughter! All he has to do is to – smile! Smiles answer him everywhere! The band strikes up, and once more he is roamin' in the gloamin' – amazing little man! The greatest compliment the world pays him is the fact that he is the only comedian who is permitted to be serious whenever he feels like it.

The good stories which he has told about himself are only outnumbered by those attributed to him.

'A gey row ye kickit up,' his mother often told him; 'the neighbours across the street heard ye roarin' an' cam' ower tae ask if ye was twins.'

And he has described at various times, as so many successful Scotsmen have described with something more than pride, the harsh poverty of his early life. A boyhood in a flax-mill in Arbroath and 2s. 1d. a week for working from six a.m. until six p.m. Then he used to sit up until midnight with his mother teasing ropes in order to earn an extra 3s. a week. How truly Scots his comment was: 'How could ever a man forget such a beginning as that? How could any man ever put on airs and hold himself above his fellows when he, within his own soul, had an experience like that? These things make one very humble.'

He worked as a pit-boy in a mine at Hamilton near Glasgow. It was here that his talents first came out in concerts and soirées. Then a first prize in a singing competition led him to his career, and he was soon touring at 35s. a week. He never looked back after his first appearance at Gatti's Music Hall, London, in March 1900. One night a bunch of Scotsmen grew hilarious in the theatre. A bonnet was flung on the stage. An attendant came to turn out the offender, who shouted to Lauder:

'Dinna let them pit me oot, Harry. I kent ye in Glesca'!'

'Dinna let them pit ye oot,' replied Lauder; 'remember ye're a Scotsman! Hang on!'

But the truest thing he ever said was: 'I stand for nationality and the simple human things which are its roots.' Therein lies his genius and his spell.

CHAPTER SEVEN

*Describes a sincere Scottish breakfast and a visit to a graveyard at Elgin. I go
to Forres and on to Inverness, where I stand on the battlefield of Culloden*

I

THERE are mornings now and then, rarer as a man
grows older, which come steeped in the lost wonder of
youth. Everything is sharper, more lovely, more desirable,
so that, alive to the very fingertips with the beauty of the
world, a man trembles, it seems, on the threshold of a
discovery. Such things are outside normal experience. It is
almost as though the spirit had crossed the boundary
between this world and the next.

On such an ecstatic morning I took the road that runs for
some way beside the Don to Inverurie. It was so early that
the autumnal mists lay over the fields in long, waist-high
streaks of silver. Thin grey veils were queerly twisted in
hollow places, lying above old watercourses like the ghosts
of the streams that once ran there. As the sun rose the mists
fell away, like spectral armies in retreat, curling off, or
streaming upwards from the earth, revealing the gold corn-
stooks ranked in the stubble in all the pride of a gay
morning. The air came sweet from the sea, ice-cold and
scented with the pungent earthiness of autumn, and all the
land smiled like a woman who has her child safe at her
heart. It hurt me to go over roads so quickly in a machine
when I would have been walking with wet boots on grass
and through the browning bracken of woods. I stopped and,
following a little footpath for a mile or so, listened to the
sound of sheep and the drone of bees out so early to traffic
in wet flowers. I saw, with a childish delight, the furry
saffron hindquarters of a bumble-bee wedged in a damp
foxglove. And I thought, as I laughed at him struggling to
get out, that he was one of the most ridiculous sights in

nature, always excepting the duck that dives, exposing two absurd paddling feet which prepare the observer for the equally amusing reappearance of him wrapped in a solemn gustatory satisfaction.

I came to a brown stream – I think it was the Deveron at Huntly – which sang a song of salmon as it slipped over its pebbles. I am sure that the fattest trout in all Scotland come out of that river, such streamy flyable waters, so rich and encouraging. And as I went on out of Aberdeenshire over the borders into Banff it occurred to me that I had not breakfasted. As if in answer to my desires, a bend in the road revealed a few cottages, on one of which was the sign which may mean anything or nothing: 'Teas and Refreshments.' What, however, was so encouraging at this moment was the strong smell of frying bacon which came out of a back door and fought a pitched battle with a hedge of honeysuckle. The door was wide open. It revealed a little parlour and a table set with a white cloth. It was all so perfect and in tune with the morning. Yes; of course I could have breakfast. Would I take porridge? No, not in fairyland, thanks! Would I take eggs and bacon? I would. The maid with the unsmiling freckled face and the exceedingly shy eyes departed, and I went out to admire the morning again. There was a tea garden attached to this heavenly cottage hidden from the road by a hedge of honeysuckle, which positively shook as the bees swung from one blossom to another. In the tea garden, among a number of dissipated-looking green metal tables and collapsible chairs, sat a black retriever with an expression like that of Pelleas and Melisande, Tristan and Iseult, Romeo and Juliet, and all other great but tragic lovers of the world. He came up and talked to me. He said that he was delighted that I had come. He would very much like to take me somewhere and show me something, but he supposed that, like most visitors to his cottage, I was firmly anchored by hunger. He snapped sideways at a bee, missed, and smiled up at me. Perhaps if he lay down on his back in the grass and looked silly I might care to rub his stomach and romp with him, at which point in our friendship the solemn maiden put her freckled face round the door and cried in a high, cheerful voice:

'Yer breakfast's ready for ye!'

Scotland is the best place in the world to take an appetite. France, with its messy mysteries and its pretentious fragments, is all very well for that dreadful creature with a bashful interior who has to be led gently to his food, but if a man has an honest hunger sharpened by open air he will satisfy it with less risk to his mechanism more speedily in a Scottish kitchen than anywhere else. I could live on Scotch broth and cockaleekie for ever! These supreme soups, the absolute monarchs of the stock-pot, are unparalleled elsewhere in the world. They are the food of the gods, not anaemic gods who sit in clouds on Ida, but hairy gods who tramp the heather with swords and howl from hill to hill. These soups appeal not only to my taste but also to my sense of colour and my love of variety. They are like a great orchestra engaged in perfect symphony. If a man encounters nothing in Scotland but broth – that porridge of the evening – thick with peas, barley, leeks, carrots, and almost everything that was in the kitchen at the time, he has not travelled in vain. He can return to his own land with the boast that he has met real soup.

It is, however, in breakfasts and teas that the Scottish genius for repletion manifests itself to perfection. I entered the front parlour and saw on the table a breakfast which I can describe only as perfectly sincere. There were eggs and bacon. There were warm oatcakes. There were warm scones. There were baps. There was toast. There was marmalade. There was jelly. There was honey. In case this was not enough, there was a plate of parkins and a currant loaf.

On the opposite wall Queen Victoria was being crowned in Westminster Abbey. The Archbishop of Canterbury was advancing with the crown, but the House of Lords had lost all interest in the historic event as it gazed down at me with expressions of surprise and envy. They were dressed up in their robes, condemned to stand in perpetual attendance, and there sat I at a Scottish breakfast. It was enough to break their hearts! Even Her Majesty, I thought, as I attacked the oatcakes, was beginning to look slightly in my direction.

I sat in the window-seat smoking, looking at French fashion papers. They contained minute instructions for the making of evening gowns and knickers of *crêpe de Chine*. How on earth, I wondered had they invaded this cottage in Banff. What a queer wind from the Rue de la Paix to find blowing about through the honeysuckle of a Scottish lane! The black retriever entered and placing at my feet an ancient bone remarked: 'Well, if you wouldn't come with me to find it I suppose I must bring it to you! This is the bone for which I have an almost sentimental affection. I show it to you because we understand one another pretty well, and you seem the kind of fellow who might have bones hidden away, too, which you would show to me if I visited your house. I'm glad you admire it; and now I must remove it! Women don't understand these things as we do, consumed, as they are, by a passion for tidiness before which the greatest treasures of our hearts go completely west. . . .'

I was soon on the way again and had crossed the Isla at Keith.

2

Elgin has a prosperous, retired-looking air. I feel that its tradesmen specialize in local gentry.

In the days when Scotland was Catholic the great Cathedral of Elgin must have been the finest example of pointed Gothic in the land. Now it is the most picturesque religious ruin north of the Border abbeys. I saw it in hot sunlight, the shapes of its fractured towers lying in broad shadows across the green grass of the nave. The old lady who lives in the gatehouse took me round and led me to the graves of the Gordons and into the chapter-house whose piscina is linked with a romantic story enlivened by that financial sequel so dear to the Scottish heart.

When Bonnie Prince Charlie was marching with the clans in 1745 a good-looking girl called Mary Gilzean in the neighbouring parish of Drainie ran away with a soldier called Anderson. They fled across the seas, where the soldier and his delicately brought-up wife lived a life of such tragic privation that it unhinged her mind. She appeared in Elgin three years later carrying an infant son in her arms. She had nowhere to go, but happening to pass through the ruins of Elgin Cathedral she found a resting-place in the chapter-house, cradling her baby in the stone piscina in which, in old times, the priest washed his hands before saying Mass. Apparently the poor woman became a local character. The boy grew up and received lessons in Elgin Grammar School in return for certain menial labours. Eventually he entered the service of the East India Company as a drummer-boy. Long years after his mother's grave had been forgotten he became Lieut.-General Anderson. He died in London in 1824, aged seventy-seven, leaving the sum of £70,000 to found an institute in Elgin for the care of ten old people and the education of 300 children. The moral of work is – education!

The collector of epitaphs might spend a useful day in Elgin Cathedral. I took down a number which were new to me. What could be more business-like than this, employed by a man in 1777 in memory of his second wife:

She was remarkable for
Exact, Prudent, Genteel Economy;
Ready Equal Good Sense;
A constant flow of cheerful Spirits;
An uncommon sweetness of natural temper;
A Great Warmth of Heart Affection,
And an early and continued piety.

Tho' these qualities, displayed daily in her manner and actions, could not fail of gaining esteem and affection, yet strict justice demands this tribute to her memory.

187

This epitaph reads as though it had been drafted by the secretary of a company and passed by the board of directors. Over the grave of a glover of Elgin is:

> *This world is a Cite full of streets,*
> *And death is the mercat that all men meets,*
> *If lyfe were a thing that monie could buy,*
> *The poor could not live and the rich would not die.*

I wonder how many can gather the meaning of this at the first reading:

> *Elizabeth here lyes, who led her life*
> *Unstained while virgin and twice married wife.*
> *She was her parents' image – her did grace*
> *All the illustrious honours of the face;*
> *With eminent piety and complaisance –*
> *All the decorements of exalted sense.*
> *David's swan-song much in her mouth she had,*
> *More in her heart on it established.*
> *Departed hence, it being her desire,*
> *All and delight, just when she did expire;*
> *By all bewailed, she in the flower of age,*
> *As Jacob's Rachael, was turned off the stage;*
> *Ane only child beside, death by his sting*
> *Unto this urn within three days did bring.*

It was surely rather unfair to complicate death by such an announcement. A classic Scottish epitaph is, of course:

> *Here lies Billy Knox*
> *Wha lived and died like ither folks.*

Another excellent one is said to be in Reid Kirkyard, Annandale:

> *I Jockey Bell o' Braikenbrow, lyes under this stand,*
> *Five of my awn sons laid it in my wame;*
> *I lived aw my dayes, but sturt or strife*
> *Was man o' my meat, and master o' my wife.*
> *If you done better your time, than I did in mine,*
> *Take the stane off my wame, and lay it on o' thine.*

Another good one is:

> *Here lie I, Martin Elginbrodde:*

Hae mercy o' my soul, Lord God,
As I wad do, were I Lord God,
And ye were Martin Elginbrodde.

(That is surely the high-water mark of the Scottish sense of social equality!) But the best of them all is:

Here lys
James Stewart
He sall rys.

3

I approached Forres, unlike Macbeth, in brilliant sunlight. Just outside the town is one of the most remarkable monoliths in Great Britain. It is over 900 years old and is supposed to commemorate a victory of Sweyn, son of Harald, over Malcolm II. The monument is a shaft of sandstone covered with an intricate pattern of runic knots and the figures of men and beasts. Another kind of stone near at hand marks the place where the witches of Forres were burnt in olden times.

These towns must have altered surprisingly during the last century. When Sir John Carr made his tour in 1809 he found prosperous Elgin idle and poverty-stricken, and he noted that over Forres poverty seemed to hang 'like an evil spirit'. Today Forres is one of the snuggest towns you will find in the Highlands. You could pick it up and plant it in a comfortable place like Devonshire and no one would ask it any questions! I shall never forget Forres because there happened to me one of those strange little incidents which occur in unlikely places. After lunch I asked the hotel proprietor if he would have a drink with me. We were standing in a bar talking to some labourers.

'Aye, I'll have a wee one,' he said.

'What will you have?'

'Vodka,' he replied.

I thought this was an obscure joke of his, but, sure enough, he produced a bottle of vodka! I discovered that he had spent many years in Russia before and during the war, and had brought back with him a supply of this drink.

Had you asked me one of the least likely places on earth in which a man dying for a drink of vodka would be likely to discover this exoticism I would most certainly have included Forres. The weird sisters would probably have welcomed a drop of it to add to the 'fillet of a fenny snake', 'the eye of newt, toe of frog, and liver of blaspheming Jew', and the other ingredients of their famous cockaleekie!

4

The road dips down from Nairn to Moray Firth and Inverness.

I have tried to describe views whose beauty has appealed to me from the Border onward, but this view on a day of brilliant sun is one of the most perfect things I know. There are glimpses through pine woods of distant blue waters. The hills round Moray Firth are that incredible Atlantic blue which almost breaks the heart – the blue of Aran and Achill Island off the west coast of Ireland – a blue so blue, and yet so soft, that to look at it is to think of the islands of the Hesperides or the land of the Lotus Eaters. It is a colour not of this world: it is a paint they use only in heaven. Beyond the Firth lie piled the distant hills of Cromarty and Dornoch, etched in the same even, tender magic; and, more remote still, lying in a haze of heat, are the clustered highlands of Sutherlandshire and the coastline that swings up to Caithness.

I dipped down into this with a queer feeling of unreality. A railway poster had come true! This was not the Scotland of popular fancy, it was not the Scotland framed in so many hearts all over the world. What is that Scotland which rises before the eyes of the exile? It is the Scotland of slow clouds steaming down a little way into the gullies of gaunt hills, the Scotland of blown mist and drizzle. Notice how in three of the best songs of exile outside Ireland emphasis is placed on the mist and the storm. Neil Munro has written:

> *Are you not weary in your distant places,*
> *Far, far from Scotland of the mist and storm,*
> *In drowsy airs, the sun-smite on your faces,*
> *The days so long and warm?*
> *When all around you lie the strange fields sleeping,*
> *The dreary woods where no fond memories roam,*
> *Do not your sad hearts over seas come leaping*
> *To the highlands and the lowlands of your home?*
>
> *Let torrents pour then, let the great winds rally,*
> *Snow-silence fall, or lightning blast the pine;*
> *That light of Home shines brightly in the valley,*
> *And, exiled son of Scotland, it is thine.*
> *For you have wandered over seas of longing,*
> *And now you drowse, and now you well may weep,*
> *When all the recollections come a-thronging*
> *Of this old country where your fathers sleep.*

The same note sings through Stevenson's 'In Exile':

> *Blows the wind today, and the sun and the rain are flying,*
> *Blows the rain wind on the moors today and now,*
> *Where about the graves of the martyrs the whaups are crying,*
> *My heart remembers how!*

Then, too, in that magnificent 'Canadian Boat Song' whose author is unknown:

> *From the lone shieling of the misty island*
> *Mountains divide us and a waste of seas —*
> *Yet still the blood is strong, the heart is Highland,*
> *And we in dreams behold the Hebrides.*

There is no sunlight in the poetry of exile. There is only mist, wind, rain, the cry of whaups, and the slow clouds above damp moorland. That is the real Scotland; that is the Scotland whose memory wrings the withers of the far-from-home; and, in some way that is mysterious, that is the Scotland that even a stranger learns to love.

I entered Inverness. Moray Firth was as blue as the sea at Capri and the light in the streets was as glaring as in

Tangier. It was very pleasant; but it was all slightly incredible!

This true story may help you to understand Inverness.

An old Highland chieftain, whose name marches through Scottish history behind a fence of pikes, came into Inverness one day and stood looking into the window of a motor-car shop. He thought it would be nice to have a motor-car, but, being as poor as only a man can be who declines to sell inherited mountains to Americans, he wondered whether he ought to afford it. He went inside the shop where he was told, to his surprise and delight, that he could have any of the cars around him by paying a small deposit and the rest by instalments. He chose a car with great deliberation and was preparing to write a cheque for the deposit when the salesman placed before him a hire-purchase agreement.

'What is this?' asked the chief.

The salesman explained.

'Is not the word of a Highland chief good enough?' he cried, insulted to the very depths of his being, as he stamped indignantly from the shop.

A city in which that sort of thing can happen is no ordinary collection of buildings. It has, obviously, one foot in the new world and the other in the old.

Inverness is as unique among the cities of Scotland as York among those of England. It has none of York's visible age, yet, strangely enough, here is a city which has swept away its antiquities without losing an air of antiquity. It is almost as though centuries of history steam upward through the soil of Inverness. Like Edinburgh, Stirling, Dundee, and Perth, it has the appearance of having been founded by a member of the Royal Academy in a landscape mood. No human communities, except perhaps the hill towns of Tuscany, are so fortunate as the cities and towns of Scotland in their surroundings. That is the virtue of a turbulent youth. Peaceful and law-abiding countries build their towns in sheltered places; wild countries fly to the protection of hills. Now that the savage seas have ebbed, these cities of

Scotland are left like great arks stranded magnificently on their Ararats.

Inverness annoys and disturbs me. I thought until I saw it that Edinburgh was the most romantic city in Scotland. Now I am uncertain. It is not right that one country should have two such candidates. Edinburgh is more magnificent, enthroned, as it is, in authentic regality; but Inverness is more – romantic. It has the distinction which a river only can give to a city, a broad, lovely river that flows through the heart of it. Is there to be seen from any other city in Scotland a lovelier coastline than that of Moray Firth curving north to Tarbat Ness and eastward to Burghead? Blue water reflects blue hills. There are the landlocked firths of Beauly and Inverness which lie peacefully at the very doors of this city. From high ground you look south-west down the valley where the broad brown Ness flows seaward from its loch; and round you the Highlands lie piled hill against hill, wood against wood, mountain against mountain, in every shade of blue. Inverness is the watchtower of the Highlands. The Castle on its high mound – not, I believe, the site of Macbeth's castle – is a window that looks out over all north-west Scotland, and wherever you turn is something perfect and unforgettable – mountain, sea, or firth. Go at sunset to the turret of the Castle and watch the sun sink below the western hills. Of all the sunsets to be seen in Scotland this is, I think, the most memorable.

'I would like to come here again,' I told the youth who took me to the topmost turret.

'Ring the bell and ask for my father, Mr Macbeth.'

'Mr Macbeth!'

'Aye!'

Mr Macbeth, doorkeeper of Inverness Castle! What puckish fancy is at play here?

I have never in all my wandering through England, Scotland, or Ireland discovered a more alluring park than that possessed by Inverness. A number of thickly-wooded islets in the river have been linked by rustic bridges so that you can walk from one to the other, never for long out of sight of the river, and never out of earshot of its music. I went there again by night. There was a fête. Fairy lights hung in regrettable festoons from the trees. Pipers in tartan, their white spats gleaming, hugged their bags of woe or victory and strutted back and forwards giving the full benefit of the music to the velvet night.

And I went in search of the Inverness accent, which was the only thing Scotsmen in London warned me to discover in Scotland. I listened attentively to the girl in the reception office of the hotel. I was charmed with her accent and intonation. Words fell from her lips as sweetly and clearly as a mountain burn falling from the hills. I complimented her on this.

'Well,' she replied, with a touch of annoyance, 'I'm English!'

And I must admit that I discovered nothing so remarkable as I had been led to expect in the accent of Inverness. I may have had bad luck. I must have provoked at least fifty inhabitants into speech at various times, but not once did I hear the superlative beauty of perfect English. Is it not just possible that the accent of Inverness has killed itself? It is conceivable that in the old days when Inverness was a Gaelic-speaking town the English learnt at school would take root in virgin minds and blossom with a certain precise perfection?

5

The hill of Tomnahurich, dark with cypress and with cedar of Lebanon, rises above the left bank of the Ness. It is a hill of death. When primeval torrents burst their way to the sea this hill, opposing them, stood firm; and the waters passed on either side of it. The people of Inverness have made of it the most beautiful cemetery in the world.

Some say that Tomnahurich means 'hill of the fairies',

others 'hill of the boat'. A Celtic eye is not necessary to see this enormous woody mound as a ship lying keel-up covered with the dark green weeds of the sea. It is, of course, haunted. It knows all about the children which the fairies steal from time to time. You are wise to keep away from it on dark nights, for that is the time when you might hear the thin piping of a fairy reel. Someone would come to invite you to the dance. That is fatal. Everyone in Inverness knows what happened to Farquhar Grant and Thomas Cumming of Strathspey, two street musicians, who were persuaded to play reels for a dance held inside Tomnahurich. When the dance was over they came out into Inverness surprised by everything round them. The wooden bridge on which they crossed the Ness was a substantial bridge of stone! People meeting them in the streets jeered at their quaint dress! The fairy dance had lasted a whole century! When the two pipers entered a church they crumbled into the dust on hearing the name of the Deity.

I was taken up to Tomnahurich by a man who admired it so much that I gathered he would positively enjoy being buried there; but he seemed to require me with him.

'Did ye ever see in all yer life, maun, a spot in which ye could lie doon more content at the end o' yer days? Look at yon trees. . . .'

I tried to keep him impersonal; but it was no good: he insisted on regarding me as a candidate for Tomnahurich, which – I don't care how beautiful a cemetery may be – is not the most cheering form of companionship.

'How pairfectly peaceful ye could lie there – could ye not? Aye, aye. . . .'

We plodded on up the circular paths from terrace to terrace between rows of tombstones. Now and then, as we mounted higher, we saw, through a screen of cypress and cedar branches, a blue flash of Moray Firth and the clustered roofs of Inverness. And on the hill of death was no sound but the piping of birds and the mournful voice of my friend going on in a kind of hushed enthusiasm.

'Aye – would ye not feel it a pree-vilege to lie here?' he asked. He began to depress me frightfully. 'With the river flawin' by so softly and the Hie'lands at your back!'

We reached the flat top of Tomnahurich and looked down on a long avenue of graves with dark trees between them. It was exactly like the scene from Maeterlinck's *Blue Bird*. There can be no burial-place, I think, in the world more peaceful, more beautiful, more drenched in the appalling pathos of death. From the top of this great mound of graves we looked west towards the mountains and east towards the sea; below us the river ran winding through the valley.

'If ye want a pairfect resting-place,' insisted my friend, 'ye'll find none better in the wor-r-ld.'

Tomnahurich is indeed perfect. It is a hill of faery and it is also a ship of death.

6

One of the world's greatest romances came to grief on Culloden Moor, four miles from Inverness. Is there a more perfect hero than Prince Charles Edward – a more daring tale than that of his attempt to place his father on the throne of the Stuarts? From the moment he landed in Scotland until he escaped, a bedraggled fugitive, from the mountains of the Hebrides, Bonnie Prince Charlie marches through romance between Don Quixote and d'Artagnan. It is surprising to remember that James Watt was already born. The world was pregnant with the new age. And this young man strides through it sword in hand on the last personal gallantry of kingship. . . .

It is July 1745.

There is a sound of gunfire at sea off the Lizard. A French and an English warship engage hotly for five hours and then limp away wounded. A French frigate of sixteen guns which has taken no part in the fight continues her voyage and puts in before a storm to the desolate island of

Eriskay at the south end of South Uist in the Outer Hebrides.

Seven men land. Among them is a young fellow of twenty-four with large brown eyes, hair richly brown and almost gold at the ends. This is Charles Edward, who calls himself 'Prince of Wales, Regent of Scotland, England, France, and Ireland, and the dominions thereunto belonging'. He comes to remove George II from the throne and to place his father there; and he comes, as his father did thirty years previously, empty-handed. But what a different young man is here! The Stuart strain is crossed with the Sobieski. Charles Edward has all the Stuart charm with some part of the Sobieski fire.

An eagle which follows the frigate flies off to the mountains, and the storm breaks. The seven men have no food. They catch flounders and, taking them to a mean hut, roast them in peat embers. The Prince sits on a pile of peat and laughs heartily at the sight. But night is coming on and the storm blows harder. They make for the small house of one Angus MacDonald and ask for accommodation. The Prince, although he has known poverty and has bought vegetables in a bag in Paris streets, has never endured the peat reek of a Highland croft. He goes outside for air, whereon the indignant MacDonald, who has noticed with glum disapproval the young man's fussiness and jocularity, cries out: 'What a plague is the matter with that fellow that he can neither sit nor stand still, and neither keep within or without doors?' That was Scotland's first word to Bonnie Prince Charlie.

In the days that follow the news speeds over the mountains. The adventurers reach the mainland. There is much coming and going of Highland chiefs. The heather is alight again! News goes out to the Jacobite strongholds that 'someone' has arrived in Scotland, and the Jacobite chiefs – a prey to various emotions – mount their shaggy ponies and ride secretly to meet a solemn young man addressed as 'M. l'Abbé'. Sometimes those who must not know too much are told that he is an English clergyman anxious to tour the Highlands, and he dresses the part, coming silently among his friends in a plain black coat with a plain shirt, not too clean, black stockings, and brass-buckled shoes. 'I found my heart swell to my very throat,' writes one who saw him. A most unconvincing cleric!

So for days the enterprise hangs fire as the chiefs weigh up the consequences of rebellion. Cameron of Lochiel is the decisive factor. If he hangs back the clans will not rise. He begs Charles to return to France. There is no hope, he says. Then Charles wins him with the first of his many heroic gestures.

'In a few days,' he says, 'with the few friends I have, I will erect the Royal Standard and proclaim to the people of Britain that Charles Stuart is come over to claim the crown of his ancestors, to win it or perish in the attempt. Lochiel, who, my father has often told me, was our firmest friend, may stay at home, and learn from the newspapers the fate of his prince.'

What could you do with such a prince?

'No,' says the gentle Lochiel, 'I'll share the fate of my prince; and so shall every man over whom nature or fortune hath given me any power.'

So the Camerons come in and war is declared. To follow up this victory Charles burns his boats – the French frigate sails back to France, leaving him at the mercy of fate!

Events march. There is much sharpening of swords as the Fiery Cross goes round. It is not always welcome. Queer details sometimes come between great events: it is harvest-time and the oats are not gathered in! But the time is as ripe as the harvest; George II is in Hanover; the British army is on the Continent. They must make haste! And at this time the news trickles south to London, where no one believes it, except the Jacobites, who rise in candlelight to drink in silence to every three letters of the alphabet:

A B C. – A blessed change.
D E F. – Damn evey foreigner.

G H J. – Get home, Jemmy.
K L M. – Keep loyal ministers.
N O P. – No oppressive parliaments.
Q R S. – Quickly return Stuart.
T U W. – Tuck up, Whelps (Guelphs).
X Y Z. – Exert your zeal.

Most of the zeal, however, is exerted in mysterious potations. If all the people who at this time lifted glasses sentimentally to 'The King over the water' had drawn swords instead of corks James might have 'sat in Geordie's chair'; but Jacobitism is a blundering tangle of 'if's'. More rumours come south, and messengers race to Hanover to bring home the King. One day, when camped among his followers at Kinolcheill, under the eye of Ben Nevis, someone shows 'the Prince of Wales' the following proclamation from London:

'We have received information that the eldest son of the said Pretender did lately embark in France in order to land in some part of his Majesty's kingdoms, we, being moved with just indignation at so daring an attempt . . . do hereby, in his Majesty's name, command and require all his Majesty's officers civil and military, and all other his Majesty's loving subjects, to use their utmost endeavours to seize and secure the said son of the Pretender whenever he shall land, or attempt to land, or be found in Great Britain or Ireland, or any of the dominions or territories belonging to the crown of Great Britain, or shall be found on board any ship, vessel or boat, being so on board with intent to land in Great Britain or Ireland, or any of the dominions or territories aforesaid, in order to his being brought to justice; and to give notice thereof immediately, when he shall be so seized and secured, to one of his Majesty's Principal Secretaries of State. And to the intent that all due encouragement shall be given to so important a service, we do hereby further, in his Majesty's name, promise a reward of thirty thousand pounds to such person or persons who shall seize and secure the said son of the said Pretender, so as that he may be brought to justice; and his Majesty's high treasurer, or the commissioners of his Majesty's Treasury for the time being, is and are hereby required to make payment thereof accordingly. And if any of the persons who have adhered to, or assisted, or who shall adhere to or assist the said Pretender or his said son, shall seize and secure him the said son as aforesaid, he or they who shall so seize and secure him shall have his Majesty's gracious pardon, and shall also receive the said reward, to be paid in manner aforesaid.

'Given at Whitehall, the first day of August, in the nineteenth year of his Majesty's reign.

'GOD SAVE THE KING'

Charles is furious. He wishes to prepare a proclamation offering thirty pounds for George II! What a splendid piece of boyishness! How they must have laughed when his anger died down and the humour of it came out! But they persuade him to raise the price, and Charles (who might have paid the thirty pounds by borrowing it from his friends!) offers the impossible sum of £30,000 for George, in the following words:

'Charles, Prince of Wales, etc., Regent of the Kingdoms of Scotland, England, France, and Ireland, and the dominions thereunto belonging.

'Whereas we have seen a certain scandalous and malicious paper, published in the stile and form of a proclamation bearing date of 1st instant, wherein, under pretence of bringing us to justice, like our royal ancestor King Charles the I of blessed memory, there is a reward of thirty thousand pounds sterling promised to those who shall deliver us into the hands of our enemies: we could not but be moved with a just indignation at so insolent attempt. And though from our nature and principles we abhor and detest a practice so unusual among Christian princes, we cannot but, out of a just regard for the dignity of our person, promise the like reward of thirty thousand pounds sterling, to him or those who shall seize and secure, till our further orders, the person of the Elector of Hanover, whether landed or attempting to land, in any part of his Majesty's dominions. Should any fatal accident happen from hence, let the blame lie entirely at the door of those who first set the infamous example.

'CHARLES, P. R.'

It is August 19.

In the narrow valley, where the Finnan flows between its high gorge, Charles waits in a small barn. With him is the Marquis of Tullibardine with the Royal Standard. Two hours they wait, and then, looking up, they see pouring down over the hills the Clan Cameron, eight hundred of them, marching in two lines three abreast. But who are these, marching unarmed, which Lochiel brings to the meeting? With the Highlanders are two companies of Royal Scots captured at Spean Bridge. Blood has already been shed for Charles! Up goes the standard; and for the second time in thirty years James VIII is proclaimed King of Scotland and Charles is made his regent.

Now begins that amazing march to Edinburgh. The heather is well alight. The tartan army moves southward. Drums beat to arms in Edinburgh and Stirling. The Lowlands are frightened to death. The savages from the hills are coming; the naked barbarians with their claymores and their terrible pipes! To arms! to arms! The British troops in Scotland are raw. Guise's No. 6 is the only seasoned foot regiment, and it is far off on garrison duty in the north. Lees', Murray's, and Lascelles' are the three youngest regiments in the army. There are two dragoon regiments – Gardiner's and Hamilton's – who have never charged an enemy. Their horses are out to grass on the Carse o' Stirling; but it's boot and saddle for them and out on patrol duty along the roads! The skirl of the war pibrochs grows louder from Perth and Dundee. They are coming – thousands of them, some armed with scythes on long poles, a terrible thought for untried cavalry! – and as the rumours grow thicker the soldiers become even more nervous than the civilians. The dragoons are ready to stampede at a rabbit. So raw are their nerves that when a trooper falls with a great clatter into a shallow pit a whole squadron wheels round and flies, strewing the road with swords and pistols! Lucky Charlie! . . .

Eleven o'clock at night. The fire-bell is ringing in Edinburgh. The clans are coming! The volunteers must arm. Out marches the city guard, but the volunteers refuse to go with them! Have they not been recruited to defend the city and therefore they prefer to remain inside it! White cockades in Perth and white feathers in Edinburgh! So the city waits all night at alarm posts. Next morning there is the terrible spectacle of cavalry in panic. The dragoons come galloping in, crazy with terror and utterly demoralized. Edinburgh catches the panic! Only the women are calm: they want to see Charlie! The magistrates meet in Goldsmiths' Hall to decide whether to fight or make terms. They convene a meeting of citizens. 'Make terms!' cry the citizens. At this point an inoffensive-looking caddie comes up with a letter addressed to the Lord Provost which had been given to him by a mysterious stranger. His harassed lordship tears it open and begins to read: 'Whereas we are now ready to enter the beloved metropolis of our ancient Kingdom of Scotland . . .' – what is this? – he turns to the signature: 'Charles, Prince of Wales, Regent of Scotland, England, France, and Ireland, and the dominions thereunto belonging.' He drops the letter like a hot scone, refuses to read it; and the meeting breaks up. Deputies are sent out to treat with the Highlanders. News comes that British troops are approaching to the support of Edinburgh. Recall the deputies! But it is too late! Another night of terror and through the darkness creep a body of Camerons with barrels of gunpowder. They lie before the Netherbow Gate, waiting. A fool sentry opens the gate to allow a coach to pass out – there is a wild rush of kilted men and in five minutes Edinburgh belongs to the Prince! Early in the

morning an Edinburgh citizen taking a walk is surprised to
see a Highlander sitting on a gun.

'You do not belong to yesterday's guard!' he says.

'Oh, no,' replies the Highlander, 'she iss relieved!'

It is high noon. The Highland army, keeping out of the way
of the Castle guns, marches through Duddingston to the
King's Park. And between crowds of excited women and
dubious men rides a young prince very thoughtful, in a
tartan coat, red velvet breeches, and a green velvet bonnet
with a white cockade in it. He passes through to Holyrood;
and from the Rock barks an indignant, futile cannon.

7

Holyrood became a Scottish court for a little while. The
clans marched out to battle. There was that half-naked rush
in the dawn through the autumn stubble at Prestonpans.
Carlyle, from his father's church tower, watched how
Cope's army ran 'like rabets', as Charles, who was the
world's worst speller, wrote to James in Rome. Then began
that magnificent but insolent invasion of England, that
inconceivable march on London with 500 cavalry, 5,500
foot, and 13 pieces of cannon. *De l'audace, et toujours de
l'audace!* That was the motto of the '45.

There was Derby, a run on the Bank of England, a ship
ready to take George to Hanover, then that retreat which
ended in an April hailstorm on the moor outside Inverness.

I went to Culloden one morning before breakfast. The
battlefield is a level stretch of heathland on the left and right
of the road. A wood of tall, slim trees closes it on one side,
and on the other the fields rise gently to a ridge. The
morning mists were still ghost-like in the trees and overnight
some great colony of spiders had covered the furze-bushes
with silver gauze.

Culloden is the only battlefield in the world which is as

the poet or the antiquary would have it. Bannockburn is merely a field; Flodden is smiling cornland; Waterloo is a place of farms; even the Ypres Salient is already obliterated by crops. On Hell Fire Corner now stands a little new house, a line of washing on posts, and chickens busily scratching in the cinders. How swiftly nature covers up the scars of battle! Culloden, alone of all the battlefields known to me, is still drenched with the melancholy of its association: it is the only battlefield I know which contains the graves of the fallen, buried in trenches as they died.

Small, weather-worn stones rise from the heath and stand among the slim trees. On these stones are written the names of the Highland clans who died for the Stuarts.

I walked over the wet grass and spelt out the names: 'Clans McGillivray, MacLean, Maclachlan, Athol Highlanders.'

That is on one stone. Not far off another bears the words, 'Clan Stewart of Appin'; another, 'Clan Cameron'; a third, 'Clan Mackintosh'.

A little burn flows in a hollow; it hardly deserves the name of burn: it is little more than a sogginess of the grass; but there is a spring near a fence and over this is a stone with these words: 'The Well of the Dead'.

During the action numbers of wounded Highlanders crawled to this spring to slake their thirst, among them a chieftain who was shot as he was raising his head. He fell with his head in the spring. After the battle the little pool of water was found choked with stiffened corpses, and from that day to this no one will drink from 'The Well of the Dead'.

A few yards farther on, at the edge of a cornfield, is the laconic inscription on a stone:

> *The Field of the English.*
> *They were buried here.*

I remembered, as I looked at this memorial, a strange

conversation I once heard in a London club. An English-man declared that this inscription was the only thing that made his blood boil in all Scotland.

'So curt and unchivalrous!' he cried. 'And they were even growing corn on them; actually making a profit out of them!'

Someone ventured to suggest that chivalry had little part in Culloden.

'Well, anyhow,' he replied, 'that stone makes me mad! I love the Scots, but when I saw that stone I said, "Blast Scotland!" . . .'

I remember wondering who was speaking, because this man's great-grandfather was governor of Fort William! Perhaps he was not responsible for his feelings.

I had no such emotion. It seemed to me a perfectly adequate memorial. There were only fifty English dead at Culloden. From the English point of view it was, as far as casualties went, a mere skirmish; but to the other side it was the Flodden of the Scottish Gael.

Sit, as I did, on a wall and re-fight Culloden, a hopeless piece of gallantry, if ever there was one. There was no road over the moor in 1746. The present wood did not exist. Culloden was just a bleak heath.

Prince Charles had 5,000 hungry clansmen wearied by a night march. The Duke of Cumberland had 9,000 regular troops. The Prince's artillery was wretched. His gunners, such as they were, had gone to Inverness in search of food, leaving the guns in the charge of volunteers who never got the enemy's range. The Duke, on the other hand, had a permanent field train of seven four-pounders and sixteen four-pounder battalion guns commanded by Colonel Bedford, one of the most brilliant artillery officers of the day.

The armies are drawn up within 400 yards of each other. Cumberland's army moves to the sound of drum-taps. There are no fewer than 225 kettle-drummers with it. The Jacobite army is furious to hear the skirl of the pipes among the enemy ranks; the pipers of the Protestant Campbells are playing their men – about 800 of them – to their position in the rear, where they have been ordered to guard the baggage. Both armies are drawn up in two lines. Behind the Royalist army the Duke of Cumberland sits his horse; behind the Jacobite forces, on a slight rise of ground exactly opposite the Duke, is Prince Charlie.

For two hours not a shot is fired as the armies form for battle. Then at a little after one o'clock the Highlanders fire their cannon at the enemy. The Duke replies with a bombardment of grapeshot which cuts lines through the clans. The second shot is fired at Prince Charles and falls among the horsemen round him, spattering his face with mud. . . .

The Highlanders wish to charge, but there is no order. When Charles decides to attack, there is some delay in carrying out his command; meanwhile the clans, furious at their inaction, begin to murmur. They want to rush the guns that bombard them! Half an hour passes. A quick shower of hailstones is blown by the wind in their faces. It is intolerable! With a wild shout the Mackintoshes break from the right centre of the line and dash for the enemy guns! McGillivray of Drumglass leads, waving his claymore. Beside him is borne the yellow Mackintosh flag. They race over the moor through grapeshot, musket fire, and a flanking fire from Wolfe's regiment. On they go like furies, their swords rising and falling! It is a stupendous charge! They hack a path through the first line, and find themselves facing the second, where Sempill's regiment, the front rank kneeling, pumps musket fire into them, mowing them to the earth. Still they press on, desperate and furious, to die on the English bayonets.

The Highland attack develops into a series of Homeric encounters. Big John McGillivray of the Markets sweeps a path with his broadsword, cuts down the English gunners, and captures a four-pounder. There is a Highland cheer! The English soldiers club their muskets, but he cuts down three of them. He tightens his kilt and leaps onward to the second line. He falls on like a fiend. A dozen more fall to his sword before he dies pierced through the body.

Through the smoke and the hail the Highland front line moves forward to suicide. There are volleys of musketry, then the clansmen, flinging their firearms away, leap with hideous shouts on the enemy, sword in hand. The slaughter is frightful. Cumberland's army stand firm, fires, re-dresses ranks, and then waits ready with the bayonet.

Gillies Macbean of Kinchyle creeps away from the battle badly wounded, to stand at bay with his back to the dike. A troop of Cobham's dragoons come up with him, and the wounded man leaps at them with his sword and slays thirteen before he is killed! Cumberland sees his death and it strikes from him the only word of chivalry which he utters during the campaign: 'I wish you had spared that brave man's life,' he says.

Wave after wave of clansmen fling themselves on the bayonets. Wave after wave go down. The moor is strewn with corpses, chief and clansman side by side in a huddle of stained tartan; and then the drums sound an advance and the redcoats move forward. The battle is over! It is lost! And even as the Macdonalds advance at last from the left of the Highland line there is the sound of bagpipes: the Frasers are leaving the field! The retreat begins! The clans fall back, and Prince Charlie, his dream over, his heart broken, gallops off towards the heather and the road that leads to Skye.

Such was Culloden. One thousand two hundred clansmen lay dead on the moor. This moor is the grave not only of Jacobitism but also of the clan system. The Highlands were never to be the same again. The traditions of centuries lie buried there; but from the green mounds of Culloden was to rise a united Scotland. Charles Edward did not know as he made for the heather that his defeat had brought Highlands and Lowlands together and had welded the Scottish nation.

In the barbarities that followed, which for ever befoul the name of Cumberland, was only one fine moment. When the Royalist army swept over the field stabbing the dying, one man was seen leaning against the dike wall, sick from wounds. He was Fraser of Inverallochy. General Hawley saw him and shouted:

'To whom do you belong?'

'To the Prince,' replied Fraser.

'Shoot that dog!' said Hawley to an A.D.C.

'My commission is at your disposal,' replied the young officer, 'but I will not shoot him.'

'Then a trooper will do so,' said Hawley.

Fraser was shot.

The young officer was Wolfe, afterwards the hero of Quebec. There was a tradition in the Highlands that when he lay dying on the heights of Abraham it was into the arms of Fraser of Lovat that he fell.

I have come across a fascinating description of Culloden as it appeared to a traveller ninety years after the battle. It is in William Howitt's *Visits to Remarkable Places*. Howitt walked to the moor from Inverness asking the way, but could find no one who could speak English! This was in 1836. He found the remains of the hut which belonged to the smith who, legend says, performed such valours at Culloden armed with the shaft of a cart.

'The country people yet tell the spot where the sturdy blacksmith dropped. His smithy stood from year to year on the fatal field, deserted and gradually falling to decay. It remained a heap of mouldering ruin till within these few years, when several fresh huts springing up on the Moor not far off, the people gradually conveyed away the stones of the walls to construct their own habitations. It is said that the forge, the tools, and heaps of rusty iron, were found beneath the ruins of the roof, which had fallen in. Such had been the horror connected with the fatal field, that none had cared to carry them away. When we saw the place every stone was grubbed up to the bottom of the foundations, and a pool of water nearly filled the hollow; but you had only to turn up any part of the floor which was bare, and you found it to consist of the cinders and smithy-slack of the brave old blacksmith's forge.'

Near this ruin was a hut occupied, much to Howitt's delight, by an English-speaking family. The son, Willie Mackenzie, gladly took Howitt over the battlefield and explained the clan graves.

'As we sate on the greensward of one of these battle-graves, we observed that in many places the turf had been broken up by digging; and our young guide told us that scarcely a party came there but was desirous of carrying away the fragment of a bone as a relic: "What," said we, "are the bones so soon come at?" "Yes," he replied, "in some places they lie within a foot of the surface." These graves have been dug into in hundreds of places, yet you can scarcely turn a turf but you come upon them. He dug out a sod with his knife, and throwing out a little earth, presently came to fragments of the crumbling bones of 1746. He told us that, in one instance, a quantity of bones that had been carried off by a traveller, had been sent back at great expense, and buried again: the person who conveyed them away being continually tormented by his conscience, and his dreams, till that was done; "and the next visitor," added Willy Mackenzie, "would most probably carry them off once more." Balls and portions of military accoutrements are still not unfrequently found about the heath. We picked up, as we walked across it, a leaden bullet, flattened by having struck against some hard body, and rendered quite white with age.'

After rambling about the field the lad Mackenzie invited the strangers into the hut and offered to play a tune on the pipes for them. Howitt then describes the scene with that curious air of describing a foreign country common to all writers on the Highlands less than a century ago.

'There is something very delightful,' he writes, 'to sit in the simple cabin of these mountaineers, and see them

converse with an easy and unembarrassed air, and with a
mixture of intelligence and local superstition nowhere else to
be found. We observed that the beds, and various parts of
the roof, were canopied with birch boughs, which had dried
with all their leaves on. These, they assured us, were a
certain protection from the plague of flies, for not a fly
would go near the birch. This, we suppose, is a fact which
experience has taught them, and if so, is a valuable one. We
had a long talk with these good people about the battlefield
and its traditions. They told us that the name of Drumossie
was not now used for that moor – Culloden had superseded
it; but was retained for a wild track at its extremity in the
direction of Badenoch. They assured us with the utmost
gravity that a battle would some day be fought *there*. We
inquired how they knew that. They replied, because it had
been repeatedly seen. On a summer's evening, people going
across that moor had suddenly on various occasions found
themselves in the midst of the smoke and noise of a battle.
They could see the various clans engaged, and clearly
recognize their proper tartans; and on all these occasions
the Laird of Culdethel, a neighbouring gentleman, was
conspicuous on his white horse. One woman was so
frightened and bewildered by this strange spectacle that she
fainted away, and on coming to herself, found all trace of
the battle gone, and made the best of her way home again
without proceeding on her original object. We told them
that these must be strong impressions made on the
imaginations of the people by the memory of the old battle,
but they only shook their heads. They were perfectly
satisfied that a battle was to be fought on Drumossie, and
that the Laird of Culdethel would be in it – though with
whom the clans would fight, and for what, they could not
pretend to tell.'

Willie Mackenzie, having tuned his pipes, played to
them.

'Our gallant piper,' says Howitt, 'never seemed weary of
playing; and it was a treat to sit in a Highland hut, and hear

such a musician, we got him to play all the interesting airs we could recollect. There scarcely was one that he was not master of; and on no occasion did we ever listen to music that so powerfully and variously affected us. He played pibrochs and marches, and spite of our better judgements, we could not help kindling into the admiration of clan warfare; but the celebrated dirge, of which he related the origin, with which Highlanders march to the shore when they are about to embark as emigrants to some distant clime:

> *Cha till, cha till, cha till, mi tuille,*
> *We return, we return, we return no more!*

it was impossible to listen to it without tears. Let no one despise the droning of the bagpipe that has not heard it as we heard it that day.'

I think that I would rather have heard Willie Mackenzie that day only ninety years ago than all the crack pipers who frequent the Braemar, Aboyne, and Inverness Games; for Willie, hugging his pipes on Culloden Moor and sending 'MacCrimmon's Lament' over those green mounds, must have been amazing in many ways, and particularly so in his unconsciousness that all he stood for had been slain on that very field.

CHAPTER EIGHT

In which I cross from east to west, sing rebel songs until midnight, enter the Land of Venison, visit a Scottish monastery, climb Ben Nevis, and see the secret portrait of Prince Charlie at Fort William

§ I

I LEFT Inverness to follow the Caledonian Canal to Fort Augustus and Fort William, two names which Fenimore Cooper might have written on the map of Scotland. These forts were, of course, built in the eighteenth century to subdue the Highlanders, just as similar forts were built in Canada to subdue the redskins.

I entered a country of glens and bens and sudden bright flashes of lake water. The Canal looks less like a canal than any waterway in the world. It is not actually a canal: it is merely a series of short cuttings which connect four lochs with each other. There are thirty-eight miles of loch and twenty-two miles of canal; and a ship on its way to or from Inverness sails one hundred feet above sea-level when it enters Loch Oich!

What scenery, what primeval wildness, what splendid solitudes, what lonely mountain-crests, what dark gloom of pine and larch, what sudden bright glimpses through trees of deep water reflecting the curves of guardian hills! If I were asked to indicate the most romantic inland voyage in Europe I would vote for the journey up and down the Caledonian Canal. The Rhine cannot hold a candle to it. The sameness of Rhineland hill and castle and scraggy vineyard palls and wearies, except through St Goar and near Bingen; but the Great Glen through which the Caledonian Canal runs is a luscious extravagance in landscape, rich in its variety, almost terrible in its wild splendour.

It is wrong to motor, as I did, along the Canal. I will some day return and glide the length of it in a steamer.

2

Here is the Land of Venison.

I became aware of it in a little hotel which is tucked away slightly off the road in the shadow of a mountain. It is the kind of hotel which Englishmen of sober age regard as a foretaste of paradise because they are left alone to lie to each other about fish and stags. No one ever interrupts them (for they come mostly without their wives), and no one ever contradicts them (because that would be ill-bred, and, in addition, when everyone is telling stories about fish or stags, who would dare to cast the first stone?).

It is rather a Spartan hotel. Draughts tear through it from back door to front. The hall is as full of walking-sticks as Lourdes of discarded crutches. Abnormal and improbable fish which seem to have been blown up with a pump by a reckless taxidermist lie in glass cases, suggesting to the generous and fair-minded that perhaps all fish stories are not apocryphal. There are deer slots mounted on wall brackets. The mild, slightly indignant eyes of stags gaze down at guests beneath perfect hat-racks of antlers. And there is no escape from them. Their glassy stare presides even over bedroom corridors.

In such hotels the casual guest feels himself to be an incidental nuisance, rather like the man who finds himself in an alien club while his own club is in process of redecoration. Conversation has a habit of lapsing in his presence. He feels that he is intruding. He is not in the secret. He is not a deer-slayer or a salmon-killer; he is merely an unpleasant reminder of the outside world.

At luncheon and at dinner it is difficult to avoid venison. Personally I hate venison. It is, to my thinking, the most overrated of all meats. I would rather eat bully beef out of a tin. It is strange that the Scots who can produce the most perfect porridge and soup seem nine times out of ten incapable of cooking meat, which is surely a much simpler thing to do. The Irish also cannot cook meat. Roast beef or mutton as served in an Irish hotel is the nearest thing to a rubber bathmat that has ever emerged miserably from a kitchen, always excepting, of course, venison in the Land of Venison. It is redeemed only by the red-currant jelly. Salmon is another story. The Scots cook salmon perfectly – when they can get it!

Luncheon in this hotel is a solitary affair. The dining-room is half full of motorists. The regular inhabitants are all out, either lying on their stomachs in heather or standing thigh-deep in water. But dinner! Behold the hunter home from the hill and the fisher from the loch!

They sit in a chill silence, terribly English, their past lives stamped on their faces, on the wide checks of their tweed jackets, or the twist of their evening bows: admirals, generals, proconsuls! The stranger looks at them, visualizing the grey lines of battleships, or the wheeling columns of infantry, the dusty squadrons of cavalry, or the arid plains and the white towns at the edge of alien oceans which formed the background of their lives. Now they lie on their stomachs in heather or wade into water and eat stonily in the evening, longing for that time when they will slink off to the little room behind the bar to drink the landlord's special Scotch and tell each other of the day's failures or successes.

Scraps of their conversation float out through a suddenly opened door.

'He was a twelve-pointer. I stalked him for three hours in the bed of a watercourse, then the wind changed. . . .'

'I cast over him. He was lying under a stone, an eighteen-pounder if he was an ounce, and, believe me . . .'

'Do you remember old Monty Maddocks?'

'The general?'

'Yes; the fellow who caught the big trout in the lounge!'

'When was that?'

'Eighteen ninety, wasn't it, Angus?'

The landlord taps his pipe out on the mantelpiece and after a reflective Scottish interval says slowly:

'Na; it wasna in eighteen ninety, 'twas in eighteen ninety-two, on the fifteenth o' September . . .'

Everyone accepts this as if an oracle has spoken, as indeed it has.

In the fields of this part of Scotland are targets. They depict running stags. Sometimes, looking up, you can pick out, far away on the bare slopes of hills, moving brown creatures, uncannily cautious even to the naked eye. Through binoculars you see a herd feeding, lifting their heads to sniff the air, moving slowly behind the stag, which every now and then flings up his arched neck and gazes round him cautiously, as if conscious that the spiky splendour which he wears is hung about with death.

You wonder which old proconsul in check tweeds is crawling forward on his stomach to bring this wild beauty to the earth.

3

The road to Fort Augustus runs for twenty-four miles beside the northern bank of Loch Ness. This is my idea of a perfect Highland loch. It is never greater than a mile in width, so that, unlike some lakes, it cannot pretend to be the sea. Here for twenty-four miles is a changing beauty of hill, woodland, and water. I have never seen inland water which looked deeper: it is actually black with fathoms – 130 fathoms, I am told.

The deepest, most sinister portion of the loch is that opposite the ruined shell of Urquhart Castle. Here the water is 750 feet in depth! And the old castle sits grimly on a bluff overlooking the deep water and sings a song of battle and siege. Weeds grow over it and try to press apart its massive stones, but the old building gazes steadily down to Loch Ness, and Loch Ness gazes back with rarely a ripple on her black face; and it seems to you that both of them have appropriate secrets. . . .

It was along this road on an August day in 1773 that the bulky form of Dr Johnson was observed by the adoring Boswell for the first time on horseback. The Doctor, Bozzy noted, rode well. It was beside Loch Ness that Johnson had his amusing interview with the Highland woman, old Mrs Frazer:

'I perceived a little hut,' wrote Boswell in his *Tour to the Hebrides*, 'with an old-looking woman at the door of it. I thought that here might be a scene that would amuse Dr Johnson, so I mentioned it to him. "Let's go in," said he. We dismounted and we and our guides entered the hut. It was a wretched little hovel of earth only, I think, and for a window had only a small hole, which was stopped by a piece of turf that was taken out occasionally to let in light. In the middle of the room or space which we entered was a fire of peat, the smoke going out at a hole in the roof; she had a pot upon it, with goat's flesh boiling. There was at one end, under the same roof but divided by a kind of partition made of wattles, a pen or fold, in which we saw a good many kids.

'Dr Johnson was curious to know where she slept. I asked one of the guides, who questioned her in Erse. She answered with a tone of emotion, saying, as he told us, she was afraid we wanted to go to bed with her. This coquetry, or whatever it may be called, of so wretched a being was truly ludicrous. Dr Johnson and I afterwards were merry upon it. I said it was he who alarmed the poor woman's virtue. "No, sir," said he. "She'll say, There came a wicked young fellow, a wild dog, who I believe would have ravished me, had there not been with him a grave old gentleman who repressed him; but when he gets out of sight of his tutor, I'll warrant you he'll spare no woman he meets, young or old." "No, sir," I replied, "She'll say, There was a terrible ruffian who would have forced me had it not been for a civil, decent young man who, I take it, was an angel sent from heaven to protect me.'"

In such a way did Johnson and Boswell enliven that romantic ride to Fort Augustus.

When they arrived there, it will be remembered, Governor Trapaud awaited them at the gates of the fort, which was built after the 1715 rebellion. There they spent the night, and Johnson, tired out with his day on horseback, fell into that dreamless slumber which he was to immortalize in his diary.

I found Fort Augustus standing where Johnson saw it, at the head of the lake, overlooked by solemn hills. It is now that strange thing in Scotland, a monastery. I walked up to the gate and rang the bell. The door was opened after an interval by a middle-aged monk. He spoke with a strong American accent. This should not have surprised me. I have heard the seminarists in Rome talking every known language, but somehow an American monk opening the door of a Highland monastery struck me as wildly improbable.

'Sure,' he said, when I asked if I could look over the place. 'Come right in.'

There was not much to see. The building is modern. Part of the old fort is incorporated in it. There is a church and a school. The monks, who are Benedictines, received the site in 1876 from Lord Lovat.

My American guide had been a man of the world. We discussed the Seven Deadly Sins, dancing, and the shortness of women's skirts; and it was strange to hear a Benedictine monk condemn the materialism and the sinfulness of the age in the voice of New York.

'Well, say, mighty glad to have met you! Guess I must be getting along. That's the bell for vespers. . . . S'long!'

I walked thoughtfully down the avenue to the road and continued my journey.

Miss Mackintosh was like a small, bright bird. She was helped in this by the hotel reception office, which formed a kind of cage for her. Whenever her plump, sharp little face shot into the glass aperture in answer to a bell it seemed that she had flown there to a cry of 'tweet-tweet' to peck a lump of sugar. She invariably appeared, however, to give a single bedroom to a commercial traveller.

Some women are the born sisters of men. Maggie was one of them. She was a dear, plump, broad-beamed, cheerful little thing with a very white neck, grey eyes, and a freckled nose. She reminded me somehow of a hen bullfinch.

I liked to watch her alone with a crowd of men – a revealing test – and I never discovered in her anything more than a genius for comradeship and a kind of rough and jolly sisterliness. She was the kind of girl to whom men confide their love-affairs.

'Maggie, come here!' men would bawl at her as if they were at home!

No man would dream of trying to fix a bachelor button if Maggie were anywhere near to sew on a real one. And I remember feeling, when she bandaged my wrist after dabbing on the iodine with a wad of cotton wool (saying 'There noo, ye're a' richt!'), that I was indeed all right, and that no tetanus germ would presume to put up a fight against the ministrations of Maggie.

'Oh, Maggie's a great girl. . . . Maggie's one of the best. Let's pull Maggie's leg tonight! I'll come staggering in and say . . .'

But no one apparently felt sentimental about Maggie. She seemed to belong to everyone's family. I suppose a film director would say that she had no sex appeal. (In other words, she was the kind of girl who suddenly blossoms out into a startling romance; who turns out to be married secretly to a gas-inspector or runs away with a visiting curate!)

Maggie's only apparent passion was a love of music. She could make a greater variety of horrible noises on a piano, and keep them up longer than anyone I have ever met. In the evenings she would come down to the smoking-room, pert, sleek, and broader beamed than ever in a flouncy black taffeta gown, and, after much chaff, would be persuaded, outwardly reluctant but inwardly delighted, to plump down at the disgraceful old reprobate of a piano which flaunted in this modern world an old red silk shirt-front given to him in the days of Queen Victoria by some manufacturer in Munich. Then Maggie would turn the thumbed pages of Scotland's musical Bible, the *Scottish Student's Song Book*, and play songs that can never grow old.

It was strange that Maggie's fingers, so sure and deft in tying an intricate bandage, sewing on a button and, presumably, in patting and smoothing into shape the invisible domesticities of a hotel, could be so damnable on the keyboard of a piano. She thought that she played well, which made it worse; but she was such a dear that one came in time to excuse the intoxicated liberties which she took with notation, and even, in time, to forgive them, as one overlooks the stammer of a friend.

I had found in Aberdeen the satisfying first edition of Hogg's *Jacobite Relics of Scotland: Being the Songs, Airs and Legends of the Adherents to the House of Stuart*. The old rebel songs are here printed with music. One night I brought these books down into the smoking-room and asked Maggie to play things like 'The Wee Wee German Lairdie' and 'The Sow's Tail to Geordie'.

I suppose had it been 1728 instead of 1928 we would all have been flung into jail for it! But it was a great evening! There was Charlie, a real Highlander from the top of his head to the soles of his feet; Sandy, a thin, spectacled Scotsman, quick as a dart and as keen; Angus, a big, slow, humorous Aberdonian; Jock, with the face of a Pilgrim Father and a heart when warmed by whisky of a Catholic (but he didn't know it!); and a man whose name I never knew. I think he was a commercial traveller or something to do with the new dock. He was a Yorkshireman, and even when slightly drunk could never unlock his heart in song. But he liked to sit shyly in a corner with a glass and a pipe, looking like a piece of furniture.

Well; we sang Hogg's Jacobite airs very badly but very loudly, until the top of the piano was covered with empty glasses, and it then dawned on us that, in some miraculous manner not quite clear to us, a long overdue magic had crept into Maggie's fingers. She awakened heavenly music from the old hack from Munich.

'Come on, Maggie,' cried Sandy. 'Let's ha'e "Bonnie Charlie".'

'Aye, "Bonnie Charlie". Are ye ready?'

'Wait now while I find the place! Now off ye go!'

> *Tho' my fireside it be but sma'*
> *And bare and comfortless with-a'*
> *I'll keep a seat, and maybe twa,*
> *To welcome Bonny Charlie.*
>
> *Altho' my aumrie and my shiel*
> *Are toom as the glen of Earnanhyle,*
> *I'll keep my hindmost hand-fu' meal*
> *To gie to Bonny Charlie.*
>
> *Although my lands are fair and wide,*
> *It's there nae langer I maun bide;*
> *Yet my last hoof, and horn, and hide,*
> *I'll gie to Bonny Charlie.*
>
> *Although my heart is unco sair,*
> *And lies fu' lowly in its lair,*
> *Yet the last drap o' blude that's there*
> *I'll gie for Bonny Charlie.*

Maggie struck a slightly inaccurate final chord, and we leaned over the piano in a mood of moist sentimentality.

'Let's sing "The Skye Boat song".'

'Na,' na'; it's awfu' familiar! Let's sing something wi' red bluid in it – "The White Cockade"?'

'Not at all!'

'The "Whigs o' Fife"?'

'Och, not at all! We'll sing "The Wee, Wee German Lairdie".'

'Fine! Come on, ma lads!'

Wha the de'il hae we gotten for a king
  But a wee, wee German lairdie!
And when we gade to bring him hame,
  He was delving in his kail-yardie;
Sheughing kail and laying leeks,
Without the hose, and but the breeks
And up his beggar duds he cleeks.
  The wee, wee German lairdie.

And he's clappit doon in our gudeman's chair
  The wee, wee German lairdie,
And he's brought routh o' foreign trash,
  And dibbled them in his yardie.
He's pu'd the rose o' English loons,
And broken the harp o' Irish clowns,
But our Scotch thistle will jag his thooms,
  The wee, wee German lairdie.

Come up amang our Highland hills,
  Thou wee, wee German lairdie,
And see how the Stuart's lang-kail thrive,
  They dibbled in our yardie;
And if a stock ye dare to pu',
Or haud the yoking o' a plough.
We'll break your sceptre o'er your mou'
  Thou wee bit German lairdie!

Auld Scotland, thou'rt o'er cauld a hole
  For nursing siccan vermin;
But the very dogs o' England's court,
  They bark and howl in German.
Then keep thy dibble in i' thy ain hand,
Thy spade but and thy yardie;
For wha the deil now claims your land,
  But a wee, wee German lairdie!

'Maggie, ye play like an angel!'

We were now wearing white cockades in our hearts. We mourned that we were born two centuries too late. What one of us would not have drawn a sword for Charles

Edward? What one would not gladly have expired on the Hanoverian bayonets at Culloden?

Hogg, in gathering these old songs, has done for the Highlands what Scott, in his *Minstrelsy of the Scottish Border*, did for the Lowlands. To my mind these are the two indispensable books on Scotland: the heart of the Lowlands is in one, the heart of the Highlands in the other. And between the lines of these rebel airs you see, or rather feel, a dim background of wainscoting and candlelight in which men rise to toast an absent king.

No political situation has been more vividly preserved in popular song than Jacobitism. To read these songs is to pass down two centuries and to breathe the very air of that time pregnant with violent prejudice, primitive hatred, scornful contempt, sly humour, and reckless sincerity. These Jacobite relics are as personal and as vital in their appeal as the *Diary* of Samuel Pepys. And as we sang them, our souls slightly uplifted from the common earth, something like the faint perfume of old love-letters rose from them. It was difficult to believe that the men and women who composed them lay dead these two centuries in Scottish kirkyards. The authors of the Border ballads are far-off and remote; the authors of the Jacobite songs were men in something like the same mood in which we found ourselves as Maggie thumped the asthmatical piano in the little Highland inn.

'Now one last song, Maggie, and then we'll away to our beds.'

So we sang I think the most beautiful of all, 'MacLean's Welcome':

> Come o'er the stream, Charlie, dear Charlie, brave Charlie,
> Come o'er the stream, Charlie, and dine with MacLean;
> And though you be weary we'll make your heart cheery,
> And welcome our Charlie and his loyal train.
> We'll bring down the track deer, we'll bring down the black steer,
> The lamb from the breckan, and doe from the glen;
> The salt sea we'll harry, and bring to our Charlie,
> The cream from the bothy, and curd from the pen.

Come o'er the stream, Charlie, dear Charlie, brave Charlie,
Come o'er the stream, Charlie, and dine with MacLean,
And you shall drink freely the dews of Glen-Sheerly,
That stream in the starlight when kings dinna ken;
And deep be your meea of the wine that is red,
To drink to your sire and his friend the MacLean.

Come o'er the stream, Charlie, dear Charlie, brave Charlie,
Come o'er the stream, Charlie, and dine with MacLean.
O'er heath bells shall trace you the maids to embrace you,
And deck your blue bonnet with flowers of the brae;
And the loveliest Mari in all Glen McQuarry
Shall lie in your bosom till break of the day.

Come o'er the stream, Charlie, dear Charlie, brave Charlie,
Come o'er the stream, Charlie, and dine with MacLean.
If aught will invite you, or more will delight you,
'Tis ready – a troop of our bold Highlandmen
Shall range on the heather with bonnet and feather,
Strong arms and broad claymores three hundred and ten. . . .

What a song!

Here is the spirit of poetry, as raw and potent as a swig of poteen dug from the peat hag. The MacLean's Welcome is the invitation of all warrior tribes to all heroes since the world began. Here in Scotland 200 odd years ago, and within 500 miles of a sophisticated London, the Clan MacLean was offering to a Christian prince the traditional pagan offerings of meat, wine, garlands, and girls, with which all tribes have rewarded all heroes since the dawn of time. You could translate this song into ancient Egyptian or Greek.

'And now just one last song – "Will He No' Come Back Again?"'

Royal Charlie's now awa,
Safely ower the friendly main;
Mony a heart will break in twa,
Should he ne'er come back again.
Will ye no' come back again?
Will ye no' come back again?
Better lo'ed you'll never be.
And will ye no' come back again?

The hills he trode were a' his ain,
And bed beneath the birken tree;
The bush that hid him on the plain,
There's none on earth can claim but he.

Whene'er I hear the blackbird sing
Unto the evening sinking down,
Or merl that makes the woods to ring,
To me they hae nea ither soun';
Sweet the lav'rock's note and lang,
Lilting wildly up the glen.
And aye the o'erword o' the sang
Is 'Will he no come back again?'
Will he no' come back again?
Will he no' come back again?
Better lo'ed he'll never be,
And will he no' come back again?

It is difficult to describe the emotion that lived in this song so late at night with the piano covered with empty glasses and a Yorkshireman asleep in a chair.

'If he came back now,' said Angus, with tears in his eyes, 'I'd follow him.'

'Angus, you're drunk!'

'Drunk or sober, I'd follow him!' cried Angus dramatically.

He was then understood to say that he'd fight anybody who contradicted him.

'Are ye wi' me or agin me, Jock?'

Jock; looking more than ever like the Landing of the Pilgrim Fathers, said solemnly:

'Good gracious me, yes!' which from Jock was almost an oath.

Sandy, shining behind his spectacles, became aggressively logical, but nobody paid any attention to him. Aye, it was the end of an auld sang! Of course nobody would follow him if he came back now! Why should they? Sentimentalism! Romanticism! Roman Catholicism! ('Will you shut up, Angus?') But, come to think of it, hadn't we all fought for the last Stuarts in the war? And rather interesting, too, that the Prince of Wales is the only prince in modern Europe whose charm recalls that of Bonnie Prince Charlie? Have ye ever thought of that now? Is it the last thin strain of the Stuart coming out? Is it? ('Shut up, Sandy!')

'The Prince of Wales!' cried Maggie, suddenly wheeling round on the red plush piano-stool. 'Oh, he's just a darlin'. We hope he's coming to open the new water works!'

That seemed to me a marvellous ending to a Jacobite evening! It remained only to awaken the Yorkshireman.

We stamped out to the porch. An autumn moon was hiding behind the hills. We could hear the burn falling down from the rock and the glassy tinkle of it where it crosses the road beneath the bridge. We all solemnly shook hands – a bad sign! A little distance down the road Charlie was singing:

> Better lo'ed you'll never be.
> Will ye no' come back again?

'Come on, Charlie, pull the heather out of your ears and come to bed.'

'Go to hell!'

5

On a bright morning I slipped away along the road to Fort William and Ben Nevis.

I pitied those comfortable tourists who believe that Braemar and Ballater are the Scottish Highlands – those lovely post cards! Here are the real Highlands. The heather was like spilt claret on the high, smooth slopes of the hills; the thick woods were stained with autumnal colour; there was a flash of lake water between trees and the splash of mountain streams falling from the heights. Imagine the best of Switzerland and the Rhine valley mixed up and poured out across Scotland in a broad, wild belt of beauty.

The road runs along the south side of Loch Oich and crosses the water again at Invergarry. Here, beside the road, I came to a strange monument placed against a well or spring. It is a pyramid surmounted by seven heads cut in stone. Round the monument is written in English, Gaelic, French, and Latin the following explanation:

'As a Memorial of the ample and summary vengeance which in the swift course of feudal justice, inflicted by the orders of the Lord MacDonnell and Aross, overtook the perpetrators of the foul murder of the Keppoch Family, a branch of the powerful and illustrious Clan of which his Lordship was the Chief. This monument is erected by Colonel MacDonnell of Glengarry, XVII Mac-mhic Alistair, his Successor and Representative, in the year of our Lord 1812. The heads of the seven murderers were presented at the feet of the Noble Chief in Glengarry Castle, after having been washed in this spring; and ever since that event, which took place early in the sixteenth century, it has been known by the name of "Tobar-nan-Ceann" or "The Well of the Heads".'

I went on to Fort William.

The placid afternoon sun was warm over the hills. I watched the paddle-steamer going up Loch Lochy. Very small and Victorian it looked nosing its way with a steady thrash of paddles through the solitudes. Its rails should have been crowded with men in side-whiskers and Norfolk jackets and women holding long-handled frilly parasols. In each hand should have been the latest 'Waverley', everyone should have been marvelling at the skill of Mr Telford. In this way the Highlands became fashionable and also civilized!

Then, as I went on, the rich Highlands faded behind me and I came into a wilderness of rock. I could, it seemed, smell the sea at last; and those dim hills to the westward must be the mountains of the Isle of Skye. There is a queer magic in those gaunt hills. It is the strange unearthliness of the west coast of Ireland. The wind blows even on a placid afternoon of sun. The heather is ripe and the wind is in it, pressing it back; the strange rocks that rise up from moors might be enchanted men, and there is something super-natural even in the grouse that bang up from the moor and settle gracefully behind the next stone wall.

The shadows lengthen, the sun sinks, the hills change

colour. I saw blue over Tweedside, blue over the Border hills; there was blue over the Ochils at Stirling and blue over the distant Grampians from Perth; but I did not know the colour of blue until I saw the western Highlands at the end of day. This blue is unknown to art. The man who could paint it truthfully would be called a raving lunatic.

I leaned over the bridge at Spean watching a devilish witches' cauldron boil and bubble. The rocky bed of the Spean is deep and full of terrible jagged caverns. You can look down far into the clear brown water and visualize depth beyond depth.

It was near this bridge on August 16, 1745, that Captain John Scott, marching to reinforce the garrison at Fort William with two companies of Royal Scots, heard a pibroch. He saw on the other side of the bridge a number of Highlanders leaping about, some armed with swords, some with firelocks. A fight followed in which two soldiers were killed. The Royal Scots, finding themselves surrounded, laid down their arms.

This was the first blow struck in Scotland for Bonnie Prince Charlie. . . .

I saw the vast bulk of Ben Nevis lying above Fort William in the gathering shadows. There were clouds over his head.

6

Fort William nestles, or crouches, with an air of pretending to be at the end of the world at the foot of Ben Nevis, the highest and most famous mountain in the British Isles. It is 4,406 feet in height, or 846 feet higher than Snowdon. Every healthy man who visits Fort William climbs Ben Nevis. No one suggests that he should do so. It is just one of Scotland's unwritten laws of decent conduct. When he has done this the climber finds that the atmosphere of Fort William warms towards him. He went up friendless; he returns to smiles and companionship. He has proved himself.

Men who previously scowled uncertainly at him now regard his torn and battered feet with approval and say, 'You've been up "the Ben"!' He finds that he has earned the confidences of other men who have climbed Ben Nevis. He learns with respectful disappointment that he has put up no new record; that hefty local Scotsmen have gone up and come down in a quarter of the time; but no matter! He went up a novice; he returns initiated as one of that noble company who know the summit of Britain's greatest mountain.

Before I set off I walked round Fort William in the hope of seeing Ben Nevis; but nothing is more difficult. I have never found it so hard to see a mountain. The Ben has a base which is said to be twenty-four miles in circumference, so that firmly seated on this rocky throne he manages to hide his crown in mist or beyond the shoulders of lesser monarchs.

As I walked singing up the glen with a heart as foolishly light as my shoes, a woman at the white farm of Achintree, holding a baby in a tartan kilt, smiled and said, 'It's a graund day for "the Ben",' and as she said it she looked up into the sky in the direction of the invisible summit. 'A graund day for "the Ben"!' They all talk about Ben Nevis as if he were an aged and irascible old gentleman whose polite reception of the stranger is by no means guaranteed!

And this, I was to learn, is the best way to regard him!

The sun shines. It is warm. The distant trees are turning goldy-brown, and as I mount the winding path the sound of the burn that curves and twists through Glen Nevis grows fainter and finally ceases.

I am alone in the sunlight with great hills shouldering the sky above me, brown with dead bracken, grey with the beautiful silvery heather stems, and soggy with peat bogs. Birds fly up from the heather; sheep look up from their grazing with no expression, and thrusting their soft bodies into the heather continue to crop the grass. Little brown peaty streams rumble from above and fall cascading between boulders down the hillside.

I am conscious that the path up Ben Nevis is the flintiest on earth. I am wearing the wrong shoes for Ben Nevis. These soles that have trod Piccadilly and Bond Street in their time have met their end; and serve them right! I am glad to rest, and to ease my knapsack on a rock, and to look down into the valley where the little roads run, thin as tape pinned round the foothills and over the fields; where the burn, sparkling like a mirror, heliographs in sharp turns and twists before it slides into its tunnel of October leaves; where the small, scattered farms, dwarfed to the size of match-boxes, sit perched on the hillsides or nestle comfortably in the rare shelter of woodland.

There comes in the climbing of all mountains a time when a man turns from such sights to face the loneliness of great hills and that solitude which never has given and never will give food or shelter to man. The hills shoulder one another as if to cut off sight of the habitable earth; the clouds loom nearer; the yellow clouds which from earth are puffy cotton-wool things are now seen to have texture, to be wind-blown in wild spirals; the darker clouds are misty and frayed at the edges with impending rain and the grass grows thinner, the rock more frequent, and the wind is cold.

So yard by flinty yard I mount slowly and painfully into a grim valley of rocks through which falls a stream. I am now on a level with the lesser mountains; I can even see above their heads beyond to hills and more hills and a hint of water.

I come to a little tarn hidden in the mountains, lying there all silent like a patch of fallen blue sky, and near it is the halfway hut.

The hut is of stone and doorless. Round it lie signs of human exhaustion – orange peel, scraps of paper that once concealed sandwiches, the metal tops of mineral water bottles – debris suggesting the bottom of a monkey's cage and the justice of Darwin's theory. And the view from the halfway hut on Ben Nevis is surely one of the greatest in the world. . . .

This is Scotland, these are the wild Highlands of Romance! Across the great, gaunt shoulder of the mountain opposite I can see Loch Linnhe, blue as the sky; to the right I can follow it between its hills to Loch Lochy, and then begins that astonishingly lovely valley, a rainbow over it, that leads the Caledonian Canal from loch to loch into Inverness.

The path now grows steeper, its zigzags more frequent, its surface rougher; and I go on full of a magnificent exhilaration, the cold air like wine. When I turn to look back I find some new marvel: a sudden gleam of the Atlantic over a mountain's head; dim, blue, far-off peaks that may be the Hebrides. Then, suddenly, I am in the valley of death. Nothing grows. The bare rock thrusts its sharp edges from the mountainside. The clouds are near. There is even one far below me, a thin grey thing, gently steaming over the face of the mountain, a stray, lost wisp of a cloud.

I am so far above the world of man that even the sunlight does not cheer this solitude. The spirit of great mountains is a wild, implacable spirit. Even the jolly golden clouds that sail so near can come before the sun and in an instant be things of horrible mystery, ominous things hiding something that might obliterate a man on a mountainside as a bird picks a fly from a wall.

Man is nowhere so alone with all the fears in his blood as on the side of a mountain.

I tramp on with bursting lungs, beating heart, and lacerated feet, my mind fixed on the summit that surely cannot be far off!

Suddenly the sunlight dies. I enter a mist: a thin, clinging mist, a cold, foggy mist. I am warm with my climb. I do not notice how cold it is. Out of it emerge two shapes. Two men come towards me muffled to the eyes. They wear gloves and their teeth are chattering, their noses are red, their ears stand out like slices of raw beef. They try to smile but the smile freezes on their iced cheeks:

'Another half mile!' they say to me. 'Is it still fine down below?'

'Yes, brilliant sun!'

They swing their arms like cabmen on a frosty morning, and, taking off their gloves, blow into their cold fingers.

'Don't lean on the wooden platform over the ravine. It's not safe! Goodbye!'

And they depart, fading in the mist. As I go on the mist thickens. There are irregular patches of snow two or three inches deep. I have come into the depth of winter. An icy wind howls round me, whipping the chill mist into my face. All the heat of my climb is taken out of me. I stoop in the wind and take out a coat from my knapsack and cover myself; but I am now so cold that I cannot feel my ears; and my eyes ache.

The mist turns to sleet, and the sleet to soft, whirling snow that dances giddily round me on every side. The path becomes level. Through the snow I see the ruin of a stone house. I go in for shelter. It is a horrible ruin, like a shipwreck. It looks as if all the fiends of the air have torn it stone from stone. I hear the most horrible sound on earth – the sough of wind coming up over the crest of Ben Nevis. It is not loud. I have to listen for it, and having heard it I go on listening with chilled blood: it is a dreadful sound; an evil, damnable sound. I am drawn towards it through the snow. I come to the jagged edge of the mountain. The snow is whirled up over the edge of it. It is as if the snow were rising and not falling; and all the time the wind comes moaning out of space over the edge of Ben Nevis.

The precipice is 1,500 feet deep. I take a stone and fling it. Seven sickening seconds and then, far off, an echo of the fall and another and another.

I stand chilled to the very marrow, watching the weird snowfall veer and shift in the wind, blowing aside to reveal dim, craggy shapes, rocks like spectres or crouching men or queer, misshapen beasts. And the dreadful ghost of a wind moaning over the precipice with an evil invitation at the back of it, moaning up out of space, through distant spiky gullies where the sun is shining, moaning with a suggestion of inhuman mirth, causes me to face the ravine as if something might come out of it which would have to be fought.

I could stay there longer if the wind would not bite into my bones and numb my fingers. I go on out of the snow and into the sleet and the mist. And on my way down a great hole is suddenly blown in the cloud, and I see, it seems at my feet, an amazing, brilliant panorama of mountains with the sun on them, of blue lochs, a steamer no bigger than a fly moving up Loch Ness beneath the arch of a rainbow. Then the hole fills with mist and I go on for an hour, stumbling, scrambling until the mist frays and stops, and the sun shines. . . .

All round me are the Highlands, magnificent among the clouds, the evening blueness spreading over them; peak calling to peak, the Atlantic like a thin streak of silver, the bare rock beneath my feet fading to brown bogland and heather.

I sit down and hold out my frozen hands in the sun, and, suddenly catching sight of those shoes which have in their time known Piccadilly and Bond Street, I roar with laughter!

'So you've been up "the Ben"!'

Before a warm fire we talk. Hitherto padlocked Highland tongues unlock themselves. Men tell the story of the strange and wonderful things they have seen on 'the Ben'; one how he saw the sun come up over Scotland; another how he saw the sun sink in splendour; a third how he saw all the Highland peaks nosing their way for a hundred miles through a white waste of motionless cloud.

I edge in and pay my tribute. I tell them of the Swiss mountains I have climbed and of the sights I have seen from the Libyan Hills in Egypt, and from the crests of the Aures Mountains in North Africa. Nothing I have seen from any mountain approached the glory of the blue hills against blue hills – the monarchs of Scotland, mile after mile, with their heads in the sunlight of an autumn day.

7

The little West Highland Museum at Fort William contains, among other relics of the '45, the secret portrait of Prince Charlie.

Few relics of Jacobitism bring back more vividly the exciting risks of those times. The portrait was painted probably as a curiosity and certainly for the dangerous toast of 'The King over the water'.

There is a board daubed with paint in a half circle. It looks like the palette of a rather careless painter. You can make nothing of the queer streaks, the dots of blue and red, the snaky spirals of brown and green. I defy anyone to recognize this mess of paint as a portrait. Notice, however, that some little distance from the half circle of paint is a white circle about the size of the base of a teacup. A shining metal cylinder about six inches high is placed on this circle and at once the crazy mess of paint forms in the shining curvature of the cylinder as a pretty little miniature portrait of Prince Charles Edward. He is wearing a brown wig, an elaborate satin coat. Across his breast is the ribbon and the star of St Andrew. It is a fascinating little picture. Get too far to left or right and it becomes distorted, but face it and look down into it, standing as you stand to drink a health, and you have before you 'Charles Edward, Prince of Wales, Regent of Scotland, England, Ireland, and the Dominions thereunto belonging!'

I believe I am right in saying that this unique relic was picked up in an antique shop for a few shillings. It was fortunate that the metal cylinder had not become separated from the wooden panel, otherwise that queer daub would have remained a mystery for ever.

A leather hood rather like a dice-box was provided to drop over the cylinder in suspicious company, or to hide the portrait until the moment had arrived for toasting 'The King over the water'.

And when you look at this ingenious freak painting the same feeling comes over you that comes with Hogg's Jacobite airs, and you call to mind oak-panelled dining-rooms and candles lit, a warm glow over family portraits, a guard over the door, and the company rising to lift their glasses to the cause that was fated to be lost.

Prince Charlie's breeks are also to be seen in this museum. They are made of Stuart tartan, very hard and fine, and leg and foot are all in one piece like a pair of tights. There are documents innumerable from the Cluny Charter Chest; brown ink scrawls appointing Highland chieftains to colonelcies of the rebel forces, orders to clansmen to report at the rendezvous, and suchlike; many of them signed 'Charles, P.R.', and all of them brown with age. There is also a lock of Charlie's hair, fine, soft, and golden as a child's.

If any American millionaire wishes to write his name on the Highlands I can think of nothing more intelligent than the building and the endowment of an adequate museum in Fort William.

CHAPTER NINE

I go by sea to Skye, walk through a gorge, meet an eagle, see the Fairy Flag of Dunvegan, and try to keep an appointment with Prince Charlie

I

IF you look at the map of Scotland you will find, high up on the mountainous north-west coast, a little port called Mallaig on the Sound of Sleat. Its harbour lies tucked away in a shelter of hills and rocky headlands: a little grey Dover full of small, sturdy ships with one red funnel apiece, and a general air – assisted by a strong smell of oil, pea-soup, and roasting mutton – of waggish sea-doggery.

This race of small ships links the scattered Hebrides with civilization. Some of them run once a week, and all of them in winter, 'weather permitting'. They slip away from Scotland to regions more remote and more foreign than any in the British Isles, to little volcanic eruptions in the blue Atlantic, which are the crests and summits of submerged mountain ranges; and wherever they go they represent the world, never more truly, perhaps, than when they nose into some craggy bay, where one white house shows on the mountain-side, to drop a small Post Office bag, and a new bicycle for Angus MacDonald.

They are the sole links with a happily marooned community, otherwise connected to the British Isles only by its war memorials. . . .

I lean over the deck of the Stornoway boat with a greater feeling of adventure than I have felt when bound for the ends of the earth. I am going to the Isle of Skye. I look out to the misty headlands, grey in a drizzle, and down into the clear, bottle-green depths where small fish swim; and all round me is the exciting bustle of departure. We are a varied crowd. There is a beautiful, long-legged girl in Harris tweed with a queer, yellow mastiff-like dog in leash, and a pile of luggage which contains golf-clubs and fishing-rods. She is, perhaps, the daughter of some clan chieftain going home to a castle on a rock.

There is a fat-faced young man wearing a religious hat of black velour, and a pair of dove-grey spats. In Ireland he would be a priest: here he is a son of the manse or a son destined for the manse. A governess sits out of the wind with four small boys, all in new suits. Her luggage contains wooden boxes of provisions. She has made a raid on civilization for clothes, and for those epicurean refinements not sold on her particular mountain-top. A commercial traveller comes aboard preceded by a pyramid of goods tied in black oilskin; artificial silk stockings perhaps, civilization's inevitable gift to the Hebrides!

Shaggy islanders walk the forecastle wearing plus fours and unpolishable boots, whose tags stick out behind against their fluffy homespun stockings. They lean on long sticks, almost crooks, and talk in Gaelic about the price of sheep. Black and white sheep-dogs, frantic with anxiety, run all over the ship in search of shepherds who are below having a drink. There is a great commotion as a wild and unwilling black horse is led and pushed aboard.

The little ship is drenched in all those smells which women try to forget as they run down to Dover in the Continental Boat Express: pea-soup, fat mutton, batter pudding. The cook's galley is on deck. He emerges in a rich, composite cloud of smell, his sleeves rolled above his elbows, says something in Gaelic to a steward, who picks up a bell and goes noisily round the ship.

Bells sound from the other little ships around us. Rival whiffs of pea-soup fight their way sturdily to us from our companion vessels. Passengers exactly like ourselves gaze at us from other decks and know that we, too, are going out into remote blueness; that we, too, carry a black horse, many shepherds, and a lovely girl in Harris tweed; that we, too, are about to eat pea-soup, fat mutton, and batter pudding drenched in treacle.

The ship is steaming up the Sound of Sleat between mountains vague in rain. The grey mists steal stealthily down their great brown flanks: their heads are lost in ragged cloud edges. Each new vista is one of hills behind hills, dim, remote. The clouds move slowly, and the sun, finding a way through a rent in them, sends a momentary golden haze into a valley or lights up, alone in all the wild, dark landscape, a mile or two of heather, and a small, white farm.

Suddenly the engines stop. Away over the desolate, green waters of the sound two men pull lustily at a clumsy boat. As they come alongside with Gaelic shouts and greetings the governess, the children, and the boxes are lowered into the boat. The children are excited. They turn to the wilderness of hill and heather that tower to the sky and wave their hands. From the great boulders at the water's edge comes an answering flash of white. A woman is waiting there for them. Behind her, over the wall of the mountain road, is a grey touring car. . . .

A bell rings and we steam on towards the mountains that close in on the Kyle of Lochalsh. We tie up to a wooden jetty covered with pink sea-anemones. I look down in the bright green water and see the pretty shell-pink things clinging to the wood like small hedgehogs. And here I change to the Skye boat, a paddle steamer.

I find myself and the shepherds are the only passengers. Mail-bags are being shot down a smooth plank; and the crew, chattering together in Gaelic, exchange jokes with the dock labourers above them on the jetty. The morning newspapers arrive! They will be eagerly read at 7 p.m.! The captain procures a copy, and his officers gather round him. They read the news in English and discuss it in Gaelic!

All round me is Gaelic: a live, vivid language. The captain, in the midst of a spirited conversation in this soft tongue, turns to me.

'Aye, we'll be an hour late at Portree, maybe! And you're Mr Morton?'

'How on earth did you know that?'

'Ah, weel, I was talking to Mr Campbell, of Sligachan, and he said he was expecting you! He's got a lot of letters for you. . . .'

If you want to be really well known go to live in the most solitary place on earth! In an island there are no secrets!

Now begins a three-hour voyage, which I will never forget. I turn my face towards the mountains of Skye, half fearful that Skye may let me down, as other places I have longed to see have done so often.

Skye. . . .

To me it is pure romance. Some stray old wind from Culloden blew, I think, into my nursery when I was a child, for almost the first stories I heard were stories of Skye and of a brown-eyed prince hiding in a cave. I suppose all boys, Scots or English, would rather be flying with Bonnie Prince Charlie than pursuing at the head of Cumberland's dragoons. I know it was so with me.

Skye, for me, has always been shrouded in the splendour of a lost cause. The sound of it is like a sword going home to its scabbard. Many's the time I have followed a little boat over a cold sea at dawn to Skye, and have seen Flora Macdonald step out on the craggy shore with an ungainly six-foot 'maid' with golden hair and a clumsy way with a skirt; and many's the time I have known that cave where a ragged young man addressed as 'your highness' sat down with a show of ceremony to cold mutton and cheese.

I feel, as I approach Skye, that I am on the way to wreck a dream. It may be almost as disappointing to see Skye as to meet in later life the girl you wanted to marry when you were eighteen! But something in the blue mountains reassures me as the clouds lift – queer, grotesque mountains, dark and heroic.

The boat steams in between the mainland and the island of Scalpay, and to the west loom giant peaks with a hint of darker, higher, and even wilder peaks behind them; and as the dusk falls infrequent lights gem the shore – the lights of little homes far from anywhere. There is no sound but the thrust of the steamer through the quiet seas; and a strange feeling comes out to me from the land, from the gaunt, black shadows that lie piled against the clouds, persuading me that I have left the world behind me.

I am glad that there is no one to talk to me. It is not often that a man feels himself hanging between this world and the next, between past and future, in some strange, timeless interlude. I am anxious not to exaggerate this feeling, because I cannot hope that anyone who has not felt the shadow of Skye for the first time will understand it. It would not have surprised me to see a galley put out from the dark shores and to come face to face with Ulysses or Jason . . .

We turn at last into the peace of a quiet harbour, where lights shine high up among the trees. It seems to me that all the population of Portree has come down to greet the link with another world. I smell the glorious sweet reek of peat.

'Your first visit?' asks a quiet voice at my side. It is the captain, and he is about to light a pipe.

'Yes.'

'Weel – ye'll come back!' he says, and flings his match into the still harbour.

2

Where an ice-white salmon stream flows through a gorge to join Lock Sligachan is utter desolation, and an hotel, called an inn, which might have been blown over from Devon. Here are salmon-fishers, deer-slayers, artists in oil and watercolour, mountaineers, and the clipped voice of that which was once the English ruling class.

I arrived there after dark over nine miles of uninhabited mountainside. I knew that I was in a wilderness. I could feel the nearness of great mountains, although I could see nothing in the mist. I could smell mountains in the wet wind as you can smell ships in a fog.

I dined and joined the varied crowd in the lounge. It

seemed to me that these people had been drawn together by virtue of the wilderness outside, much as those in *The Decameron* were drawn together by the plague. You cannot stand on etiquette in a mountain hut, and this place, in spite of its hot baths, its aquatints, and its garage, was spiritually a mountain hut: the only place of warmth and shelter in the abomination of desolation.

We were banded together in a conspiracy of friendliness. And the wind howled at the windows and the rain fell. Our cheerfulness over coffee brought home to me the abnormally cruel wilderness which I knew to lie outside, mile after mile. When English travellers – and particularly Englishwomen with daughters – melt to a chance acquaintance one suspects a reality equivalent to a war! It must, I thought, be an appalling thing out there in the dark which has broken down an English tradition; and I looked at the drawn curtains, shuddering apprehensively, and went alarmed to bed. . . .

I was awakened before the sun was up by the rush of a stream over stones. I drew the blind on a still, clear, lemon-coloured sky and a sight that made me gasp. Right in front of me a tremendous Vesuvius called Glamaig shot up in the air, a colossal cone, with queer, grey-pink ravines searing his gigantic flanks. The rising sun immediately behind him covered him in a weird, reflected light, that hung over his vastness like gold dust. All round him, shouldering him, were other mountains, vague in morning mists, enormous shadows with white clouds steaming over their crests. Gentler moorlands, brown with heather, formed the reverse slope of that wild valley through which the ice-white stream tumbled beneath a stone bridge towards the silver waters of Loch Sligachan.

No words can tell the strange atmosphere of this place, which is unlike Scotland, unlike Norway, unlike Switzerland, unlike anything else on earth.

I dressed – but with no idea of the shock that awaited me outside!

The inn is built at an angle which, when you stand on the steps, cuts off the view to the right. You remain there, mesmerized by Glamaig, in whose shadow you stand. He is in the shape of Vesuvius. He looks as though he might at any moment give a terrible explosion and belch flame. You take a step towards him. You clear the boundary wall, and instantly out of the corner of your eye become aware of something tremendous to your right. You turn . . . the sight of the 'Black' Coolins hits you like a blow in the face!

I have spent nights in the Sinai Desert, I have slept in the Valley of the Dead in Egypt, I have seen the sun rise from the summit of the Silvrettahorn in Switzerland, I have stood all night on a ship in a great storm off the coast of Crete, I have been impressed by a number of other experiences, but I have never in all my life seen anything like the 'Black' Coolins standing, grape-blue and still, in morning sunshine.

I gasped. I lost my breath. These expressions are generally untrue. You seldom gasp or lose your breath. It is a figure of speech. But when you come suddenly for the first time on the Coolins your mouth opens and you really do gasp.

Imagine Wagner's 'Ride of the Valkyries' frozen in stone and hung up like a colossal screen against the sky. It seems as if Nature when she hurled the Coolins up into the light of the sun said: 'I will make mountains which shall be the essence of all that can be terrible in mountains. I will pack into them all the fearful mystery of high places. I will carve them into a million queer, horrible shapes. Their scarred ravines, on which nothing shall grow, shall lead up to towering spires of rock, sharp splinters shall strike the sky along their mighty summits, and they shall be formed of rock unlike any other rock so that they will never look the same for very long, now blue, now grey, now silver, sometimes seeming to retreat or to advance, but always drenched in mystery and terrors.

It takes time for the mind to adjust itself to the Coolins. Some minds, I imagine, never become reconciled to them, but feel always that a spectre is walking at their side. I can imagine a neurotic person flying from these mountains as from the devil.

I understand, and feel, the fascination which they exert over others.

I walked a little way up the glen. That word is too gentle. The Glen of Sligachan is a gorge. It lies dark in a hollow of the grim mountains. Rocks lie piled up in it and show their heads above the peaty moorland where the heather stems are now as silver-grey as olives on the plains round Avignon.

The sun rose; and the pale clouds above the Coolins took fire and hung, the colour of apricots, above the jagged spires of the Sgurr-nan-Gillean. As the sun came up over Glamaig, the light spread out fanwise in enormous beams above his mighty back. I walked on in an enchanted silence, broken only by the cries of birds in marsh and heather and by the silver music of streams falling over blue pebbles.

I believe that Skye is the strangest place in the British Isles. It is one of Scotland's greatest enthusiasms. I have heard of the spell of Skye from the first moment I entered Scotland. Men who are not subject to hallucination have told me of the hauntedness of Skye. And it is all true! Skye is something outside normal experience.

It cannot be compared with anything. I thought that possibly it might fall into line with Aran off the west coast of Ireland, another Gaelic island of strange beauty, where life is different. But Skye stands alone, one of Nature's supreme experiments in atmosphere.

The thought came to me as I went through the glen that Valhalla might be like this gorge of Sligachan. It is Norse. All Skye names are a mixture of Norse and Gaelic. It was Viking land in remote ages. The Norsemen colonized it; and many a Skye man reverts to the pale hair and blue eyes of his ancestors. The Viking named the hills, the lochs, and the mournful peaks. Even now the shadow of his long boat falls across the craggy estuaries, and the ghost of Thor surely walks the Sgurr-nan-Gillean when the lightning cracks from peak to peak and the thunder rolls and rocks from Alasdair to Dearg.

Even on this lovely October morning the glen is weird. In the loneliest solitude I feel that I am watched. It is not 'fey' as the west coast of Ireland: it is gnomish. You would never hear fairy harps in Sligachan, but you might hear the sound of hammers in the earth below the oddly-shaped hummocks of heather; and someone might step from behind a stone to place a sword in your hands – a Viking sword.

No wonder Skye is a mass of carefully guarded ghost stories. No wonder its people are locked away in an aloof reticence. No wonder they tell still of strange things seen by shepherds on misty mornings on hill and in glen. You have only to look at the epic sight of peak against peak along the dark ridge of the Coolins to feel that a man climbing those awful mysteries alone would have no eyes did he not meet some heathen god crying for blood from hill to hill, or, on entering the darkness of a ravine, did not discover Fingalian warriors crouched against the rock picking great bones of venison, their swords upon their knees.

The fascination of these mountains is, I think, the mystery of something which can be seen, approached, touched, but never understood. We look at the volcanic rocks, we trace with our fingers the ice-scratches of glaciers that in remote times smoothed, polished, and rounded them. We have a dim perception of the inconceivable eruption which flung them up out of the bowels of the earth. They come down to us wrapped in the wonder of the men who have seen them and lived under their uncanny influence; imagination has flung a veil of mystery and terror over them as thick as the mists which so often hide them from our view.

And we stand on them, climb them, and pretend that we have conquered them, knowing all the time that they are as remote from conquest or understanding as the mountains of the moon.

3

Your first thought on awakening in the Isle of Skye is to tap the hotel barometer. You go downstairs to find that Colonel X., who killed five salmon last week, is glaring at the instrument as at a defaulter.

'Going up, damn it,' he says. 'Need rain, heaps of it, no water in the river.'

Major B., who shot a 'Royal' last year, comes along, packing the first pipe of the day.

'Going up,' he says; 'that's the stuff.'

The colonel grunts like an enraged boar.

Mr D. A., member of the mountaineering club, thunders downstairs like a shire horse, wearing enormous dubbined boots, embroidered with crab-like nails. He smacks the barometer in the eye and remarks: 'Ah! Going up. I'm afraid it's going to be misty, but as long as the rain holds off. . . .'

Salmon-fisher and deer-stalker regard him with brief but intense dislike.

Then arrives Miss Y., who wages a desperate battle with Skye and watercolours.

'Is it really going up, Colonel? How enchanting. Now I may get Loch Coruisk in ideal light. That blue, you know, like those grapes they give you when you've been frightfully ill.'

The colonel, who desperately requires rain in great sheets, and privately regards Miss Y.'s conflicts with nature as contemptible, makes a noise like a bull already frightfully ill, and hides his feelings behind an Indian cheroot.

All the time servants pile the hall table with packets of sandwiches wrapped in butter paper, mutton sandwiches, cheese between fractured biscuits, jam between biscuits, buttered scones, and hard-boiled eggs. Outside, in the wilderness of moor and mountain, the dour, bearded ghillies assemble, some with guns and telescopes, some with rods, some with shaggy mountain ponies, and at this moment, just as the gallant company is about to spread itself over the mountainside, the weather does exactly what the barometer said it would not do, but at least somebody is sure to be delighted.

I decide to walk twenty miles.

I sling a haversack full of rations over my shoulders, make sure I have plenty of matches, take a map, a strong ash-stick and strike off over the hummocky moorland into the Valhalla of Glen Sligachan.

Autumn lies over Skye like a lullaby, not the soft lullaby of English stubble fields and rich, fulfilled maternal orchards, but the sad, wild, Gaelic lullabies, with the sea wind and the hill wind in them, which the Hebridean mothers sing to their little ones.

The Coolins lift their jagged heads clear of mist, but already the clouds which these mountains seem to pull out of clear skies are edging up from the blue. The Coolins fascinate and thrill me. They are frightful. They are stupendous. As you look up at their incredible, fantastic summits, so still and yet so weirdly alive, you feel that some day these heights will shout together and announce the end of the world.

But was ever a mighty spectacle cursed with a more piffling name? 'The Coolins.' It is like the sound of a small lawn being mown. It is like an instalment-system villa in Beckenham. You can see the name on a garden gate. The Gaelic name 'A Chuilionn' looks better, so does the modified Cuillin. The names of the peaks, however, have the authentic thunder which they deserve – Sgurr-nan-Gillean, Sgurr Mhic Coinneach, Sgurr Ghreadaidh, and Sgurr Alasdair.

I walked for about five miles with the Coolins solemnly moving round at my right, rather like a deity keeping an eye on a fly. Great mountains, brown with dead heather, shouldered the sky on my left, and in the valley were the sound of innumerable streams, the colossal kiss of my feet in a peat-hag, and a winding path of sharp rocks.

High up on the mountains to the left I saw a stag. I lay in the heather and watched him through field-glasses. He was grazing with five hinds. They followed obediently, lovely, long-legged, graceful things. He was a big fellow, a fine, yellow body, a perfect hat rack of a head, and a great, shaggy chest. Every now and then he would lift his magnificent antlers and taste the wind suspiciously, and go on grazing.

Rounding a big, peaty hummock, I came on three men glued to the earth in the position of a joke in *Punch*. One was a deer-slayer, and the other two were helping him with telescopes. I sank into the heather beside them with the idea that I might hear a ghillie work off a joke on the man with the gun. But nothing like this happened. They had been wriggling since early dawn, and had no jokes in them. One old ghillie, with his beard all mixed up in the heather, kept whispering as he observed my poor stag: 'A graund nine-pointer, a graund nine-pointer.'

Deer-stalking holds all the elements of eternity. Fishing is a brisk sport compared with this crawling whispering vigil. At length they decided to struggle up a dead watercourse, and one by one slipped like large brown caterpillars through the heather. I went on wishing that I could have sent a telegram to the stag.

The end of my walk was a long climb into the heart of the mountains above Loch Coruisk. This is surely the grandest and most gloomy view in the British Isles. Mountains all round me, the sinister Coolins forming a gigantic barrier to the west, and below, like some deep, dark jewel, the rock-bound waters of the loch, pale green at the edges and green-black in the depths, fretted by wind into a million ripples.

Away out over the waters of Loch Scavaig and the open sea lay those islands which sound like a new cocktail – Rum,

Eigg, and Muck – but I could see only the vague shape of Rum like a blue whale in the sea-mist.

I clambered still higher in the hope of finding among the great boulders some place free from icy wind, and, turning a corner, I came to a level ledge on which an eagle had just finished a meal. We were both surprised and both a little startled. He was not thirty yards from me. He acted first, but he was too heavy with food to rise, and I was surprised to see him run some distance, just like an aeroplane taking off, before he could launch himself. Then with a beat of enormous wings, wonderfully curved at the tip, he lifted himself, circled near me, so that I could hear the wind in his feathers, and slowly flapped his way below me into the gorge, to become lost in the black fastness of the jagged peaks and the splintered terraces.

It was inexpressibly weird sitting up there. The bird of prey was like the spirit of these mountains. The solitude was fearful. The mists steamed over the crests, now hiding and now revealing them, and the Coolins never the same for five minutes, now iron-grey, now blue, now black. . . .

Dusk was creeping through the glen as I went back, bone-weary and wind-blown. I passed the bloody stone where the Macdonalds were slaughtered – or was it the Macleods? – and the wind howled like the ghosts of the dead.

On the sharp stones of the twisting track I saw a drop of blood, then another and another. I shivered. It was exactly the track to follow through this grim valley. For three miles I followed it, until it ended in men and a white mountain pony, with my stag over its back, limp, bleeding, and hardly cold.

'It's a graund nine-pointer,' said the old man with the beard.

I suppose I am no sportsman. I touched his rough skin and wished that he was on the heather again with his hinds, proud in his lovely grace and strength.

All round us the wild hills rose, cruel and bloodthirsty hills, seeming to approve and to gloat in the blue shadows over this latest death, and the atmosphere of the Coolins is such that I looked up to their fretted ridges and their cavernous ravines, wondering from which one some old god, hungry for sacrifice, would creep that night to smell the warm red blood that stains the stones of Valhalla.

4

Every man who bears the name of Macleod – which must be rather like going through life wrapped in a plaid – has heard of the Fairy Flag of Dunvegan Castle. I suppose it is the first story told to little Macleods among the pines of Canada, in Australia, New Zealand, and, in fact, wherever little Macleods happen to be born. . . .

Dunvegan Castle, for over a thousand years the home of the Macleod of Macleod, is the oldest inhabited dwelling in Scotland. Everything you have read about enchanted castles, captured princesses, wizards distilling the Water of Life, victims dying of thirst in dungeons, mermaids swimming up in moonlight to lure a man to his death, men beaten back to a whistle of swords and a hail of arrows, comes true as you see the turrets of Dunvegan lifted in the dusk above the trees on a spur of rock that leans over an arm of the sea in Skye.

The castle is surrounded on three sides by water and on four by ghosts; and no wonder! The little village that hides from the wind near by has had nothing to do for centuries but to remember things about Dunvegan Castle, to improve on the memory in the Celtic fashion, and to add to it. The past of Dunvegan dominates the west of Skye. It stands there like a grey ghost from which there is no escape. It is the Iliad of Skye: it is a saga in stone. The very name smells of blood, fire, and things done long ago in the dark.

I am not surprised to know that many a grown man from the village will not pass the castle alone in the night, and that no local girl will stay there long as a servant.

Today Dunvegan is untenanted for most of the year. The

twenty-third chief, the Macleod, is over eighty years of age, and he lives in England. That also is understandable. It is possible for a house to be in a family for so long that its memories are insupportable. For a Macleod to live in Dunvegan must be rather like sitting down to dinner in a vault which contains the remains of all your ancestors.

Twice a week the castle is opened for those who wish to see the Fairy Flag.

I crossed a bridge built over the ancient moat and rang a bell. A middle-aged Englishwoman opened the baronial door. She lives, to the astonishment of Dunvegan, alone in the castle, sometimes with her sister.

'I would not mind staying here alone one bit,' she told me, 'but it is rather lonely in the winter! I have never seen a ghost, but perhaps that is because I am not a Scotswoman! A local man, only the other day, asked me how on earth I could live here as I do. He said: "If the Macleod of Macleod came to me and said: 'I leave my castle to you and all that's in it!' I would say: 'Ye can keep the castle – I wouldna have it as a gift!' " '

We went through room after room completely furnished, but with the chill of loneliness over them. From every window a view of the sea and wild headlands; in every room a red gleam of mahogany; big chairs waiting, it seems, for someone; tables round which, one imagines, when the house is silent, the ancestors, stepping from their gilt frames, might gather and bridge their distant centuries until cockcrow. In the cold emptiness of Dunvegan the faces of the Macleods gaze down from walls, men in old uniforms against alien backgrounds, men in tartan of antique cut; elegant beauties in high bodices, grave and austere beneath powdered wigs, their shoulders shining from white satin.

Such a one, explains the guide, was a good man. He retrieved the family fortunes. There is another as a young man; there he is again in middle life, the same eyes and mouth, the same insolent air of pride, but no longer

untouched by living, no longer innocent, no longer expectant. There, in tartan, hangs the wicked Macleod who, so
they say, kept his pretty wife in a dungeon in the rock. . . .

You feel that Dunvegan is the mausoleum of a family. No
man would dare to shatter the continuity of its portrait
gallery; no man would dare to take these men and women
from their ancestral walls and store them in the dark; no
heir could possibly enter these halls without first uncovering
to the dead men and women in possession and . . . May I?
Should I? Do you think it right for me to do this, or that?
Would you object if I did so and so? A Macleod could never
be alone in Dunvegan! That is its terror; those are its ghosts:
the calm, watchful eyes of ancestors.

In a glass case is a tissue-frail bundle of fabric, brown
with age, which looks like a yard of tussore silk. This is the
famous Fairy Flag.

The caretaker tells you the story.

In remote ages when the heir was born to Macleod of
Macleod the nurse left the turret in which the child was
sleeping to join in the festivities. The Macleod ordered her
to go up and bring down the child in order that he might be
shown to the assembled clansmen. When she regained the
turret she found the child wrapped in the Fairy Flag. As she
carried the infant, still wrapped in the flag, to the hall
instantly voices were heard chanting that the flag would
save the clan in three great dangers. It was to be waved
three times, but only in dire necessity. It is an historic fact
that it was waved twice, first when the Macleods were hard
pressed by the Macdonalds, who, having landed a strong
force at Waternish, had sacked the church at Trumpan. As
soon as the flag was waved the Macdonalds thought
themselves faced by a much greater throng and, faltering,
were slaughtered to a man. The second waving ended a
cattle plague.

'There was also a tradition, which is believed in to this
day,' says the guide, 'that if the flag was waved for some
trivial reason a dreadful curse would fall on the Macleods:

the heir would die; the "Three Maidens" (the rocks at Dunvegan) would be sold to a Campbell; and when a fox had young in a turret of the castle the glory of the Macleods would depart, much of the estate would be sold, and in time there would not be sufficient Macleods left to row a boat over the loch.

'Well now; in the year 1799 Macleod's factor, a man named Buchanan, decided to test the curse. He employed an English blacksmith in the village to force open the iron box in which the Fairy Flag was kept, and he waved it and put it back again. It may have been coincidence, but in a short time the heir was blown up in H.M.S. *Charlotte*; the Maidens were sold to Angus Campbell of Esnay; a tame fox in the possession of a Lieutenant Maclean, then staying in the castle, had young in the west turret, and the Macleod fortune began to decline. The present chief and his father re-established them, but today there are only three Macleods left, not enough to row a four-oared boat over Lock Dunvegan. . . .

'It may be all a coincidence, but – it's strange, isn't it?'

What is the Fairy Flag? I am the last person on earth to doubt its origin! It has been described as a Saracen banner taken in the Crusades, and the silk is certainly fine and may have come in ancient times from Damascus. There are little bunches of embroidery on it. They are known as 'elf spots'.

I went up the winding stone stair to the Fairy Turret where the child was lying when fairyland came to Dunvegan. The room now, like the old rooms in this castle, is lost beneath Georgian panelling. I thought of a very unfairy-like person – Dr Johnson. He spent a night in this room during that amazing journey to the Hebrides. How the enormous doctor managed to squeeze himself up the narrow spiral staircase to the Fairy Room is one of the mysteries of that journey.

It is surprising that Boswell has not, so far as I remember, given us details of this going to bed. No doubt his devotion blinded him to what must have been an undignified occasion. . . .

In the inn at night I was discussing the story of the Fairy Flag with a man from Glasgow. There were five or six men in the room, big farmers, lean, red, and shaggy as Highland cattle. I did not think they were paying the slightest attention until one came over and said, with the excessive solemnity and conviction possible only to a Scotsman:

'Ye're wrang when ye say that the flag will no' be waved a thurr-rr-d time! It will! When the last Macleod dies the flag will be waved for the thurr-rrd and last time, and – it will crr-umble and vanish awa'.'

He delivered this information with the authority of a prophet, and then stamped out of the room. All the other farmers looked up from their talk and nodded solemnly.

5

I sit in candlelight in the inn at Portree waiting for a ghost. It is a wild, gusty night. The rain beats up in sudden fury against the window. It is just such a night as that, many years ago, on which Prince Charlie said goodbye to Flora Macdonald in this room. . . .

It was nearly midnight. The wind shook at the window, and the rain fell, as rain can fall only in Skye. Into the candlelight of this room came the Prince, flying from Kingsburgh House, and no longer disguised as Flora Macdonald's Irish maid. On his way here he had gladly entered a wood to step from the flowered linen gown and the quilted petticoat which he wore so clumsily. He put on Highland dress – a tartan coat, waistcoat, filabeg, hose, a plaid, a wig, and a bonnet.

He was drenched to the skin. He called for a dram of spirits, and then changed into a dry shirt. The innkeeper had no idea of his rank, or, if so, kept his mouth shut, as everyone did in the Highlands. He set before the visitor fish, bread, and cheese. In those awful days after Culloden

Prince Charlie seemed to have a song or a laugh always on his lips. He joked with the good man, and trying to change a guinea could get only thirteen shillings for it!

Half a mile away a rowing-boat beached in the dark pointed to the island of Raasay. Men came secretly to the little room and implored the Prince to go. There was £30,000 in English gold on his head, and though the poorest man in the Highlands would not have touched a penny of it, who knew what dangerous Hanoverian might seek shelter in the Portree inn on such a fiendish night? The Prince listened to the rain and the wind. Perhaps he walked to the window, as I have just done, and saw the dark bay below, sheeted in blown mist, and the trees bent back from the land. Could he not stay the night and set out in the dawn? Impossible! They would not hear of it! All right, he would come, but – first he must smoke a pipe of tobacco!

Can you imagine how they fumed and fretted as the young man calmly lit his pipe, and how every creak on the stairs must have seemed like the step of some enemy creeping in the dark; and how often did they tiptoe to the door to listen with their thoughts on the window and the drop beneath?

He knocked out his pipe and rose. He was ready! He turned to the brave woman who had saved his life and said goodbye. He gave her his miniature and repaid a small sum of money which he had borrowed from her. Then this wet, hunted prince smiled and said, magnificently, that in spite of all that had happened he hoped some day to welcome her to St James's!

Is there a more operatic farewell in history? Think of him standing there in the candlelight, hunted, beaten, bedraggled, in borrowed clothes, £30,000 on his head and all England after him, holding a parcel containing four clean shirts, a cold fowl tied in a handkerchief, a bottle of brandy on one side of his belt, a bottle of whisky on the other, going out in the rain with an invitation to Court on his lips!

So Flora Macdonald watched him leave the candlelight for the dark of the stairhead, heard the cautious steps and the shutting of the inn door and the tramp of feet beneath the window.

I wait for the ghost. I wait for the door to be flung open; but all I see is a vision of my own making: Flora Macdonald standing there, holding the miniature, still warm from his hands.

This town of Portree, the capital of, and the only town in, Skye, is as different from Sligachan as Hereford from Cornwall. All the wildness of vast mountains that lies piled up at Sligachan fades nine miles to the north in the gentleness of Portree – which might be the sister of Polperro.

A handful of houses stands among trees above the bay. Below is the wooden jetty to which the paddle steamer ties up each night with a ruby-red lamp on her masthead – our only reminder of the world. Life is quieter than in any capital I have known. The sound of Portree is not the roar of wheels, but the lowing of kine in the morning and the bleating of sheep at night. There are about 900 inhabitants, a few lamps which are lit on the coming of winter-time; one street of those satisfying shops full of sweets, aniseed-balls, humbugs, boots, groceries, postcards, jumpers, tobacco, and everything you can possibly want in this life; a tremendous square with its war memorial; a police force consisting of an inspector, a sergeant, a constable; and a jail which would certainly collapse if they found a prisoner for it!

Just now the clever young dentist from Aberdeen is paying his quarterly visit. His forerunners – which sent a thrill of interest through the capital – were a foot-drill done up in brown paper, a box of instruments, and other articles of torture, which were carried from the jetty to the inn. All the gumboils of Skye, and all the aches saved up since last June, are now being paraded on the inn stairs, not in the apprehensive hush of the average waiting-room, but with

Gaelic vivacity. I feel that the dentist is a social occasion. His visit is almost a levee. Not to have a cavity, or at least a gumboil, is to argue yourself out of the swim!

So, on the way up to my room, I pass through a crowd of varied people: ancient crofters about to part from their final molar, sitting there with their inseparable sheep-dogs, women with plaid shawls over their shoulders, pretty young girls from the capital, smart in silk stockings and cloche hats, and an occasional fisherman in a blue jersey.

The gentle, white-haired sheriff, the Lord Chief Justice of Skye, who holds an occasional court, is off on circuit to some remote portion of the Hebrides. Someone there, perhaps, may have coveted a neighbour's sheep. But probably not. . . .

I imagine that in order to understand the Hebrides a man would have to settle down here and found a family. His children might understand; but that may be a swift conclusion!

The mainlander is always an outsider. If hungry he is fed, if cold he is sheltered; but that does not lead to confidences. The Highlander has a proud, locked heart, and the only key to it is kinship. I am told that an islander once married a girl from the mainland a few miles off. She lived with him for fifty years and died beloved and full of good deeds.

'I hear,' said an islander to his friend, 'that the foreign woman is dead at last!'

I believe it is a fact that when the minister leaves certain remote islands to spend a weekend on the mainland a notice is put up over the church porch: 'No service on the Sabbath: the minister has gone abroad.'

The Celt is fated to be misunderstood by the Saxon. The stage Irishman and the stage Scotsman exist only in the brain of the English. The Highlander possesses all the virtues and the vices of the Celt. He is an extremist. He is either hard as steel or soft as water. He is an almost dangerous sentimentalist. His pride is nearly always greater than his poverty. Appeal to him and you find the aristocrat;

offend him and you find the eternal warrior. I see girls in Skye who could in a few weeks take a place in society and betray their origin in no word, thought, or action. I see men who could, and frequently do, rise in the world unhampered by a peasant tradition.

There is no servility in Scotland. A man has always been as good as his master. The Celt, unlike the Saxon, never knew the feudal system and never touched his forelock to a baron. The clan was a family, not a social hierarchy. However, I am straying from Portree. . . .

The great event of our day is the arrival with the dusk of the *Glencoe*.

An hour or so before she arrives we gather on the jetty. Visitors must feel that the whole town has turned out in their honour; but Portree is merely anxious to know what strange things the incredible world has washed up on her shores.

Suddenly the steamer turns into the bay and comes through the dusk, batting the water with her paddles, the light shining on the mast-head. Her stalwart captain directs the process of tying up and we stand, following every order, the ring of every little internal bell, the movement of every man and beast. She brings two new visitors. English! Where from? Probably Glasgow! Where to? Probably Sligachan! Not interesting! A flock of Cheviot sheep from Dingwall. Many mailbags. Those new mudguards for Maggie Macpherson's old bicycle. She *will* be glad! Three crates of whisky. Better still! Cans of oil and petrol. And what is that large box by which Mr Macdonald waits so anxiously? Most, *most* interesting! What can it be? We must find out! Mr Macgregor is bound to know. . . .

So we speculate until the sheep are driven forth in a dim, grey wave, with the dogs snapping, but never biting, at their tails. . . .

All night the *Glencoe* lies at anchor, with her red eye unwinking at the mast-head, reminding us beyond our ken is a restless place known as Scotland. Much farther away is

also a place called England. Both of them form a place
called Britain which, every now and then in the course of a
century or so, requires recruits; and gets them every time.

6

The boat leaves Skye for the mainland soon after sunrise. I
pack by candlelight and go down to the jetty where the
Glencoe lies, her riding-lights growing pale in the grey dawn.
Sheep are being taken to the mainland for winter grazing.
Flocks of smooth Cheviot and horned mountain sheep are
driven aboard by small black-and-white dogs, who grin as
they snap at the silly tails, and above the creak of the derrick
and the rumble of the donkey-engine sounds the click of
innumerable feet as the white wave narrows to the gangway
and scatters in bleating confusion over the forecastle.

Sheep are unfortunate creatures. They are destined to be
messed about. There is always a dog exercising superior
mentality on them or a man with a stick. I feel sorry for
them as I watch their incredibly stupid faces and their
nicked ears lifted in panic, the foolish struggles of those on
the flanks to climb over others into the soft safety of the
flock, and the sudden shrinking as the crane swings a box
over them to the darkness of the hold.

Portree is awakening behind its trees on the cliff. Blue
smoke rises from chimneys. The glimmer of candles shines
in many a window. I hate to leave Skye. I place it with
Lindisfarne, Tintagel, and Connemara among the magic
regions of this world. As I stand in the chilly dawn I
remember the blue mountains of Sligachan, the misty glens,
the little sea beaches where the seals play, the sweeping
uplands with their dark ramparts of peat, the white crofts
whose thatches are weighted with stones, the small fields
where the corn is stacked in honey-coloured crinolines, the
slow salmon streams, the desolate peat-hags where the
peewit cries, the little gardens in which summer lingers still

in patches of bright flowers, and the still lochs with mirrored mountains in their depths.

I remember my arrival at night and the captain's question: 'Your first visit? Ah, weel, ye'll come back!'

This is true of Skye. It is one of those places to which a man must some day return.

The shepherds count their sheep, the dogs retire to the saloon deck and sit there watching their charges, ready to leap down at the first whistle from a shepherd, and the *Glencoe* is ready to pay her daily visit to another world.

A sergeant of the Cameron Highlanders has a great send-off.

'Give our love to Piccadilly,' shout his friends on the jetty as the paddle-wheels revolve. Piccadilly and Portree! Could any two places be more remote from one another? So, edging out into the bay with our alarmed cargo, we turn towards a troubled sunrise and mountains lost in mist.

The sergeant waves until Portree disappears behind a hill, a fine figure in kilt and snow-white spats. Then he lights a cigarette and becomes reflective. He tells me he is retiring on pension. His war ribbons prove that he has earned it. He expects to feel a bit lost at first – every fellow must when he leaves the Army. He has been recruiting in Skye. I tell him how surprised I was to find a resident recruiting-sergeant in this small island, but he says that some of the finest soldiers in the Army come from Skye.

'When we do get one,' he says, 'he's a good lad.'

He goes into details about the local chest-expansion. Skye, he says, is a grand spot for a man, full of good fellows, but it's no place to take a wife who has been used to towns. He is sorry in a way to leave, but his wife will be glad. Women don't like solitary places. While an old soldier can settle down and make himself at home almost anywhere, a woman grows restless and begins to sigh for shops and cinemas and crowds. It's only natural, after all. . . .

So we lean over the deck-rail and watch the enormous

bulk of Glamaig hiding in cloud and, behind, the sinister outline of the Coolins, also dim in mist.

We move slowly out into good weather, the sunlight bright over the wind-dark hills of Inverness. We look back and see the Skye mountains under their cloud-caps, wrapped about with mist and rain, queerly withdrawn, remote, mirage-like.

Skye has its own private supply of weather!

The *Glencoe* ties up for a few minutes to the wooden pier of Broadford. Small boys and the local policeman give a hand with the ropes.

The sheep bleat, thinking they are about to land and feel their feet on heather again. Postbags are flung down to us, also many bulging sacks which scrunch strangely as they are lowered gently on deck. I am interested because I see that they are labelled 'London'. What traffic can London have with this strange little backwater?

'Whelks,' says the captain.

'Do you mean to say that Skye sends whelks to London?'

'Millions.'

'What a hungry stomach that place has!'

'Aye,' says the captain, 'and what a big one!'

He tells me that it is impossible to eat lobsters in Skye because they all go to London.

Who would have imagined that the whelk could be romantic? Now I will never again encounter a whelk-stall in Bethnal Green or Shoreditch but I shall see it overshadowed by the mystic gloom of Skye. Whenever I observe the Cockney on holiday spotting his little saucer of whelks with vinegar from a bottle with a hole in the cork, I shall see the jetty at Broadford and the mountains behind. . . .

Now we near the mainland. We can see the smoke of a railway engine. A rustle of anticipation goes through the small ship. We are about to link our destinies with the wide world once more. The sergeant stepping into it with his freedom, two servant girls with tin trunks on some professional adventure, a commercial traveller going back for more silk stockings, the shepherds, disliking the mainland intensely, frowning at it, and myself anxious to take the road in Scotland once again, but sorry to leave behind me the mystic communion of mountain and mist and the magic of those winds which blow through Skye from the land of fäery.

There is a slight shiver as we touch the pier at Kyle and someone offers to sell us yesterday's newspaper.

We are indeed back in the world.

CHAPTER TEN

How I break the Sabbath and depart for the Gloomy Pass of Glencoe. I meet a goddess and plunge into a storm, pick up a wet Highlander and hear a strange story before I go on into the Land of Rob Roy

§ 1

IT is the Sabbath.

I lie in bed for a time listening to it. You can feel the Sabbath in the Highlands of Scotland just as in cities you can feel a fall of snow: the world is wrapped in a kind of soft hush; normal early morning noises are muffled or absent.

I sing in my bath; then, remembering with a shock that I am breaking the Sabbath, stop and feel criminal. I slink down to breakfast and eat, gazing across the narrow street at the closed shop fronts opposite and the big bow-fronted parlour windows with the sun on them. I can see inside. Shafts of sunlight lie over horsehair sofas, or, wandering, splash the walls with light, illuminating the hideous coloured photographic enlargements of grandfather and grand-mother which gaze grimly down from so many Scottish parlour walls. Grandfather looks out from a hedge of whisker with an expression like a granite quarry; grand-mother, wearing a lace cap on her thin, parted hair, looks down on the younger generations with an expression which is something between a rebuke and an accusation. The older Scottish generation must have been singularly alike. I would guarantee to take away these pictures of grand-parents and replace them with other grandparents lower down the street and no one would notice!

The rooms are all empty. The little town is lying reverently in bed.

There are footsteps in the street. I look down with interest. A young man comes along dressed in abnormal clothes. There is a small boy with him wearing a kilt. They

261

have the appearance of being strangers, but they are merely dressed for the Sabbath.

I feel restless and uneasy. I pick up the *Autobiography* of the Rev. Thomas Guthrie and come at length to this:

'On first going to Ross-shire to visit and preach for my excellent friend Mr Carment, of Rosskeen, I asked him on the Saturday evening before retiring to rest, whether I would get warm water in the morning? Whereupon he held up a warning hand, saying "whisht, whisht!" On my looking and expressing astonishment, he said with a twinkle in his eye, "Speak of shaving on the Lord's day in Ross-shire, and you need never preach here more!" In that same county Sir Kenneth Mackenzie directed my attention to a servant girl, who, if not less scrupulous, was more logical in her practice. She astonished her master, one of Sir Kenneth's tenants, by refusing to feed the cows on the Sabbath. She was ready to milk but would by no means feed them; and her defence shows that though a fanatic, she was not a fool. "The cows," she said – drawing a nice metaphysical distinction between what are not and what are the works of necessity and mercy that would have done honour to a casuist – "the cows canna milk themselves, so to milk them is a clear work of necessity and mercy; but let them out to the fields, and they'll feed themselves." '

I cannot read. I drift restlessly round the little hotel. It is deserted. I ring the bell near the reception office. Miss Campbell comes clothed in a neat coat and skirt and wearing a discreet black hat.

'Good morning. Can I have some cigarettes?'

'Are ye gaun' tae the kirk?'

'I don't know. . . .'

'Mr MacLean's preaching the day. He's a graund preacher.'

As she hands me the cigarettes I observe in the background a Sabbatarian calm over the kitchen; and one of the chambermaids likewise garbed in coat and skirt and discreet hat. The whole place is pervaded by an air of solemn preparation.

'I think I will go to church. Can I come with you?'

'Aye, ye can that.'

I immediately repent. I think there is time to print some photographs of Skye. I go up to my room to discover that I have no hypo. Never mind, I will run over to the chemist and persuade jolly old Mr Macintyre to give me a handful. I go out in the street bareheaded, ignorant of the crime on which I am bound. I come to the chemist's shop. It is shut, but I ring the little bell at the house door to the side. The old boy will probably be glad to see me and will invite me into the shrouded shop and crack a joke or two. I hear his footsteps descending the stairs. The door opens, but only for two or three inches, and in the narrow slit I see the face of Mr Macintyre, but – what a changed Mr Macintyre!

He wears a black cut-away coat, a waistcoat that exposes almost as much boiled shirt as an evening waistcoat; a big, pure, shining expanse punctuated by two gold studs. His neck rises from the kind of collar which used to distinguish labour leaders, and inside the wings of this collar is tucked a mournful little squirt of a black tie. In one hand he grasps a Bible.

An awful foreboding of disaster comes upon me as I observe the steely grimness with which Mr Macintyre is regarding me. My old friend has somehow become engulfed in a kind of caricature of himself. The change in him is as remarkable as that which now and then came over Mr Hyde.

'Weel?' he said through the wooden slit.

'Good morning,' I cry brightly. 'I'm so sorry to trouble you, but I've run out of hypo and –'

Mr Macintyre's mouth is set in a hard line. I feel that I never knew him until this moment.

'D'ye no' ken it's the Lord's Day?' he asks, as if rebuking a child of two.

'But. . . .'

There is no but about it: the door is shut and I hear his returning footsteps.

I feel terribly snubbed and hurt. My first instinct is to kick the door down and tell him that he is an old fool. Then I realize that I have put my foot, so to speak, right through his Calvinism. I have committed a deadly sin. I have not only paraded myself as a Sabbath-breaker: I have also tried to involve him in my crime against God's commandments. The iniquity of it sinks into me. I want to apologize to him; but I am only making it worse by standing there without a hat.

I visualize generations of Macintyres going back to the time of John Knox, all in black, all with icy eyes, all holding Bibles, becoming suddenly different and forbidding on the seventh day. To think of old Macintyre dressed like that sitting up in his parlour in an orgy of Hebrew prophesy! I want to smile. Yet there is something about his grim Sabbath self almost startling to one who had known him only on weekdays.

As I turn from the door I notice that Mr Hulme, the haberdasher opposite, is gazing down reflectively into the street from his parlour window. I feel ashamed that he should have seen my humiliation. Then I wonder – was he meant to see it?

The little town is stirring to life.

Strangely enough, the mountains look exactly as they do on week-days. Why has no one thought of hanging crêpe on the trees? Sinful berries are wearing red on rowan-trees. A bell rings – a tinny insistent bell. Doors open, families slip out discreetly; doors shut. Each member holds a hymn book in gloved hands. Children look miserably clean and tidy. They walk slowly along the narrow pavements, bowing distantly to friends and relatives. The whole town is in mental mourning. It is locked up in the Sabbath tradition. Everybody is pretending to be remote from carnal things. What is the God they worship? I feel certain that he wears elastic-sided boots and puts all the cherubim in kilts.

I go back and tell Miss Stewart that I have changed my mind about kirk. I cannot go. The sight of Mr Macintyre would be too much for me. I will go out and look at some honest week-day cows. . . .

On my way back I run right into the returning stream of Calvanism. I am not a self-confessed pagan. And whom should I see but Mr Macintyre walking with a Sabbath stride as slow and distinct as the march to the 'Flowers of the Forest' at a Scottish military funeral. He is – I can hardly believe it – wearing black gloves. The pipe which he loves is not in his mouth nor, I feel sure, even in the pocket of his black cut-away. I feel about him as Sir Toby Belch and the others felt about Malvolio when he began to go off his head in the garden. Should I cross the road or ignore him?

'Guid day,' says Mr Macintyre to my astonishment. He is almost human again.

'A good sermon?' I ask.

I gather from his manner that our earlier meeting must be ignored.

'Aye; no' sae bad at a'.'

Still I do not understand him in this religious mood. I can think of nothing to say to him. Suddenly he looks at me with a real quick week-day eye.

'I was sorry,' he says, 'tae be compelled tae refuse ye a while back'; then lowering his voice he adds, 'if ye still want the hypo *come roond tae the back door*!'

He leaves me standing speechless and continues his black, majestic progress down the little High Street.

2

Along the road from Ballachulish where the river Coe pours into Loch Leven is a comfortable little village which boasts the most grotesque signpost in the British Isles:

THE VILLAGE OF GLENCOE
SCENE OF THE FAMOUS MASSACRE
TEAS AND REFRESHMENTS, TOBACCO AND CIGARETTES

This statement relieves the feeling of gloom with which a traveller approaches the scene of the clan massacre. The only writer who found Glencoe cheerful was Andrew Lang. Macaulay's description is well known, so is that by Dorothy Wordsworth; perhaps the best, however, is the not so familiar letter by Dickens in Forster's *Life*.

'All the way,' wrote Dickens, 'the road had been among moors and mountains with huge masses of rock which fell down God knows where, sprinkling the ground in every direction, and giving it the aspect of the burial place of a race of giants. Now and then we passed a hut or two, with neither window nor chimney, and the smoke of the peat fire rolling out at the door. But there were not six of these dwellings in a dozen miles; and anything so bleak and wild and mighty in its loneliness, as the whole country, it is impossible to conceive. Glencoe itself is perfectly *terrible*. The pass is an awful place. It is shut in on each side by enormous rocks from which great torrents come rushing down in all directions. In amongst these rocks on one side of the pass (the left as we came) there are scores of glens, high up, which form such haunts as you might imagine yourself wandering in, in the very height and madness of a fever. They will live in my dreams for years – I was going to say as long as I live, and I seriously think so. The very recollection of them makes me shudder. . . .'

I went on into this mountain pass ready, even anxious, to shudder at it. But, alas, the sun was shining! Glencoe in this mood – the mood that Lang must have known – is not frightful: it is awesome, it is stark, it is, like all the wild mountains of Scotland, a lesson in humility. Man has never existed for it; it is, at least in sunlight, not unfriendly so much as utterly oblivious of humanity. A man suddenly shot up into the moon might gaze at the cold, remote mountains with much the same chilly awe that he looks at the Pass of Glencoe. Here is a landscape without mercy. So far as Glencoe is concerned the first germ of life has never struggled from the warm slime. It is still dreaming of geological convulsions. Glencoe in sunlight does not make a man shudder because it is beautiful. It rather encourages him to sit down and look at it for a long time as you sit down in the sand and look at the Sphinx, wondering what he – for the Sphinx is masculine – can see in the sky. Perhaps it is God. Glencoe has the same expression.

The worst road in Scotland winds its way through the solitude. The iron-grey mountains fret the sky on either hand. Half the pass is in sunlight; half in cold shadow. Tough grass and soggy bogland fill the narrow valley. There is no sound but the running of icy water, brown with peat; no movement but the wind in the long grass and the slow wheeling of some sinister bird high over the hills.

The volcanic heights are gashed by sharp gullies, broadening as they descend, in which water has in the course of centuries found its way to the valley. In some of these gashes trees try to hide from the wind like men sheltering. Mostly they are great slashes in the rock, as if giants had sharpened their swords on the hills. . . .

The sun is covered by a cloud. The light dies in Glencoe as suddenly as a light is switched off in a room. The pass has changed colour. It is grey and hopeless. Now you see why Macaulay called it the 'Valley of the Shadow'. As you look up at the mountains, at the queer gullies and the dark glens they seem a fit abode for naked devils. It was surely in such a place as Glencoe that the Gadarene swine met their end.

I came across a young shepherd walking behind sheep which moved softly like a grey wave over the grass on invisible feet. His collie would sleuth ahead and turning in the direction of the flock, crouch in the grass with his long nose showing, watching his charges with bright, critical eyes. If any sheep strayed or nibbled too long at the grass he would spring out like a brown and white dart, and in a second the offender would be pressing his way into the grey wave and the flock would have resumed its right formation.

The shepherd gave a low whistle. The dog, which

appeared to be obsessed by the sheep, heard and instantly responded, bounding in long, graceful leaps towards his man, to stand, head on one side – blue tongue out, eyes on his eyes, one of the most beautiful pictures of intelligence I have ever seen.

The shepherd said something which I did not understand. The dog immediately wheeled round and turned back the flock. The shepherd, proud to show off his dog to me, whistled and said something else, and the dog headed the sheep back again! Another whistle and the dog raced ahead and lay obediently in the grass.

'He's a goot dog, but not so goot as his mother wass!' said the shepherd carelessly, not wishing to praise his own property.

A gunshot echoed round the hills. We looked up. They were shooting today, explained the shepherd, and the roads over the mountains were closed. His journey to market, which on an ordinary day would have taken him a few hours, would by the main road get him in at nightfall. But sport in the Highlands takes no count of ordinary people.

3

A white inn gazes out towards the Moor of Rannoch. Two figures plodded towards it with slow mountaineering steps. One was a young man and the other was a young girl. But, heavens, what a girl! She was a Diana in breeches. She wore no hat. Gold hair was blown about her head. Her blouse was open at the throat. She wore a tweed coat and tweed breeches. It sounds terrible. It rouses recollection of regrettable maidens seen in transit through lakeland villages in Cumberland, moving onward on either fat or stumpy legs in breeches terminating in hideous, insecure worsted stockings. But this Diana of Rannoch Moor might have stepped into some modern outfitter's from a Greek fresco. The boy was obviously her brother, but she was the taller by four inches.

They stumped into the white inn, and her enormous dubbined boots, with their woollen over-socks, did not take away from the beauty of her long, slim limbs. She slipped a bulky rucksack over her strong shoulders, ran her hands through the gold hair, and sat down to eat mutton. Health and youth shone out of her like light. Her voice was that, I think, of Edinburgh, but her face was the face of Greece. I have never seen the eating of mutton lifted into the regions of art. I was enchanted. I did not want to know whence she came or where she was going. I was content just to watch her. And when she had swung her green rucksack on her lovely back and had taken up the stick she carried and had tramped off with a grind of boots on the grit of the road, I knew that real beauty was going through Glencoe, and it would not have surprised me to hear even those old and awful hills shout in welcome.

I will never see her again and she will probably never see this. She might not recognize herself. But a man knows when he meets a goddess suddenly among the hills.

4

I met a man outside this inn, a quiet old man with a velvet voice. We sat at a table and talked. He told me that he 'had the Gaelic' and would rather talk in Gaelic than in English, because not only could he find better words in that language but the way of expressing ideas came easier to him.

We talked together about the massacre of Glencoe. I asked him to describe it to me and he did so with that queer trick of graphic narrative which I have noticed also when the Irish tell stories of things that happened long ago. It almost seemed that he was talking about people whom he had met.

It was in the depth of winter in the year 1691 that all the Highlands were required to take an oath of allegiance to William III before the year was out. Every clan took this oath but the Macdonalds of Glencoe. Old MacIan, their chief, held out until the last moment. But he saw how foolish it was – or perhaps the women told him; anyhow, the old man set off through the snow-drifts to swear loyalty before the magistrates at Fort William. When he got there he discovered that the oath should be taken before the sheriff at Inveraray. So the old man goes on through the hard weather. The passes are deep in snow, the wind is bitter, and he does not reach Inveraray until January 6th. He takes oath, and the sheriff tells the authorities at Edinburgh that the clan has fallen into line.

Now, the authorities in Edinburgh – and notably Sir John Dalrymple, Secretary of State – are anxious to stamp out the Macdonalds. They are Papists. They are Jacobites. They are thieves and robbers. It would be easier to rule the country were they exterminated. When the register goes to the Privy Council in Edinburgh the name of Macdonald of Glencoe is found to have been obliterated, and the clan is formally liable to punishment. Now Dalrymple had written to a friend in Scotland expressing his delight that the time of grace expired in the depth of winter, because, as he put it, 'that is the proper season to maul them, in the cold, long nights.' He wrote to the commander-in-chief in Scotland on January 11th, 'My Lord Argyle tells me that Glencoe hath not taken the oaths; at which I rejoice – it's a great work of charity to be exact in rooting out that damnable sect, the worst in all the Highlands.'

So fellow Scotsmen plan the great 'work of charity'.

At the beginning of February – four weeks after the old Macdonald had taken the oath – a detachment of a hundred and twenty men of the Earl of Argyle's regiment – all Campbells and hereditary enemies of the Macdonalds – set out from the garrison at Inverlochy under the command of Campbell of Glenlyon. This man is a relative by marriage of the old chief's. The troops march through the snows and into the valley, where they express friendship for their victims and are received with true Highland hospitality. So murderers and victims settle down together.

Every morning the commander calls at the humble house of the old chief and takes his draught of usquebaugh. In the evenings he plays at cards with the family; and all the time in his pocket is the savage death-knell of the clan: 'You are to put all to the sword under seventy. You are to have a special care that the old fox and his son do on no account escape your hands. You're to secure all avenues, that none escape; this you are to put in execution at five o'clock precisely, and by that time, or very shortly after it, I'll strive to be at you with a stronger party. If I do not come to you at five, you are not to tarry for me, but to fall on.'

At five o'clock of the dark winter morning the signal is given and the foul massacre begins. In every little hut scattered throughout the glen the same awful treachery occurs: guest murders his host and host's family. Lieutenant Lindsay comes with his men to the chief's house. The old man gets out of bed to receive him and is shot dead as he dresses. His wife, shamefully treated by the soldiers, dies next day. The whole glen echoes with the cries of the murdered and the shots of the murderers. One family receive a volley of shot as they sit round the early morning fire.

When light comes to Glencoe the snow is bloody and the smoke of the burning houses is going up in the frosty air. Thirty-eight Macdonalds have been murdered.

Colonel Hamilton, commanding officer at Inverlochy, arrives at breakfast-time to see how the 'act of charity' has panned out. He finds one old man mourning over the bodies of the dead. A Campbell catches sight of him, levels his flintlock and shoots him as he kneels so that his body falls on those of his kinsmen.

The Campbells march out of Glencoe, driving before them two hundred horses, nine hundred cattle, and many sheep and goats. . . .

Men still talk of this in the Highlands and remember details of it. The old man who spoke Gaelic before the inn at Rannoch Moor grew mournful and indignant as he told how the Campbells fraternized with the Macdonalds before the massacre. Glencoe was, for him and for everyone in the district, I suppose, still haunted.

It was London, not Edinburgh, that demanded a full inquiry into this deed. In a letter from London dated March 5th, Dalrymple scents the coming storm and pretends to deny knowledge that the clan were slaughtered in their beds. The Government was forced to hold an inquiry. That inquiry wrote down the massacre of Glencoe as the most foul and barbaric deed in the history of clan murder.

There had been savage blood-feuds in the Highlands for centuries; the history of Rob Roy's clan, the Clan MacGregor is full of them.

The Macdonalds, too, had to their discredit many deeds almost as fearful as the massacre which exterminated them. For instance, in the year 1588 young men of this clan wandering far from Glencoe carried off a deer in the forest of Glenartney. The under forester, Drummond of Drummonderoch, caught them and sent them home with cropped ears.

One day, not long after, Drummond found himself surrounded by Macdonalds, who slew him and cut off his head. They went to the house of the dead man's sister, Mrs Stewart of Ardvorlich, concealing the head. The woman received them and, apologizing because she had no food ready, put bread and cheese before them and left the room to cook a better meal. While she was gone the Macdonalds placed her brother's head on the table and stuck a piece of bread and cheese in its mouth. The woman returned, saw this, and rushed from the house insane. She was pregnant. She wandered about the hills and forests for a long time, and her son, a man of wild and ungovernable passions, was the James Stewart who murdered his friend Lord Kilpont.

But nothing in the history of Highland barbarism – for it can be called by no softer word – was more inhuman than the massacre of Glencoe. Had the Campbells marched boldly in and declared war no one could have said a word, but to shelter under the sanctity of hospitality and then – as the old man with the velvet voice said: 'Ass long ass the hills stand men will remember Glencoe.'

5

The sky grew dark and rain fell.

It was thin and slanting and cold, more like the edge of a cloud than rain; and this wilderness whose skyline I knew by heart became suddenly hidden and mysterious, its heights veiled, its distant prospects concealed.

I moved in a small circle of mist, and just as twilight can fill a well-known house with imaginary terrors so a cloud on a mountainside or mist in a valley can transform a sunny landscape into something chilling and fearful.

When a strange man suddenly materializes out of the greyness of a London fog and melts again into the greyness he is for one brief second a startling apparition. The eye concentrates on him and records the least detail of him. Mist in the Highlands invests immediate objects with the same uncanny significance. I found that my eyes, withdrawn from hill-crests and horizons, fixed themselves eagerly on the grey boundary line of vision, noted cloudy shadows which were vague rocks, and then became, as I approached them, startlingly clear rocks, veined like marble and shining blackly with the rain. But the very limitation imposed on the senses gave a special importance to them, so that I almost expected to see men step out from behind them, or perhaps they would not be men but spirits left in these hills from the youth of the world.

The little burns that slipped through the heather over brown stones were somehow important; the heather stems pressed backwards in the wind, vibrating with a wiry motion, were significant; and the eye watched for them and noted them as the mist revealed them. Once I came suddenly to the edge of a cold tarn like a plate of silver, steaming soup.

I suppose everyone who has been alone in mist on mountains or in lonely places has felt at some time that queer panic which causes a man to turn and look behind him. It is almost as if an invisible presence were at one's elbow and might at any moment reveal itself. It is not difficult to realize why the ancients gave to each hill and stream its guardian spirit.

And now, as I was longing, as so rarely happens to me, for human companionship, I heard the sound of distant thunder. It rolled round the hills angrily like some blind beast awakened from sleep to lumber round the solitudes in search of someone; and the silence that followed was already ominous with the next roar. There was a sudden flash in the mist like the flash from a gun; and then, still far off, a deeper sound of thunder in the hills.

The thin mist changed to rain and I could see the vast blue shapes of the mountains and, far away to the northward, a blackness in the sky where the storm lay.

I put on speed and slid on over the mountain road. I dislike a motor-car most of all in a storm. And, with the crack of a whiplash and an instantaneous flash of lightning, the storm leapt through the air from the mountains of Ross and broke over the Grampians with all the force of its artillery. Thunder spoke with the ear-splitting crack of heavy guns and then seemed to rumble away through the rocky defiles, exploding with diminishing fury from glen to glen. In the terrible silence of the second after I heard the rain falling, and each small burn, now swollen by the cloudburst, splashed itself across the road and fell in miniature Niagaras over stones and through heather.

I was filled with an insane exhilaration. I have known the same reckless frenzy in a storm at sea. It is almost as though one is possessed by an elemental fury. The storm cracked and thundered above me. The glens caught up the thunder and flung it from one to another like giants playing ball, and at each clap I cried out: 'Louder, louder!' and each flash of lightning seemed to light a new excitement in me.

As I swung round a corner a figure leapt up from behind a stone and waved its arms at me. I saw it with the tail of my eye: a tall figure black with rain. But I was travelling so recklessly that I was round another corner before I could pull up. Was it a figure? Was it not some queer rock shining in the deluge? But I could swear that it shouted. I looked back and, sure enough, a man came stumbling and splashing to me round the corner.

'Not an inch of shelter,' he shouted. 'Are you going to Crianlarich?'

'Go anywhere you like!'

'Thanks. I'm wet through.'

He got in and sat like a water-rat next to me. He was hatless and the rain had combed his hair straight over his forehead. His macintosh was wet inside and out. Beneath it he wore a shirt open at the neck and a tartan kilt. He was about thirty-five.

A terrific clap of thunder seemed to sound directly above us:

> D'ye ken John Peel with his coat so gay?
> D'ye ken John Peel at the break of the day?

I sang at the top of my voice. My companion, with a quick glance at me, ceased mopping his head with a wet handkerchief and joined in the song with a fine deep voice; and I knew that we were going to like each other:

> Peel's view hallo-o-o-o would awaken the dead . . .

We roared it! Crack went the thunder! Down came the rain! Cross-winds hit us! Water slewed itself across the wind-screen, and we were very happy.

Then gradually the thunder receded, the rain became less violent and ceased – the sun was shining! The storm was over.

'Do you know the William Tell overture?'

'Tiddle-om-tiddle-om-tiddle-om-pom-pom?' said my companion.

'Yes; well isn't it extraordinary that the end of a storm can be so like it? Here we are now among the wood-wind. . . .'

We looked round, and ahead of us towered the great mass of Ben Dorain and Ben Odhar; away to the north, glistening in rain, ran the windy waste of Rannoch Moor; and there was the sound of water: the rush of torrents, the tinkle of burns, and the satisfied gurgle of gorged streams.

'Wasn't that grand?'

'Aye, it was,' said my companion, rubbing his head vigorously; 'there's nothing like a storm in the Highlands.'

'A storm? You call that a storm? It was like the beginning of the end of the world. . . .'

A little gold cloud came smiling over the head of Ben Dorain, as if there was no such thing as thunder in the laboratory of heaven.

And now the sun was almost warm, wet boulders were swiftly drying, and the sky, it seemed, would never weep again.

The stranger and I decided to share our sandwiches. He was a big-boned, shaggy Highland bull of a fellow. I was sure his name was Mac Something. The only dry thing about him was his kilt, which is the only sane country dress for a man: it keeps him cool in warm weather, warm in cold weather, dry in wet weather, and at all times it gives him an air of nobility. He removed his wet shirt and ran about over the heather clothed only in his kilt, holding the shirt out to dry in the wind.

I remembered that I had in my bag a bottle of Talisker whisky, that remarkable drink which is made in the Isle of Skye and can be obtained even in its birthplace only with difficulty. This seemed to me an occasion. When my companion saw the bottle of Talisker he ceased to leap about and, becoming solemn, he said:

'Talisker? Ye don't mean to open the bottle? It's a shame to waste it; but, man, it's a grand whisky!'

We settled down.

He had a tin mug in his rucksack; I had one of those idiotic so-called drinking cups which you place firmly on a stone with the result that the whole thing telescopes and spills the liquor. We poured the amber-coloured Talisker into our mugs, and descending to an amber-coloured burn in the heather we let a little ice-cold water into the whisky.

There is, so it is said, a time for everything, and the time for whisky is after physical fatigue in the open air among great mountains. This Talisker drunk below the great, windy clouds in the shadow of Ben Dorain was as different from the whisky which a man drinks in his club as Lachryma Christi drunk in the shadow of Vesuvius differs from the same wine in Soho. This drink filled us with good nature and enthusiasm.

My friend, perched picturesquely on a stone, told me a lot about himself. He was something in a city. He always spent his holidays in his native Highlands. He loved to wear the kilt for two or three weeks and to run wild in the heather. As the Talisker burned in him it lit fires of patriotism, and I listened with delight as he spoke of his love for the hills and the glens and the peat-hags and the great winds and the grey mists.

I told him of my journey through Glencoe and of the old man outside the inn at Rannoch who spoke of the treachery of the Campbells as if it had happened only the day before yesterday. My friend smiled as he lit his pipe.

'I can tell you a true story,' he said, 'because it happened to me. My name's Campbell, you know! It must have been in nineteen-nine or nineteen-ten – anyway, I was just a boy – and I took a day excursion from Edinburgh to Glencoe – you know the sort of thing: up at five a.m. and back at nine p.m., and all for about six bob. . . .

'In the train I met a businessman who was going to visit his parents. They still lived on a small croft in the glen. When he knew that I had nowhere in particular to go he invited me to walk up with him and see the old folks.

"What's your name, laddie?" he asked. "Campbell," I told him. I thought he seemed a bit worried. "Look here," he said, "don't mention that to the old people. . . ."

'I went up the glen with him and we came to a humble little but and ben. The father, quite a poor crofter, was a grand old Highland gentleman with a head on him like a king and – you know the fine manners of many of these old people! He said to me: "Welcome to my house, sir." And after a spell of the usual Highland hospitality, the old gentleman, looking at me, said, "You'll be from the Highlands, sir?" I told him that I came from Edinburgh but that I was of Highland descent. "Where did your father come from?" asked the old man. "From Dingwall," I told him. "Was he a Fraser?" asked the old man. "No," I said. "Was he a Grant?" "No," I said. "Well, what was his name?" he demanded.

'All the time that this was going on I could see the son looking across at me and silently imploring me to lie about my name, but the old man had cornered me, and – anyway, I'm proud of my name, and I said straight out, "Well, sir, I see no shame in my name: my father's name is Campbell!" At that the old man stood up! He was more than six feet high! He seemed to fill the little cottage! He pointed to the door and said, "There shall no Campbell sit by my hearthstone!" The son pleaded with the old man; but it was no good! He stood there pointing to the door. I got up, bowed, and left. And that was in nineteen-nine or ten! I shall never forget it!'

He took another drink of Talisker and shook his head.

'The Highlands have a long memory,' he said, 'and I can't tell you the feeling of anger and shame that came over me as I went back through Glencoe like a scapegoat. . . .'

I bade farewell to Campbell on the outskirts of Crianlarich, and he stood on a stone with his kilt blowing about him and waved me out of sight.

I came down through Crianlarich and Balquhidder to the clean town of Callander, which is the gate to the Trossachs.

What a country is Scotland for presiding memories. The Border is Scott, Ayr is Burns, Edinburgh is Mary, the Highlands are Prince Charlie, and the Trossachs and Loch Lomond are Rob Roy.

Scotland is a baffling country to describe. You think that you have summed her up, that you have assessed her values and reached a decision about her when without warning she suddenly flings a surprise at you. The Trossachs are not fair. A man spends months touring a country, penetrating its remote mountains, enduring heat, cold, fatigue, high teas, Sabbaths, kirks, and at the end comes suddenly on the whole thing in concentrated form, boiled down to the very essence and spread out over a small compass conveniently near to the cities of Glasgow and Edinburgh. No wonder most travellers in Scotland never get farther than the Trossachs. I repeat: they are definitely unfair and should be abolished in the interests of more distant places.

The Trossachs are like a traveller's sample of Scottish scenery. They remind me of those small tins of biscuits which firms send out beautifully packed to indicate a range of manufactures. If you like them you can order larger quantities.

This synopsis of Scotland known as the Trossachs can be, and no doubt is, taken by Americans in a hurry. They can truthfully return and say that they have seen quite a lot of Scotland. In the Pass of Leny you have a taste of real Highland bleakness; on the Braes of Balquhidder you have a bit of everything.

How many times have I said to myself, 'That is the finest sight in Scotland.' Once again I said it on the shores of Loch Earn, as the sun was setting in a smoulder of fiery cloud, Ben Vorlich and Stuc-a-Chroin changing colour as the light goes from the sky, a water-bird winging its way to the reeds of the shore, low over the water, jet-black against the brightening silver of the loch. There is only one book for the Trossachs: *The Lady of the Lake*.

In Balquhidder Churchyard is a grave they call Rob Roy's, but I should have said that the tombstone carved with a cross, a sword, and a kilted man is much older than the eighteenth century. Someone had placed a bunch of flowers on this stone. I cannot help feeling that excellent as Scott's *Rob Roy* is, and high as it stands among his novels as a literary achievement it does not do justice to its hero. The introduction is admirable, and the Highland scenes perfect. But how sparingly Scott used the Rob Roy legends! What annoying restraint he employed!

I re-read the novel before I entered the MacGregor Country.

Rob Roy seems to sum up the Highlands just as the Trossachs sum up Scotland. How surprised Addison or Pope would have been, as Scott remarks, to know that a character who blended wild virtues with the subtle restraint and the unrestrained licence of an American Indian existed with them in the polished age of Queen Anne and George I! Imagine Robin Hood or Hereward the Wake in the England of that time! Rob Roy was the Robin Hood of Scotland, and he died as recently as 1734! He left the world just two years after James Watt entered it; it is extraordinary to think that the steam engine and Rob Roy almost coincided!

A man who steals from the rich and gives to the poor is certain of immortality, no matter what his own generation think of him, and Rob Roy's name will live as long as there is a Scotsman left to remember the stories told to him as a child. And most of the stories about Rob have the ring of truth about them. How I wish Scott had gone easy with Osbaldistone and his anaemic love-affair and had given us more about the outlaw.

There are, for instance, so many fine stories of the attempts made to capture Rob Roy from time to time by the forces of the Crown and also by private individuals.

There was a stout fellow who swore that with six men he would go through the Highlands and arrest the terrible Rob and bring him to jail at Stirling. The party, armed with cudgels, arrived at the public-house at Balquhidder and asked the way to Rob's house. The landlord, of course, sent word that a party of strangers was on the road so that Rob might be ready for them.

When the brave messenger arrived at the house he pretended to be a traveller who had lost his way. He was shown politely into a large room full of swords, battle-axes, hunting-horns, and trophies of the chase. When the door shut he screamed with terror to see hanging there, and intentionally placed there, the stuffed figure of a man. The enormous Rob calmly told him that it was the body of a rascally messenger who had come to his house the night before and there had been no time to bury him!

The affair ended for the messenger, as so many attempts to capture Rob Roy ended, in the river!

Surely the most extraordinary event in Rob's adventurous life was his visit to London. I cannot imagine why Scott made no use of this. The story of this visit is given in *Historical Memoirs of Rob Roy and the Clan MacGregor* by R. Macleay (Edinburgh 1881), in which the author writes:

'The numerous exploits of Rob Roy had rendered him so remarkable, that his name became familiar everywhere; and he was frequently the subject of conversation among the nobility at court. He was there spoken of as the acknowledged protégé of Argyll, who often endeavoured to palliate his errors; but that nobleman was frequently rallied, particularly by the king, for his partiality for MacGregor. On several occasions His Majesty had expressed a desire to see the hardy mountaineer; and Argyll, willing to gratify him, sent for Rob Roy, but concealed his being in London, lest the officers of state, aware of the king's hatred, might take measures to detain him. Argyll, however, took care that the king should see him without knowing who he was, and for this purpose made Rob Roy walk for some time in front of St James's. His Majesty observed, and remarked that he had never seen a finer-looking man in a Highland dress, and Argyll having soon after waited on the king, His Majesty told him of his having noticed a handsome Scots Highlander, when Argyll replied that it was Rob Roy MacGregor, His Majesty said he was disappointed that he did not know it sooner, and appeared not to relish the information, considering it as too serious a jest to be played upon his authority, and one which seemed to make him, among others, a dupe to our hero's impudence.'

Rob Roy in his kilt loitering at the bottom of St James's Street is a fit companion picture to that of Prince Charlie in the Strand!

Rob seems to have made financial profit out of his visit to England, and this is at least very convincing:

'On his way from London at this time,' writes Mr Macleay, 'he was accidentally introduced into the company of some officers who were recruiting at Carlisle. Struck with his robust and manly stature, they considered him a fit person for the king's service, and wished to enlist him; but he would accept no less than treble the sum they offered, to which they agreed. He then remained in the town a few days, paying no regard to them, and when he was ready to continue his journey came away, the military being unable to prevent him; and the enlisting money paid his expenses home.'

One of the finest stories is that of his death. It is said that when he lay ill, old, and worn out by his active life, a man whom he had no cause to love called on him:

'Lift me up,' cried Rob Roy; 'dress me in my best clothes; tie on my sword; place me in the great chair. That fellow shall never see me on a death-bed.'

He received the visitor with formal civilities, and when the interview was over fell back, crying:

'It is over; put me to bed! Call in the piper! Let him play "Cha till mi tuille" as long as I breathe!'

He died at his farm among the Braes of Balquhidder, and the Highlands did not long survive him.

So a saga as old as the hills was sung on the threshold of the modern world; a scene from the Iliad was acted in Balquhidder even while ebony canes were tapping delicately over the pavements of Mayfair.

7

Loch Lomond.

Here is one of the world's glories. The hills lie against one another fading into the blue distance; the autumn leaves, russet, red, and gold, go down to the edge of the water, and Loch Lomond lies for twenty-four miles in exquisite beauty.

The 'bonnie, bonnie banks' are the hail and farewell of the Highlands. If you go north along the west coast it is 'Ave!' that Ben Vorlich shouts to you as he lifts his great head to the sky; if you go down from the north over the mountains it is 'Vale!' that he cries – farewell to the Highlands of Scotland! And in Loch Lomond are gathered a million beauties: soft green banks and braes; a whisper of woodland; regal mountains with the ermine of white clouds round their purple shoulders; and always, mile after mile, silver water widening to the south where islands lie at anchor like a green flotilla.

As you stand at the edge of this greatest of all British lakes watching the small waves break on the brown stones, listening to them too, marvelling that all this should be so near to Glasgow, it seems to you that Glasgow should never lose its soul. There is no excuse for it with Loch Lomond on the doorstep and Ben Lomond standing midway above the waters like a fanfare of trumpets.

A man can go out from Glasgow and climb this mountain and see Scotland; he can see his own country lying for miles in a chain of dim blue monsters. Where the eye fails him the mind can carry on, leaping in imagination from peak to peak across the Grampians, leaping from far

Ben Nevis to the peaks of the Western Isles, and back across the sea to Cairn Gorm and over Scotland to those guardian ranges of the east which sometimes lie at the edge of the sea painted in the blue of heaven. What a spiritual adventure is Ben Lomond on the doorstep of Glasgow? . . .

As you go beside the lake the great city reveals itself in a number of ways: there are small pleasure steamers anchored at a pier, there are, bowered in trees, or hidden round the bend of a carriage drive, those establishments known as hydropathic to which the country which gave whisky to the world seems queerly attached. Along the last few miles to Balloch there is a definite feel of a city in the air, and, soon after, a tram-line, a policeman, and a chimney.

CHAPTER ELEVEN

I sail up the Clyde into Glasgow, enter the City of Reality, learn how to make Scotch broth, and attend the birth of a ship

I

A WISE old Glasgow man, whose ripe memory goes back over half a century said to me:

'Go to the Firth of Clyde and sail right up to the Broomielaw. We have an old saying: "The Clyde made Glasgow and Glasgow made the Clyde"; and it's true! If you havna seen the Clyde you havna seen Glasgow. . . .'

I thanked him and went off to hire a motorboat for a day. . . .

Now, early in the morning I embarked thirty miles down the Clyde in a windy place of hills and headlands. It was cold and misty. The motorboat was rising and falling on a pretty swell. A man with a red face, whose name was quite inevitably Jock, was sitting in the stern smoking a pipe, with a yachting cap at a Beatty angle cocked over his left eye.

'Guid day tae ye!' said Jock, spitting neatly into the Firth of Clyde. 'It's to Glesca yer're gaun?'

'I am that,' I replied.

He said something which sounded like:

'Ay-he!'

He gave the reluctant engine a turn or two and we went chugg-chugging over the Firth, nose in air like a swimming rat.

The fog lay low over the water. Ahead of us came a wild and melancholy sound like some giant cow calling to its calf.

'That's the Cloch Lighthouse!' explained Jock.

The awful moo became louder as we went on, until suddenly the mist parted and we saw the lighthouse, tall and white, above us. We tied up to a little jetty and listened. Sailors all over the world know the Cloch as well as you

285

know the lamp that stands in front of your garden gate. It is
the last milestone to Glasgow on the road from anywhere.
Lights from Ayr to Bute beckon the ships on up the Firth,
handing them on to the Cloch, whose great sword of light
sweeps the water, pinning ships, great and small, ghostly
white as moths in the glare of a headlight, for one second in
its circular beam. And when the fog lies over the sea the
Cloch bellows like a bereaved cow; but to sailors this sounds
like:

'Come along, my children, come home to ole man river!
But keep your eyes skinned past Dumbarton, for – the
Clyde's not grown any wider since you went to Singapore!'

And the man who works the light, and also the moo, is a
Highlander from Skye. We talked to him, we argued with
him, we pleaded with him, we asked him to remember his
dear old mother away back in Dunvegan, and for her sake
to let us over the Cloch. But he stood there like a bit of his
native Coolins and said:

'No, no; it iss against regulations when the horn is
blowing. I cannot do it!'

I have learnt enough about Scotland to know that it is
useless to argue with a determined Highlander. If the King
arrived wearing the State Crown, and holding the Sceptre
and the Orb, he would be turned away by the Highlander
when the 'horn is blowing'. So:

'Push off, Jock!' I said. 'We could only get in there with a
brigade of artillery!'

We slipped away, and the Cloch returned to its mists.

Now, as we chugged along I was to learn more about
Glasgow in four hours than I would have learnt in a library
in four days.

Ships passed us: little pert steamers stacked with herring
boxes off to get 'Glasgow magistrates' for breakfast; stately
miniature liners on tour round the rugged coastline; great,
humping cargo boats slouching off to the end of the world
via Belfast; and those cunning little tugs who fuss and hoot

round the big C.P.R.s as they nurse them home to berths in the shadow of the Broomielaw.

But the strangest thing I saw upon the Clyde was 'Hopper No. 20'. She was not a beauty, but she looked well-meaning. Her funnel was right aft, and she seemed to have swallowed a gigantic iron wheel, whose rim stuck up over the bulwarks amidships. Her complexion was rust red. (I was to meet the other nineteen 'hoppers' during my voyage up the Clyde!) Jock explained to me that these craft take the Clyde mud from the dredgers and dump it out to sea:

'Why are they called "hoppers"?'

'Because they're always hoppin' aboot,' said Jock; but I think he was guessing!

And this is the first lesson the Clyde taught me. Ole man Clyde is not a river: he is an excavation! Those of you who think that the Clyde was placed by Nature next to Glasgow for the building of ships are sadly wrong. Nature never meant the Clyde to be more than a shallow salmon stream! Here enters the character of Glasgow. When Glasgow decided to build ships she had first to make the Clyde in which to launch them! She had to deepen it. She had to keep it deepened. For over a century she has dredged the channel. Probably on no other river in the world have men exercised such grim and relentless determination.

The second lesson of the Clyde is that it can keep no secret. Unlike the actor, it can never pretend to be 'resting' when idle. Its shipyards, which begin at Greenock, are open to the sky. There is either a ship on the stocks or there is not; there is either a devilish clamour of hammers or there is silence – a silence in which men draw the dole and talk politics at street corners.

I looked at Greenock. It was not too good. Port Glasgow, higher up, was a wee bit better; but even here many a forest of gaunt poles and many a company of tall cranes stood above an emptiness which in good times holds the skeleton of a ship. . . .

So we went along, dipping and bowing in the wash of

'hoppers', past the romantic Rock of Dumbarton until the river at Old Kilpatrick seems suddenly to end and to run on to Glasgow between made banks like a little Suez Canal. And now on either side, right into Glasgow, run shipyards, the greatest and the most experienced in the world. The sky is fenced with the ragged outline of their davits, their vast poles, and their iron-grey electric cranes, which pick up a few tons of boiler in a claw and carry them in a wide arc as gently as a girl takes home a new pair of non-stop silk stockings in tissue paper.

There is smoke. I can feel the nearness of Glasgow. The stream is now so narrow that I can hear men shouting on the banks. It is not beautiful, but it is inspiring, like all the troubles and difficulties of Man.

In a few miles I see twenty, perhaps thirty, ships in their cradles, some just keels, like the skeleton of a whale in a museum; others gaunt hulls, rusty red or smeared with vermilion paint; a few almost ready for a bottle of champagne, and one – the *Duchess of York* – terribly young and inexperienced, lying in dock with years of the Atlantic Ocean ahead of her.

And the sound of the Clyde is that of a thousand hammers echoing in the empty belly of a hull; the fiendish chatter of electric riveters and a sudden squeal of metal tortured in the service of the seas. When I look up I see tiny men in flying cradles pressed against a mountain of steel-plate, hitting a white-hot rivet with a hammer, and at each stroke a million gold sparks fly hissing earthward to die of cold as they fall.

'This is wonderful,' I tell Jock. 'I thought the Clyde was idle!'

'It isna wonderful,' says Jock. 'It isna as guid as it looks!'

He explains to me that many a ship in these days is built at cost price just to keep the yards open. He tells me that the Clyde could turn out a hundred times the present volume of work; and then, becoming political, he curses the Treaty of Versailles, and I lose track of his argument.

'A Glasgow bookseller once told me, Jock, that when a big ship is laid down he sells more books!'

'Aye; and a cakeshop wull tell ye that they sell mair scones.'

'Then a new keel is like a large glass of whisky on a cold day: it warms the very core of Glasgow's heart. She even feels it in her fingertips!'

Jock licked his lips and looked intelligent.

'Aye, that's a verra guid compairison,' he said gravely; 'but whusky's no' what it was in the auld days!'

What an incredible river! Who would have believed that this canal could give birth to navies? All the young ships lie at an angle. If they were launched straight ahead they would hit the opposite bank!

What a romantic river! I saw a flat-bottomed boat on the stocks, which looked as though it will someday slide round the bend of the Nile to Luxor under a full moon with a fringe of American college girls on deck saying: 'Gee, I feel I could kinda pick that moon outer the sky and eat it like a peach!' In the next yard was a big ship which will someday bring majors and their livers home on leave from India; and side by side was the cargo boat which someday will glide into white towns among palm-trees, leave them petrol, and take away sugar, slipping off, always slipping off, to the horizon and leaving no address.

And all the time, as the hammers beat above ships that are not yet born, the Clyde-built argosies come creeping gingerly to Glasgow from the seaways of the world. There is salt caked on their smoke-stacks and experience bitten into them from the keel up.

They pass the very yards in which they once lay helpless and unengined, and as they berth in narrow waters the ring of hammers comes to them and a fire of sparks; for, in spite of all the woe and hardship of winning a great war, old Father Clyde is still sending his children out over the oceans of the world. . . .

I saw a city through a haze, heard the sound of traffic, slipped in under a bridge, and climbed an iron ladder to the Broomielaw. I was in Glasgow.

Jock's head appeared over the edge of the jetty.

'A'm thinkin',' he said reflectively, 'that was a graund simile o' yours.'

'What?'

'Aboot the whusky!' said Jock.

2

Glasgow on a November evening. . . .

The fog which has tickled the throat all day relents a little and hangs thinly over the city, so that each lamp casts an inverted V of light downward on the pavement. The streets are full of light and life. Pavements are packed to the edge with men and women released from a day's work, anxious to squeeze a little laughter from the dark as they move against a hazy blur of lit windows in which lie cakes, watches, rings, motor-cars, silk gowns, and everything that is supposed to be worth buying.

The sound of Glasgow is a human chatter punctuated by tramcars – coloured in broad bands like Neapolitan ices – grating round a bend to Renfield Street. There is a sharp clamour of bells, the asthmatic cough of an express engine clearing its throat on the road to London, and most characteristic of all, the sudden yelp of a tug in a Clyde fog – the yelp of a terrier whose tail has been stepped on – as she noses her way down the narrow stream.

And the Glasgow crowds in perpetual and puzzling flux go, some home to flats in Pollokshaws and – wonderful name! – Crossmyloof, where the Queen of Scots once sat a palfrey; some to take the astonishing meal of high tea which Glasgow's cafés and restaurants have elevated to the apex of the world's pyramid of indigestibility (for I still cannot believe that tea agrees with fillet steak); some to dance for 3s. in surroundings for which we pay 30s. in London; some to the theatre; but most to drift up and down the golden avenues until the last Neapolitan ice takes them home to Camlachie or Maryhill.

I go on through the crowds. George Square – Glasgow's Trafalgar Square – which looks like the centre of the city but is not, lies in graduated greyness, rather empty, a little removed from the main surge of life, the splendid Municipal Buildings wrapped in that same aloofness from the trivialities of a night which comes upon Westminster when Piccadilly is gay.

This and Trafalgar Square in London are the two most impressive and well-balanced squares in Great Britain. Walter Scott is its Nelson skied on a great pillar with his plaid over the wrong shoulder and a lightning conductor sticking like a dart from the back of his neck. Here, among stone horsemen, are some of Glasgow's few trees.

I am amazed by the apparent size of Glasgow. Her million and a quarter people are squeezed into a lesser space than that occupied by several other great cities, and this compression gives a feeling of immensity. You do not suddenly leave the main streets to plunge into dark and trackless valleys of the dead as you do in Birmingham, Manchester, and Liverpool. Here are miles of main streets, all wide, all marked by a certain grim and solid quality – shops as fine as any in Bond Street; clubs as reserved and Georgian as any in Pall Mall – and in a few yards you leave a street in which you could spend £1,000 on something for a woman's throat, to enter a street, equally broad and almost as well lit, in which perhaps the most expensive thing is a cut from the sheep whose corpse hangs head down, its horns in blood and sawdust. . . .

This meeting of extremes is characteristic of Glasgow. The splendour of riches and the abjectness of poverty, seen so close together, appear sharper than in most great cities. East and west ends run into one another in the most grotesque way. In London, for instance, crowds are local. You know exactly the kind of people you will see in

Piccadilly or Oxford Street. You know that the Aldgate Pump to Strand crowd at night will never go the extra yard to Cockspur Street; just as the Piccadilly-Leicester Square crowd will never cross the invisible frontier of Charing Cross. In Glasgow there are no frontiers.

This gives a rich and exciting variety to the crowds. My eyes are held by the passing faces. Sooner or later in the Bond Streets of this city, with their business heads under the biggest assembly of bowler hats in Great Britain and their crowds of perfectly lovely, fresh young girls, I shall see the stooped shoulders of some ancient wreck, the insolent swing of a youth with a cap over his eyes, the slow walk of a hatless woman from a neighbouring tenement bearing, much as the kangaroo bears its young, a tiny face in the fold of a thick tartan shawl.

This close-togetherness of Glasgow is one of its most important features. It means that a million and a quarter people live nearer the heart of their city than in any other social phenomenon of this size. This, I believe, explains Glasgow's clean-cut individuality. There is nothing half-hearted about Glasgow. It could not be any other city. And it is not a suburban city like London.

One of the charms of London is that there are no Londoners. Millions belong to the twenty-eight metropolitan boroughs who know as little about London as they do of Atlantis – perhaps not so much in these days of cheap encyclopædias! London, to the average Londoner, is a place to dash to and dash from, with infrequent, and often puzzling expeditions at night in search of gaiety. It is easier to go from Liverpool to New York than from Hampstead to Penge! So it happens that millions of Londoners could not pass a simple topographical examination on their own city!

But Glasgow is – Glasgow. She is self-centred. She is the greatest, closely-knit community in Great Britain. She is the least suburban of all great cities. She has become the most populous city outside London without dissipating her individuality in distant suburbs; and in no other city of this magnitude do more people know each other, at least by sight. To know a man by sight in Glasgow is to ask him to have a coffee at eleven a.m. If the Clyde ever runs dry, sufficient coffee is consumed in Glasgow every morning to float the biggest Cunarder yet built.

There is a Transatlantic alertness about Glasgow which no city in England possesses. Glasgow can be almost oppressively friendly. In one thing is she supreme among the cities in Great Britain – accessibility. Her civic leaders and her businessmen are always ready to welcome the stranger. The important doors of Glasgow fly open to him. (I suppose if he is wasting time he flies out as swiftly as he entered!) I have found more senseless ritual, more pompous obstructionists in livery barring the way to some negligible grocer with a chain round his neck in a tin-pot English town than I have found in those marble halls where the Lord Provost of Glasgow directs the destinies of the 'second city'.

Glasgow plays the part of Chicago to Edinburgh's Boston. Glasgow is a city of the glad hand and the smack on the back; Edinburgh is a city of silence until birth or brains open the social circle. In Glasgow a man is innocent until he is found guilty; in Edinburgh a man is guilty until he is found innocent. Glasgow is willing to believe the best of an unknown quantity; Edinburgh, like all aristocrats, the worst!

But the great difference between Scotland's two great cities is not a cultural versus a financial tradition. It is something deeper. Both these are poses. Edinburgh pretends to be more precious than she is; Glasgow pretends to be more material than she is. Hence the slight self-consciousness of the one and the slight roughness of the other. The real difference between these two cities is that Edinburgh is Scottish and Glasgow is cosmopolitan. That is why they will always secretly admire each other; also why Edinburgh is definitely the capital.

Glasgow is a mighty and an inspiring human story. She is Scotland's anchor to reality. Lacking her, Scotland would be a backward country lost in poetic memories and at enmity with an age in which she was playing no part. Glasgow, facing west to the new trade-ways of the world, rose after the Union, calling to Highlands and Lowlands to forget old scores and to take a hand in the building of that new world which was to begin on a Sabbath afternoon in the spring of 1765 when James Watt walked over Glasgow Green occupied with sinful week-day thoughts. The new age began sinfully on that Sabbath, for James Watt had solved the problem of the separate condenser; and as he walked over Glasgow Green a changed world lay pregnant in his brain: a world of steel and iron, tall chimneys and speed.

All over the world the last candles of the eighteenth century guttered and died. Glasgow rose: a Liverpool and a Manchester in one; a monument to the genius and the vigour of the Scot.

3

Let us now turn to food.

The fearful standardization of this age is making one place so like another that there will be no point soon in leaving home. Architecture, dress, and food as prepared by the gigantic hotel combines in their exactly similar restaurants and grill rooms, are becoming the same the world over. I write like a fat man or an epicure: I am, thank heaven, neither: I care very little for food, but I care enormously for individuality.

In the hotel which is said to be the best in Glasgow, which means that it is the most expensive, I asked the foreign waiter one day to bring me a haggis. Had I asked him to bring down Sir Walter Scott from the top of his pillar he could not have appeared more obviously sorry for my state of mind. He bent towards me a gaze in which obsequiousness was queerly mixed with pity.

'An 'aggis, m'sieu?' He smiled and shrugged his shoulders

exactly as he would have done had a cannibal asked for his favourite joint. He was insulted and surprised when I got up and went to a restaurant.

Here I met once again that divine brew – Scotch broth, of which I have not written enough. I have learnt how to make this heavenly soup in order that I may eat it at frequent intervals all my life. I intend to give the secret as a wedding present to all brides of my acquaintance who deserve happiness; for the ability to make Scotch broth must enormously increase the chance of domestic bliss. No unintelligent woman could make this soup. Its appearance is itself a guarantee of a wife's taste and skill: it is a perpetual compliment to her judgement. I have learnt to make this soup not from cookery books, which are the least comprehensible branch of literature, not excepting works on metallurgy, physics and mathematics, but I have gone down into a kitchen, rolled up my sleeves, put on an apron and made this soup with my own brain and my own hands. And this is how it is done.

The night before take a quarter of a pound of Scotch barley and allow it to soak until the morning. Scotch barley is not the inadequate, microscopic pearl barley common in England but fat generous grain almost as large, when softened, as a pea. At the same time take a quarter of a pound of dried peas and soak them in a similar way. If you like peas, throw in an extra handful. Now the cookery books, which as an earnest student of Scotch broth I have, of course, read, tell you to use fresh peas when they are obtainable. Do not be misled by such nonsense: dry peas are infinitely better, and, as I like them slightly hard, I decline to soak them overnight. When you have made this soup once or twice you will be in a position to decide for yourself whether my taste is yours. I think that the slightly hard peas give to the soup a richer accent!

The important day dawns. You are about to make divine soup. You find in the kitchen the barley and the peas soaked and ready. Now take half a pound of mutton, and if anyone says that any other meat will do give them a crack over the head with the nearest frying pan! This is rank heresy. The mutton to use is called in Scotland 'flank' and, I believe, in England 'the best end of neck'. Place this half pound of mutton in a fairly roomy saucepan and cover it with cold water. Throw in a tablespoonful of salt and bring to the boil. Then let it simmer at the boil for one hour.

During this hour take two, or even three, leeks, two carrots, one fine turnip and a good-looking young spring cabbage. Chop the carrots and the turnip into small squares, chop the leeks and the spring cabbage and mix them all up together in a basin. You now have a beautiful raw, red, white and green salad.

When the mutton has been at the boil for an hour take the barley and the peas, which, you remember, are already soaked, and empty them into the pot; then add the pile of chopped leeks, carrots, turnip and cabbage. Give them a stir with a wooden spoon. You are now well on the way.

The soup must now boil for another hour. Soon it will begin to smell like Scotch broth and you will become ravenously hungry. The great temptation at this stage is to dip into the brew with a spoon and start reducing the number of peas; but resist the temptation because you may upset the balance of power. Instead, during this second hour and in intervals of watching the soup, take a small handful of parsley, chop it finely and keep it ready on a plate. Take also a carrot and crush it over a grater into a pink mush. Keep this ready on another plate.

At the end of the hour which elapsed since the introduction of the vegetables add the chopped parsley and the grated carrot (this carrot merely gives the soup a delicate pink flush) and stir gently. In fifteen minutes the soup will be ready. The cookery books tell you to skim off the film of fat. Nonsense!

Scotch broth when properly made should be firm, yet not

too thick to stir with ease. When you dip down into it and take out a spoonful you should find a representative selection of all its ingredients in the spoon: there should be barley, peas, cubes of carrot, turnip, pieces of leek and cabbage and a hint of parsley. If not, the soup has been unfairly mixed and you must try again until the symphony is perfect.

It was this soup which Dr Johnson loved when he was in Scotland. 'At dinner,' wrote Boswell, 'Dr Johnson ate several plate-fulls of Scotch broth, with barley and peas in it, and seemed very fond of the dish. I said, "You never ate it before?" Johnson, "No, sir; and I don't care how soon I eat it again." '

This, I regard, as one of his greatest pronouncements.

Now the haggis.

Englishmen claim to see something funny in the haggis. I do not know why. It is a joke, perhaps, assisted and kept alive by the Scotsman's trick of laughing at himself. Every time the haggis is piped in on Burns Night in the Savoy Hotel the innumerable Scotsmen in Fleet Street slip into the newspapers the same weary old jokes about it.

Many Englishmen, confusing the haggis, no doubt, with the musical honours which accompany it, believe this dish to be some kind of musical instrument. The haggis, of course, is one of those puddings made of offal and grain – like the 'black-pudding' of Lancashire – invented by poor and frugal nations. Its fame is due to Burns who immortalized it in one of his poems as 'great chieftain o' the puddin' race'. Many Scotsmen, strange to say, have never tasted haggis, but it is made in Glasgow and sold in hermetically sealed tins to be exported to soothe the pangs of exile.

The best thing written about the haggis is to be found in a cookery book – a perfect cookery book which is absolved from all the sins of its kind: *The Scots Kitchen*, by F. Marian McNeill.

'The name haggis,' says the writer, who gives three

recipes for this dish, 'is commonly thought to be derived from the French *hachis*, which is the form used by King Jamie's Scottish cook in *The Fortunes of Nigel*. Jamieson, however, derives the word from *hag* (S.) to chop (E. hack), and it is very possible that the name was converted into French in the same way that Ayrshire embroidery became *broderie anglaise*. The theory that the haggis is one of the nobler legacies of France may in any case be dismissed. The composition of the dish alone disproves the assumption, and the French themselves allude to the haggis, which appears to have been commonly sent to Scots in exile as long ago as the days of the Auld Alliance, as "le pain benit d'Ecosse".

'The choice of the haggis as the supreme national dish of Scotland is very fitting. It is a testimony to the national gift of making the most of small means; for in the haggis we have concocted from humble, even despised ingredients, a veritable *plat de gourmets*. It contains a proportion of oatmeal, for centuries the national staple, whilst the savoury and wholesome blending of the cereal with onion and suet (met with in its simplicity in such dishes as Mealie Puddings, the Fitless Cock, and Skirl-in-the-Pan) is typically Scottish. Further, it is a thoroughly democratic dish, equally available and equally honoured in castle, farm and croft. Finally, the use of the paunch of the animal as the receptacle of the ingredients gives that touch of romantic barbarism so dear to the Scottish heart.'

Most Glasgow restaurants serve haggis, which arrives escorted by mashed potatoes, and looking remarkably like a piece of boiled grey granite. When I have time I must discover how and when the haggis became comic. I have never seen any food which looks less humorous.

You either like haggis or you give it up and try to hide it under the potatoes. It is no good persevering. I happen to like it, but in small quantities. It is, like porridge and Scotch broth, a sturdy, reliable food designed to sustain men; never, I think, to play the modest part of entrée to a meal.

4

Glasgow Cathedral, marooned by time away from the heart of the modern city, holds in its magnificent crypt the bones of St Mungo, patron saint and founder of Glasgow. I think Edinburgh people, who jibe at the newness of Glasgow, forget that St Mungo died in sanctity in 603 A.D. before their lordly crag had struggled out of the historic mists. His bones are surely the only Catholic relics preserved in any Scottish cathedral.

When I went to a service I was charmed by the best choir I have heard outside Westminster, or so it seemed to me. It is perfect. There are women's voices which give to it a richness and a beauty more appealing to me than the cold sexlessness of English Church singing.

At the back of Glasgow Cathedral is the surprising Necropolis. The Scottish habit of erecting heavy monuments over the departed is there seen in perfection.

This great city of the dead is to me one of the most remarkable sights in Glasgow. When you see it at first in a poor light, lifting its obelisks, towers, memorials, and minarets against the sky it appears to be a fantastic city: a thing like a mirage, utterly foreign to all around it, something that might vanish in a puff of wind.

But it must be the most solid cemetery on earth. You walk its sloping paths surrounded by surely the most ambitious symbols of grief erected since the Pyramids. John Knox, who is buried under a public highway in Edinburgh, stands guard above the Necropolis wearing his Geneva cap and gown; but the only sentimental moment for me was the discovery of the grave of William Millar, who wrote rhymes for children and the lovely 'Wee Willie Winkie' which I have known all my life.

The subject of graves reminds me that there is a grave in a Glasgow street over which thousands of people walk every day. I wonder how many have noticed it. It forms part of the pavement opposite St David's (Ramshorn) Paris Church. There is a cross and the letters R.F. A.F.

If you have never seen the launching of a ship there is still a thrill in life for you. . . .

You go through the shipyard gates. Everyone is smiling. They will not admit that they are excited. They will, in fact, tell you that it is all in the day's work, that they are so used to it that it is just a matter of routine, but – don't believe them! No man with a heart in his body could be unmoved by the birth of a ship; and when you have been hammering at her for eight months; when you have been sitting up in a bos'n's cradle playing hell with a pneumatic riveter; when you have been standing in the remote intellect of an electric crane swinging the proud body, plate by plate, into position – not excited? I refuse to believe it.

She lies, marvellously, naked, high and dry on the slipway. She has no funnels, no masts, and no engines. Her bridge is there, unpainted and innocent of glass. High on her decks men run, shouting and peering over the edge of the steel cliff to the distant shipyard. Everything is ready, waiting for the Clyde.

Her stern, with its innocent propellers, is lifted high as a house above the water; five minutes' walk back along her hull, in the shadow of her forecastle head, is a little railed-in platform covered in scarlet cloth.

It is charming to see men who have riveted her flanks performing a last service by delicately knocking tacks into half a yard of red bunting!

The tide oozes on. Men look at their watches. Pretty girls arrive in motor-cars and stand in the shadow of workshops, gazing up at the ship, reading her name – *Empress of the East*, shall we say? – printed in big bronze letters high on the sharp prow. Groups of men in dungarees, who for eight months have worked on the ship, gather and gaze up too, laugh and joke and smoke cigarettes and admire the beauty chorus.

In the shadow of the hull men, creeping about in the mud like rats, loosen great blocks of timber until at the moment when the tide is high a few swift hammer blows along the length of her keel will send her downward to the water.

Every minute is now important. There is a laugh from the workmen as a fellow, high on the forecastle head, flings down a rope which dangles above the scarlet platform. But it ceases to be a common rope as it nears the platform: its last few yards are coloured red, white, and blue. An official of the shipyard, very important, mounts the steps of the platform bearing a bottle of champagne disguised in a tight overcoat of red, white, and blue ribbons. This he attaches to the hanging rope, and he stands there steadying the dangling bottle.

The time has come! The guests move out from the work-sheds and mount the scarlet platform. The woman who is to launch the ship stands nervously fingering the hanging bottle.

'What do I do?' she whispers to the helpful official.

'Well, ye see, tak' the bottle like this and fling it har-r-rd as if ye'd break the ship and – try and hit this bolt-head!'

He walks forward and puts his finger on the steel plates. The Clyde is high. . . .

A woman's hand in a brown suéde glove, trembling a little, holds the champagne bottle. The shipyard becomes silent! Work stops! Cranes become still! You can hear the hammering of other yards across the Clyde. The tug that is waiting out on the flood tide for the new ship sounds her siren three times in salute: 'Come along, come along, come along!' A piercing whistle rings out from somewhere, there is a great shout, the sound of hammers on wood beneath the ship, a tremendous air of frantic but invisible effort, and the vast monster seems suddenly to fill with life! She does not move; but you know that in one second she *will* move! In the tremendous suspension of that second the brown suéde glove tightens on the champagne bottle and a woman's voice says:

'Good luck to the *Empress of the East*!'

Crash! The champagne bottle hits the steel plates fair and

square with a smothered tinkle of splintered glass, and great bursts of white foam fly left and right to fall like snow and to fizz a second and vanish on the scarlet platform; and now – off she goes! She moves! Hurrah! Good luck to her!

We see a wonderful thing! We see the great ship sliding backwards to the water! She makes no noise. The enormous thing just fades smoothly Clydewards, leaving behind her two broad wooden tracks of yellow grease. Silent as a phantom she is! Her stern takes the water, dips, dips, deep down. (Will she ever rise?) You watch her breathless as she dives into the Clyde to the distant sound of spray: and then her movement slows up as she meets the resistance of the water. She is almost afloat! She lies almost at the end of the two parallel grease tracks. She floats! She bounces gracefully and goes on bouncing, very high and light in the water, bouncing her great steel body as if enjoying the first taste of her buoyancy.

'Hurrah! Good luck to the *Empress of the East*!'

We lift our hats. Among a group of workmen an old man lifts his cap for a second as his eyes follow her out to the Clyde – lifts his greasy cap to eight months' wages:

'Goodbye and – good luck!'

But it is not yet over. As she floats we hear for the first time an unforgettable sound: it is the crack and creak of breaking wood, the falling asunder of the great timbers beneath her as she crushes them and drags them with her until the river all round her is alive with heavy spars, which leap up in the water beneath her hull.

Then suddenly gigantic iron chains, whose links are the thickness of a man's arm, begin to move. Until now they lay on either side of the slipway in twelve-foot heaps. They move slowly at first, but gather amazing speed. The mighty things roll over and over in clouds of dust and rust, and go bounding down to the riverside as if to pull the ship back to her birthplace, thundering after her, leaping through the mud until they take the strain, tighten out and hold her steady in the narrow stream. . . .

I stand there with the feeling that I have seen the coming to life of a giant, the breaking-away of all the shackles that held it from its element, and the glad acceptance of its fate.

I look down through the stark skeleton of poles which cradled her from the beginning, and I see her framed in the vista, still bouncing a little as if amused by the water – the symbol of Glasgow and the Clyde!

She will go to many places in her busy life, carrying the name of Glasgow across the oceans of the world. Men may love her as men love ships. On her bridge, so bare and inexperienced now, men will stand guiding her through storms to various harbours. She will become wise with the experience of the seas.

But no shareholder will ever share her intimacy as we who saw her so marvellously naked and so young slip smoothly from the hands that made her into the dark welcome of the Clyde.

CHAPTER TWELVE

In which I encounter men who melt steel. I visit the saddest house in Scotland. I go to the Land of Burns, stand in his cottage, and join a sing-song in the Globe Inn at Dumfries. Then – Goodbye to Scotland

I

IN the town of Motherwell, adjoining Glasgow, is a famous steelworks. The first person you meet there is a commissionaire who marched with Roberts to Kandahar.

He keeps a picture of Lord Roberts hanging on the wall of his little office. If, as it has been said, the pillar-box is the last temple of romance, surely a commissionaire posting letters must be the most romantic sight on earth! These old men with their medals – we meet them everywhere and take them for granted – are to industry as ships are to a city: they bring into normal life a flavour of great adventures and a spice of history.

I went into an enormous city of steel. They told me how many miles of railway track it contained, but I have forgotten. They told me how many acres it covered, but I have forgotten.

I could see only the drama of Man, with his soft little body and his puny white arms, torturing this terrible metal into life, heating it until it screamed, letting it out in livid rivers that spat at the cold air with a cascade of sparks, training the fearful stuff into required shapes, standing, blue-spectacled, in the entrails of great machines and pressing a button that shoots ingots, fiercely hot as the very core of the earth, over rollers, back and forward, giving them a meaning and a shape, making them ready to bear locomotives in West Africa, to bridge a river in South America, or to form the skeleton of a battleship or a liner.

Men stood at the mouth of furnaces with long rakes, like devils at the mouth of hell. They gave me blue glasses, and I went as near as the heat would allow. Sixty tons of steel were seething like boiling porridge. Big white eyes would open and shut, slowly, lazily, all over the moving pool, and the very bricks of the furnaces glowed pink with the heat that melts iron and makes steel.

Steelworkers at home are probably kind to their children and to their wives. They probably love dogs and grow vegetables. There is nothing human about them at work! They are merely the fingers of uncanny machinery. They come rumbling down the length of a shed, driving an electric battering ram which shoots a hand into a furnace with a ton of metal in it; they go creeping up to furnace doors with iron bars; they stand in the steam of cooling steel, bringing down levers which shoot incandescent rails from one end of a shed to the other. On their faces is the sweat of heat, and in their casual bearing the contempt of familiarity.

But now and again, when the furnace is gorged and the roar of the fires drops an octave, they roll a ball of paper and dribble it to one another and talk about the Rangers and the Celtic. It is very reassuring. It proves them to be human after all!

I went on through the city of steel, and they told me how many gigantic things have been born there out of the fire: the Tay Bridge, part of the Forth Bridge, the tragic *Lusitania*, the *Aquitania*, the *Olympic*, H.M.S. *Hood* – the greatest battleship in the world – countless locomotives, miles of steel railroads, girders, and boiler plates without number. . . .

When you visit a steelworks you are, to make an unpardonable pun, always on your mettle. You become aware of approaching heat. You look round. Nothing there! The heat increases. In pure instinctive self-protection you look upward, and there you see above your head, making a bee-line for you, a twenty-ton ingot of white-hot steel with minute salamanders sparkling and dying all over it, swinging past in an iron claw! You duck, and fifty yards away a blue-spectacled devil sitting in a travelling crane laughs over his levers at you as he brings the incandescent mountain to rest on its roller bed as softly as a maiden's sigh!

There is the innocent-looking ingot from which you recoil as if bitten. It looked tame and blue! You might have leant on it; but when a yard from it you felt the heat alive in it – a villainous heat that would have seared your flesh in an instant.

'Come along!' said my guide, looking at his watch; 'it's time they tapped a furnace!'

We went round to the casting side of the great melting shop to see the most impressive sight in the routine of a steelworks. Sixty tons of bubbling liquid steel were to be drawn from a furnace by way of an inclined channel into a ninety-ton ladle. Men worked at the tap-hole with iron bars, picking gingerly at the thin, heat-resisting film that stood between us and the inferno of blazing metal; then – a shower of sparks twenty feet high falling over a radius of thirty yards and a blinding flash of light as the steel came pouring out!

It was impossible to look at it with the naked eyes. Even through dark blue glasses the searing whiteness of the live metal was dazzling. It ran with a thick, oily motion down to the vast cauldron, where it oozed and settled and bubbled, winking volcanic eyes, gathering a white-hot skin on its surface. . . . Steel! But who could think of it as steel? Who could imagine it cooling into plates and ingots? Sixty tons of steel like a vast bath of white cream!

And I stood back under the shower of sparks and watched the men who make steel: Scotsmen with solemn, grimy faces, standing girt about with leather aprons, and leaning on iron bars; Scotsmen, peering through sparks from the glass windows of overhead cranes, waiting to pull the giant ladle with its amazing broth of steel out over the casting bay to the moulds. Every child should see this as part of its education, for a steelworks is the matrix of the modern world. The ladder of civilization is made of metal; from stone, man advanced to bronze, then iron, and now steel. It is with these metals that he has fought his way step by step from the swamp and the jungle. . . .

Outside in a yard I came on a great pyramid of old iron. There were iron gates separated from their parent stoves in some tremendous domestic convulsion; there were ancient iron pots and kettles, lengths of iron pipe, bits and scraps of iron which had played an incalculable part in life and had at last met some man shouting down a road with a barrow. My foot turned out of the pile a foot-high, iron effigy of Mr Micawber!

Yes; something was at last going to 'turn up' for him! He was going back with the shattered and tattered company into the purity of fire. All their worn-out shapes were to be obliterated in the furnaces, their identity was to be lost for ever in the bubbling cauldrons, substances were to be added to them, giving them the virtues of steel, and, resurrected but unrecognizable, they would pour out again into the world.

I wonder on what railway, in what boiler plate, in what locomotive, in what liner the humorous little thing that was once Mr Micawber would begin a new and anonymous existence!

In a laboratory chemists were testing steel, bending over thin glass tubes, peering through spectacles at changing colours, tabulating, weighing, estimating carbon, phosphorus, and sulphur.

And, last scene of all: three men in a room stand with books before a gigantic machine. A sample strip of steel is put into the machine and the metal is pulled with tremendous power until it snaps with the report of a pistol-shot:

'Forty-two!' says one of the men, writing in his book.

A new strip is clamped in the machine, another bang: 'Forty-two!'

So they go on measuring the tensile strength of the metal and putting on record, in terms that I cannot understand, something like this: 'Tensile strength 38/42 tons per square inch with a limit of Proportionality of not less than 16 tons per square inch'. (I believe Lloyds know what this means!)

In the office the men who direct the making of steel filled me full, and brimming over, with statistics; smiling at me with great kindness because they could see I did not understand one word of it.

All I know is that at Motherwell they seem to have a volcano under complete control.

2

A few miles from Glasgow are the chimneys of Hamilton and those pits through whose gloaming Sir Harry Lauder once roamed with a miner's lamp in his hand. Over the Clyde, winding here in almost a country mood, the sullen stacks of Motherwell's steel furnaces lift black fingers to the sky. In the middle of this is the saddest house in Scotland. It is the ancient home of her premier dukes, the ancestral seat of the princely family of Hamilton, Brandon, and Chatel- herault in France; but it belongs now to an Edinburgh contractor, who is pulling it stone from stone. I wonder what it feels like to pull up the roots of history. . . .

Hamilton Palace was perhaps the most regal home in Great Britain. They say that when King Edward, as Prince of Wales, stayed there in 1878 he said to his host: 'Ma mither has mony a fine hoose, but nane sae fine as yon!'

His Royal Highness may not have put it quite like that, but those are the words as repeated to me by one who lived through those times as a stable-boy; and who am I to polish a verbal tradition?

In its prime Hamilton Palace must have looked rather like the big brother of Buckingham Palace, standing there in its park, magnificently Georgian, with its gigantic portico upheld by Corinthian pillars, its long sweep of solemn windows, its gigantic stables, riding-school, and outbuild- ings.

A stairway of black Galway marble, as famous in its way and as rare as the crystal staircase of dead old Devonshire House, led up to the throne-room in which the dukes, who once stood next to the Crown, held their state, seated on the ambassadorial throne which the tenth of their line, Alexander, brought home from St Petersburg. And now the sky is its ceiling and the stars at night its candelabra. Bits of gilded cornice, damp with rain, fall through the skeleton floor, to split in the entrance-hall at the feet of two colossal bronze caryatides made by Soyer, the Frenchman.

I do not know a more dramatic conflict in Great Britain between the old world and the new. There are mine-shafts beneath the palace; and the smoke-stacks creep nearer year by year. Yet in the woods the pheasant still whirrs upward from the grass, and the rabbit flashes his scut within sight of the pit-head. If you look hard you will see, running for miles in the fields, a stretch of brighter grass, twice as wide as the Mall, going straight as a knife between two stiff ranks of trees: it is the ghost of that mighty entrance drive which once knew the creak of state harness and the jingle of many a brilliant cavalcade. . . .

I wandered through the dead Palace of the Hamiltons. There was no sound but the drip of the rain and the crash of falling stones. The tenth duke – Alexander – employed the people of Hamilton in the rebuilding of the old palace during the trade slump that followed the Napoleonic wars. It is recorded that 22,528 horses drew to it 28,056 tons of stone; 5,153 horses drew 7,976 tons of stone for the stables; 1,024 horses drew 1,361 tons of lime, sand, and slate.

The enormous Corinthian columns, twenty-five feet high and three feet three inches in diameter, each hewn out of a single block from the quarry at Dalserf, eight miles off, were drawn in an enormous wagon pulled by teams of thirty Clydesdales. How amazing are the events of a century! How little did Duke Alexander dream that this mighty effort was built on the quicksands of change!

The Egyptian Hall, in which he kept his coffin – a black

basalt sarcophagus of an Egyptian princess for which, bidding against the British Museum, he gave £10,000 – was dripping with the rain; and when I looked up at the cry: 'Mind yer heid!' I saw, striding the lath and plaster of the floor above, a man with a pick preparing to send down in dust a few hundredweights of the library.

But the full tragedy of Hamilton Palace is in the mausoleum, perhaps the most magnificent private tomb in Great Britain. Duke Alexander built it at a cost of £130,000 to hold his embalmed body and those of his family, as he thought, for ever. When the estate was sold the town of Hamilton, in a moment of sentiment, I think, bought the mausoleum for a mere song. It would make a war memorial which would be famous from one end of Scotland to the other.

This massive building stands quite near the palace looking like Hadrian's Mausoleum in Rome. The man who cares for it now, on behalf of the town, was for eighteen years in the service of the Hamilton family. His task was to polish the great coffins in the vaults where, until recently, eighteen dukes and their ladies slept in darkness. I think no one has felt the pathos of Hamilton Palace more keenly than this valet of dead dukes. Reverence for the old branch of the Hamiltons is so much a part of him that he, brought up from birth to regard the palace as the very centre of the solid earth, seems now among its ruins like someone who has survived Domesday. He took a key, and we went into the empty tomb.

It is an astonishing place, built like a fortress to defy time. Above the vaults is a circular chapel with a great dome. The floor is a mosaic of glass-smooth stone: jasper, white, and yellow marbles, and red and green porphyry divided by bands of black Galway marble. The echo in the chapel lasts for six seconds. The faintest whisper is carried up to fly round the whispering gallery of the dome. Opposite, as you enter, is the big block of black marble on which the body of the builder, Duke Alexander, used to lie in the £10,000 sarcophagus from ancient Egypt.

The man who had polished it for so many years described it minutely. It must have been one of the finest sarcophagi in the world. It belonged, he thinks, to a daughter of the Pharaoh Rameses I. It was of black basalt. Lid and coffin were chiselled to the shape of the princess. It was so perfect, he said, that her finger- and toe-nails were modelled in the granite-hard stone. From head to foot it was covered with Egyptian hieroglyphics.

'Where is it now?'

He told me how, after the sale in 1923, the bodies of the dukes were taken from their niches, piled in a cart, and buried in a field next to Hamilton cemetery! The bodies of the eleventh and twelfth dukes were, at the request of the Duchess of Montrose – daughter of the twelfth duke – taken to Arran and buried there. But sixteen Hamiltons were buried in the field, and among them the Duke Alexander in his now priceless basalt sarcophagus.

'Did you ever hear the like of it?' said the man.

I went to the cemetery. The field has now been included in the burial-ground. The big grave is headed by a joint memorial tablet to the sixteen Hamiltons. Among them is that Duke of Hamilton who was killed in a duel in Hyde Park with Lord Mohun in 1712; the sixth Duke, who married one of the beautiful Gunning sisters; and Alexander, tenth duke, the creator of the shortlived glory of Hamilton Palace, high steward at the Coronations of William IV and Victoria, the holder of two marquisates, three earldoms, and eight baronies, who married, at the age of forty-three, Susan Euphemia, the youngest daughter of William Beckford, author of *Vathek*. He lies in the common grave in a coffin which is worth probably £50,000 today. A few yards away, over the cemetery wall, is a smoking slag-heap and the great wheel at a pit-head. . . .

I shook myself clear from this lesson in the futility of human ambition and went to the neighbouring Cadzow

Park, in which the last herd of the wild, white cattle, which roamed Scotland in Roman times, is still to be seen. Cadzow Park is one of the most remarkable sights in Scotland. You leave the industrial world and plunge into a fearful solitude. It is the last vestige of the great Caledonian Forest which in old times stretched from the Clyde to the Border. The oak-trees are colossal. Half of them are mere shells. One, the 'Wallace Oak', contains a cavity in which eight persons can stand. They stretch their venerable, stricken arms against a rainy sky, and I thought, as I splashed on through the soggy grass, that here is the perfect 'blasted heath at Forres'.

I came to a gate with 'The Cattle are Dangerous' written on it. I climbed it and went on. The wild cattle were elusive. I must have walked at least three wet miles in search of them. I discovered them suddenly. They looked as dangerous as wild cattle can look! They are pure white, save for black ears, muzzles, and hoofs. They are more like buffalo than Highland cattle.

Their claim to be the last of their race is shared, I think, by a herd at Chillingham, Northumberland, but this herd is not as true to type as the Cadzow herd, because the distinctive black marks were eliminated years ago in favour of an accidental pink-eared strain. I am told that every calf in Cadzow Park which is not perfectly marked is killed.

3

Near the stately little town of Ayr, and not far from the Brig o' Doon, stands an old clay biggin' against the road. Here Burns was born in 1759.

This cottage, with its low, white walls and its close-cropped thatch, can be compared as a place of worship with the Birthplace, Stratford-on-Avon, but Burns means more to Scotland than Shakespeare means to England. Shakespeare is reverenced in England; in Scotland Burns is loved.

Shakespeare worship in England is cold and academic

when it is not downright lip-service – where is the
Shakespeare Theatre, by the way? – but Burns is in
Scotland today a warm, living force; he is part of daily life. I
think of him whenever I see a kettle steaming gently against
a Scottish fireside; he has sung his way into all the lovely
common things of life. Had Burns been a playright a chain
of Burns Theatres would link one end of Scotland with the
other because Burns is not a tradition: he is a living force.
Scotland spoke in every word he uttered.

It is an extraordinary experience for an Englishman to
encounter a real bard. We use the word a lot in England,
but we do not know what it means. We have many poets
but no bards. We have poets of the first class, finer, as poets,
than Burns. But not one of them has influenced our lives as
Burns has influenced the lives of Scotsmen. It is, of course,
impossible to compare Burns with Shakespeare: one was
universal, the other was parochial. You might possibly
compare Burns with Dante; the Italian was the poet of a
city; the Scotsman was the poet of a parish. Dante wrote in
the Tuscan; Burns in the Doric.

He interpreted Scotland to herself, whereas Scott interpreted Scotland to outsiders. Everyone in Scotland has
grown up with Burns; many quote him who have never
read a line of him, because his songs are in the air, his verses
are something heard round the fireside; and it is never
possible to tell when a man of humble birth and education
quotes the poet whether he is quoting from the printed page
or merely remembering something which he has known all
his life. There is no English poet whose songs have curled
up like an old dog on the hearthstone. As I say, England has
no bard.

Burns was the Pan of Scotland. (I believe Henley thought
of this before I was born!) He pricked his ears to every lusty
paganism. He was a natural reaction to Calvinism. I can
imagine with what unholy joy, had I been a sufferer from
the extreme holiness of the old-time Presbyterianism, I

would have read his ungodly praise of wine, women, and song.

Centuries of repression spoke in him; he was Scotland's only great expression of animal humanity since the Reformation. He snapped his pagan fingers at the gloomy kirk-made, ugly, vindictive, narrow-minded, key-hole gazing tradesman's god and opened his arms to the beauty of the earth. He was a faun born in an age of elastic-sided boots. He sinned and he sinned again, yet now and again there shot through him – for so strong is heredity – a twinge of respect for the ethics of gloom. More than once his wenching must have been interrupted by a faint prophetic smell of brimstone. Yet where on this earth is a Scotsman treading the 'primrose path to the everlasting bonfire' who does not at some moment pause in his journey and seem to hear the sound of the kirk bell? Burns was magnificently Scottish! It would have been better for him could he have concealed his little pantheisms and have walked solemnly to the kirk on the Sabbath; but he was not that common type. Only two men in Scottish history have committed adultery in a loud voice: Burns and Bothwell. Bothwell was careless of public opinion and Burns was careless of himself. There was no other resemblance; it is just an interesting coincidence.

Burns is the most attractive and in some ways the most pathetic figure in Scotland, fit to stand beside Mary, Queen of Scots, with whom, by the way, he would have agreed exceedingly well. He went through life in a kind of childish mental nudity. No one is competent to judge him until he has read his letters and his unexpurgated poems. Even when he is posing he is revealing himself in his pretences. He was a peasant who had to bear the pain of voicing the inarticulateness of centuries of peasants. In his voice, clear and unhesitant, one heard all the joys and sorrows which lay unspoken for generations in the heart of men who work with their hands. This great silence he broke magnificently. He sang in thirty-six years all the things that men like him in every other particular but that of expression had failed to sing for centuries. No wonder he died young. It was a great strain on the throat. Critics say that he was born out of his station, that had he been in Byron's position his life would have been happier. Surely Burns was first and last a peasant. Surely Byron's possibilities would have meant no greater happiness for him and as short a life.

Burns is humanly the most lovable son Scotland ever bore. Generations of black-tied tradesmen have striven desperately to bring him into line with the pulpit, but with only humorous results. It is impossible to make Burns respectable as the churchwardens understand respectability. The immoralities of Burns, the rape of Mary, Queen of Scots, and the drunkenness of Bonnie Prince Charlie's later life are three facts which a nation which prides itself on facing facts refuses to dwell upon. It is not done. The Catholic intolerance which transferred itself to the old-time Calvinism refuses to argue about them, unless a case can be made out for virtue, which in the instance of Burns at least is hopeless. One might argue that Prince Charlie had every provocation to beat his wife and get drunk, but there was no reason why Burns should have indulged in illegitimate children. The least he could have done was to pursue his passions without publicity, and make it easier for posterity to admit him into suburbia. Strangely enough, I cannot but believe that John Knox would have understood Burns much better than he would understand the average church elder of the old régime.

It is a curious commentary on the extremism of the Gael that this country of Scotland worships the God of Calvin and the pantheism of Robert Burns. Which is the real religion? It is impossible to reconcile them. An honest church elder should ban Burns from his house. What right has this loose-living, wine-bibbing seducer beside the godly hearth? Yet who will say that the General Assembly is an occasion more popular throughout Scotland than Burns's

Night? I must not write more in case I suggest that Pan and not Moses is the prophet of the north.

Burns, as an artist, is a puzzle to most Englishmen. His works are the only proof that the Scots are a foreign nation. The average Englishman cannot understand him, even with a glossary, and what the average Englishman cannot understand he distrusts.

Now that the wireless has been added to the list of modern tyrannies it seems clear that the British Isles will hear annually on the 25th of January a Burns Club dinner broadcast from Scotland. Listeners in England hearing, against a tinkling background of glasses, a flood of rolling eloquence rich in its r's will wonder if this is only the Scotsman's excuse for a drink or if they really mean all this. England gives itself over to after-dinner patriotism only on the anniversary of battles. It seems remarkable that Scotland – so hard-headed a country too – should make such a fuss of a poet! How impossible to imagine a number of English businessmen headed by the local baronets, the bigwigs of the Chamber of Commerce, and the clergy, rising to drink the health of Shakespeare, Milton, or even Shelley.

I must admit that to a stranger the Scotsman's habit of forming literary societies is, at first sight, puzzling. There are Burns Societies, Stevenson Societies, Scott Societies, and no doubt whenever a sufficiently great Scottish writer passes on a few admirers will meet in Edinburgh or Glasgow and decide to band themselves together under his name. Perhaps even Sir James Barrie is, although removed, not safe from his countrymen.

It appears to some Englishmen who, like many Englishmen, take their ideas of Scotsmen from jokes in *Punch*, as an uncanny perversion of tradition, that so practical a nation should worship its idealists. It would be understandable, for instance, if Scotsmen formed Macadam Societies or Mackintosh Societies in honour of the inventor of the waterproof, or, better still, and more in line with *Punch*, if they held a national Patterson Club Dinner to commemorate the founder of the Bank of England! But the organized admiration of literature, accompanied by a fanatical determination to whitewash the personal characters of the various gods, strikes a detached observer as a peculiar and an interesting aspect of social life in Scotland. No independent observer can probably estimate whether this semi-official admiration leads to a better understanding of a genius or whether the members of these admiration societies are too busy attending dinners in honour of their saint to read his works; but the fact remains that these societies flourish, and there must be an explanation.

I have already suggested that the Scots have a genius for national memorials. The mind of every Scotsman is a national memorial. Add to this the clan spirit and an intense local patriotism and you can conceive a man who is even unable to read becoming an ardent member of a Stevenson Society.

How pitiful are the humble birthplaces of genius. The little cottage which father Burns made with his own hands beside the road at Alloway stands now with an expression of mild surprise beside a modern building in which all manner of unconsidered trifles connected with the poet are piously preserved under glass.

I passed through a turnstile. An elderly man came with me and, removing the flannel coverings from show-cases, pointed down to autograph letters and manuscripts. He could quote Burns backwards, and never have I heard the poet quoted with such meaning and sympathy. He gave value to every word. Part of the original manuscript of 'Tam o' Shanter' is here preserved, so also is the family Bible, and the pages in brown ink whereon the poet described that Highland journey with its milestones of bright eyes.

Someone entered and called the man from the room. I was left alone with a typically odd jumble of things – old

books hallowed by the poet's hands, scraps of correspond-
ence, bits of glass on which he had written with a diamond
– all the odd trifles in whose association posterity strives
with a certain pathos to draw nearer to genius. What a
poem Burns could have written on the Burns Museum!

The man returned to conclude his recitation. I felt that he
had lost interest in me. Before he had been called from the
room he was determined to show me everything; but now
he had, I felt, changed his mind. I thought that he wanted to
get me out so that he could lock up the place. We came to a
relic, or was it the poem 'To Mary in Heaven'? He stopped
and began to recite it:

> *Thou ling'ring star with less'ning ray*
> *That lov'st to greet the early morn,*
> *Again thou usher'st in the day*
> *My Mary from my soul was torn.*
> *O Mary! dear departed shade!*
> *Where is thy place of blissful rest?*
> *See'st thou thy lover lowly laid?*
> *Hear'st thou the groans that rend his breast?*

I became impatient. I preferred to hear this man's fine voice
quoting the vernacular poems. I was prepared to cut him
short with a polite excuse when, looking up, I saw that tears
filled his eyes. He stood there with his hand in a patch of
late sunlight which slanted through the window and fell over
a glass-case; and he was shaken with a terrible emotion
before which I was startled and ashamed. He gripped
himself and went on to the second verse, the third, and then
the last; and I think no man has ever put more pathos into
this lament. His voice was raw with feeling, and I stood
there helpless in the spell of his grief, unhappy because I
knew that this was not his ordinary recitation, uneasy as a
man must always be in the presence of a stranger's heart.

> *Still o'er these scenes my mem'ry wakes*
> *And fondly broods with miser-care;*
> *Time but th' impression stronger makes*
> *As streams their channels deeper wear,*
> *My Mary! dear departed shade!*

Where is thy place of blissful rest?
See'st thou thy lover lowly laid?
Hear'st thou the groans that rend his breast?

The tears gathered in the corners of his eyes and fell.

'You must forgive me,' he said. 'I hae just had a message to say that my wife is dead. . . .'

I left him as quickly as I could. He told me that she had died under a surgeon's knife, and turning so that I was spared the sight of his eyes, he said:

'There is something in Burns for every moment of a man's life, good days and bad. I shall find his sympathy here. Burns would have known what I feel now. . . .'

And he looked round the museum, pulled a shade over a case of manuscripts, looked up at a picture of Highland Mary, and, as if shaking himself from a dream, pointed the way to the cottage.

'Ye'll not mind,' he said, 'going by yourself today.'

I went down the path only too glad to intrude no longer, thinking that in a moment of sorrow which comes but once in the lives of most men Robert Burns had received a tribute which passes the cold understanding of critics.

4

I have said that the birthplace of Burns stands beside the road with an air of surprise over it. The same resigned surprise can be detected on the face of the Birthplace, Stratford-on-Avon. Both of these humble-dwellings have been taken up out of a workaday world, for which they were so excellently designed, and dedicated to the piety of the ages.

They accept their sanctity uneasily. This white cottage with its poor flagstones once of no account and now so important to the world, with its chairs, its humble odds and ends, its alcove bed in which Burns was born, all expensively and religiously restored, has such a queer air of unreality about it. A great and historic mansion when empty is not so lonely as these obscure cottages which from the moment of their building have been dedicated to work. Idleness is natural to a mansion; to a cottage it is a kind of death. One can imagine if there are ghosts here that they would be puzzled, worried ghosts: Mrs Burns wondering – guid sakes – what had come over the old home that it should lie under so unnatural a spell. How laughable, too, to see men and women of the world touching tenderly the old armchair, the windows, and gazing with moist eyes into the gloom of the recessed bed opposite the fire! Suppose you could tell Mrs Burns, who slaved here, that the Burns Society bought the old clay biggin' for £4,000. Would she be more angry than amazed, or, like a good Scotswoman, would she call it a wicked, sinfu' waste?

And the family Bible fetched £1,700!

It was in this cottage that Keats wrote a bad sonnet and a letter which contains the most striking thing ever said about Burns.

'We went to the cottage,' wrote Keats, 'and took some whisky. I wrote a sonnet for the mere sake of writing some lines under the roof; they are so bad I cannot transcribe them. The man at the cottage was a great bore with his anecdotes. I hate the rascal. His life consists of fuzy, fuzzy, fuzziest. He drinks glasses five for the quarter, and twelve for the hour; he is a mahogany-faced old jackass who knew Burns: he ought to have been kicked for having spoken to him. He calls himself "a curious old bitch", but he is a flat old dog. I should like to employ Caliph Vathek to kick him. Oh, the flummery of a birthplace! Cant! cant! cant! It is enough to give a spirit the guts-ache. Many a true word, they say, is spoken in jest – this may be because his gab hindered my sublimity; the flat dog made me write a flat sonnet. My dear Reynolds, I cannot write about scenery and visitings. Fancy is indeed less than present palpable reality, but it is greater than remembrance. You would lift your eyes from Homer only to see close before you the real Isle of Tenedos. You would rather read Homer afterwards than remember yourself. One song of Burns is of more worth to you than all I could think for a whole year in my native country. His misery is a dead weight upon the nimbleness of one's quill; I tried to forget it – to drink toddy without any care – to write a merry sonnet – it won't do – he talked, he drank with blackguards; he was miserable. We can see horribly clear, in the works of such a man, his whole life, as if we were God's spies.'

Apart from the magnificent phrase 'God's spies', surely this sentence is the first and last thing to be said about Burns. What need is there to write his life? His personality is alluring, he positively invites biography; but why do what is done so superlatively well already: the verse of Burns is his autobiography. And we, reading it, are indeed 'God's spies'.

I left this little white cottage with the thought that if a poet could come to earth again to write one poem I would like to know what Burns would write could he sit for an hour in his little clay biggin against the road at Alloway.

5

The Burns enthusiast is happy among the world's literary pilgrims. If you go in search of Shakespeare you walk in a half light.

With Burns, however, you walk in no half light but in the full glare of topographical facts. Ayrshire and Dumfriesshire are studded with that which booksellers call by the dreadful name of 'Burnsiana'. When you tire of visiting buildings hallowed by contact with the bard, you can go round placing flowers on the tombs of his characters. Never has a poet left so many visiting places for posterity.

'Burnsiana' begins at Kilmarnock. Here his first volume of poems was issued by John Wilson in 1786. The Low Church in this town (rebuilt since the poet's day) was the church of the poem 'The Ordination', and the Angel Hotel in Kilmarnock is mentioned in that poem as 'Begbie's'. In the churchyard is an epitaph by Burns on 'Tam Samson'. In

Kay Park is a Burns Memorial and a museum in which they show you the poet's draught-board.

The next cluster is round Mauchline. Here are the 118 acres which Burns tilled with Gilbert, his brother. The very field which he ploughed is pointed out. Not far away is Ballochmyle House, mentioned in 'The Braes of Balloch-myle' and the 'Lass of Ballochmyle'. Hard by is Catrine House in which Burns dined on the eve of his famous social and literary triumph in Edinburgh.

A few miles farther on is Tarbolton, where Burns became a Freemason. Here also he founded the 'Bachelors' Club'. There is a mill just outside the village which they say is the mill mentioned in 'Death and Dr Hornbrook'. About half a mile from Tarbolton, on high ground, is the Castle o' Montgomery, where that mysterious person, Mary Camp-bell, Burns's 'Highland Mary', worked as a dairymaid. There is a monument near the junction of the Faile and the Ayr at a point which, so it is said, the poet parted from Mary. This is the scene met with in many a Highland cottage: Burns on one side of the stream and Mary on the other pledging their faith on an enlarged Bible.

Near Auchincruive is Leglen Wood. Wallace hid in this wood and Burn paid it a devout visit.

We come to Ayr. Here is the Tam o' Shanter Inn. There are the Auld Brig and the New Bridge. At Alloway is the birthplace and the museum and the Burns Monument, the beautiful curved Brig o' Doon, and the 'auld haunted kirk'. In the kirkyard of Kirkoswald are the graves of 'Tam o' Shanter' and 'Souter Johnnie'. The real name of the first was Douglas Graham and of the second John Davidson. They enjoy together the strangest of all immortality, rather like that of the fly in the amber: the fame of having blundered into the orbit of genius.

Ayr shares the glory of the poet's birth; Dumfries that of his unhappy death. Here is his house and his tomb. There are two taverns in which undoubtedly he drank: the 'Globe' and the 'Hole in the Wa''. A few miles from Dumfries is

Lincluden. Burns here saw his 'Vision of Libertie'. Here also is the farm, Ellisland, where the poet worked and wrote. He composed 'Mary in Heaven' here.

This is just a brief summary. I have no doubt that a zealous Burns pilgrim could wear his boots out in a conscientious endeavour to visit every bank, brae, burn, and 'howff' associated with the poet in the counties of Ayr and Dumfries. Compared with the topographical ubiquity of Burns, Wordsworth in Lakeland seems like a lodger. So thoroughly did Burns identify himself with this part of Scotland that he has driven from the memory of man all its previous inhabitants.

Thank goodness Walter Scott had the luck to live on Tweedside. Had he been added to Ayr and Dumfries the mind refuses to contemplate the kind of literary Hampton Court maze of association which would have complicated the map of Scotland!

6

It was dark when I went through the streets of Dumfries to look at the old bridge. I think this must be the oldest bridge in Scotland. It was built by the widowed Queen Devorguilla who established Balliol College, Oxford, as a students' hostel at some time in the thirteenth century. What queer links there are between towns in an ancient country!

The dark waters passed through the six arches, and a little way off, at a different angle, the new bridge crossed the Nith. It is curious that all three rivers associated with Burns – Ayr, Doon, and Nith – possess an old and a new bridge side by side.

I walked back through the cattle market to the High Street, and there I found the Globe Inn. They say – but I do not believe there is documentary evidence – that Burns after a carousal in the 'Globe' collapsed on a step in the snow and caught a chill which hastened his end.

The inn is a kind of temple to the conviviality of Burns.

Drinkers, like the vestal virgins, have kept alight an alcoholic enthusiasm in the bar for generations. After I had done my bit according to custom I was shown over the inn. This place is an extraordinary monument to the piety roused by Burns. It has been in the same family for generations, and so great is the reverence of the innkeeper that nothing has been altered. An enlargement of the bar would seem like an insult to the bard. This is a genuine and not a financial reverence; and it is so sincere that I felt much nearer to Burns in this public-house than ever I did in the swept solemnity of the old clay biggin' at Alloway. There was all the difference between the deserted temple and the living church.

I was shown the poet's chair, which is protected from the unworthy posteriors of this earth by a wooden bar. There is a punch-bowl, several other relics, which are brought out and handled gingerly, and there is also that reckless writing on a window-pane in praise of a woman.

'Some Americans are awfu' doubtful,' said the man who showed me round. 'I mind one aud dame who saw the writing on the glass and said, "But I thought Burns was too poor to have a diamond." Fancy that now. . . .'

'And what did you say?'

'Weel, I looked at her and I said: "Maybe he was like yersel', madam; if he hadna a diamond o' his ain perhaps he's a friend wi' one!" '

That, I felt, should have crushed the American dame.

As I came downstairs again and saw the light on wine-dark Spanish mahogany I had the feeling that this public-house should be an annexe to the Burns National Memorial. It has not changed by so much as the flicker of an eye since his day. If he came back in the cold and the wind with his excise books under his arm and his nag in a lather he would find this spot exactly as he left it in 1796. And, as if in answer to my fancy, there issued from the bar a sudden wild gust of laughter and the sound of money banged down on wood. I went in. The bar is very small. There is more room behind it where the bottles stand on shelves than there is on the side of custom. And the bar was full, that is to say, there were perhaps nine men present. They were with one exception in the thirties. Most of them wore caps. One, whom I shall call Jock, wore a black neckcloth round his red throat. He was, I learnt later, a road-worker. There was also a gentle fellow with a great sense of humour and the sad smile of the sightless; he had been blinded at, I think, Ypres. All, with the exception of the old man, were ex-soldiers and the talk was about the war and the difficulty of reaching Scotland on short leave from France.

The landlord, immense, muscular, and splendidly a Scot, stood behind the bar, his sleeves rolled above the elbow, calling everyone by his Christian name.

Humour, sympathy, and good nature shone from him. He was a man after Burns's own heart. He busied himself with the tankards and the glasses, turning to salt the conversation with many a good story.

It is not easy for a stranger to become admitted to such a gathering. I don't know how it happened, but quite soon I had accepted a drink from someone, and soon I was paying for a round of amazingly varied alcohol: Jock was drinking rum with a chaser of beer, the others were drinking beer or rum, and someone was drinking whisky escorted by a half of bitter. I was indeed in the heart of the Burns country!

I brought the conversation round to the poet, not quite sure how it would be received. (Had I mentioned Shakespeare in a public-house in Stratford-on-Avon there would have been no response!) There was, however, an instant reaction. We were suddenly all talking about Burns! An Englishman will hardly believe me when I say that every one of these men was to some extent an authority on the bard and could recite quite a lot of his verse. The innkeeper made us smile with stories of the curious people who come to the inn during the tourist season. He astonished me by stating that among the most enthusiastic foreign Burns pilgrims are the Japanese! The Japanese students, said he, always insisted on dining in the panelled room. I could hardly believe, but he assured me that it is a fact, that Burns is translated into Japanese! And on the occasions when Japanese students dine in the panelled room of the 'Globe' they invariably recite Burns.

'What on earth does it sound like?' I asked in some amazement.

'Och, it's no' sae bad!' he replied generously.

'It canna be sae bad as Jock here recitin' "Scotch Drink".'

This was – Jock will, I think, forgive me – quite the most appropriate thing he could at that moment have voiced; and he rose at once and declaimed, with an accent as sturdy as a Scotch fir:

> Let other poets raise a fracas
> 'Bout vines, an' wines, an' drunken Bacchus,
> An' crabbit names an' stories wrack us,
>   An' grate our lug –
> I sing the juice Scotch bear can mak' us,
>   In glass or jug . . .

He ploughed deliberately on through the poem, sometimes closing his eyes, the better to remember it, and while he did so one of the men said to me:

'D'ye ken the meanin' o' lug. Aye, it's an ear! And "Scotch bear", d'ye ken that yin? That means whusky! "Bear's" barley, ye ken.'

Jock meanwhile had come to grief somewhere round about verse eight, and he subsided, in a general peal of laughter.

'Ye can aye tell when Jock's a wee bit fou',' someone whispered. 'He insists on recitin', and sometimes ye canna stop him! But he's no' fou' enough yet!'

At the sound of Jock's voice the door had opened and there was a cry for a pianist. I was told that every Thursday night there was 'a wee bit o' a sing-sang at the "Globe".' The blinded ex-soldier was haled out enthusiastically and led to an outer room in which was a piano and a larger gathering sitting drinking their beer at wooden benches against tables. The sightless man sat at the piano and played with remarkable feeling. No inn piano is up to Albert Hall standards, but this man knew exactly what that piano could not do. One of his friends told me that he had become a pianist 'for something to do' after his blindness.

It was a strange sing-song. The latest vulgarity of the music-hall, sung with gusto, was followed by one of the eternal songs: 'Annie Laurie' or 'Loch Lomond'. In the silence, or the partial silence, that followed, the fingers of the blind pianist would wander fancifully over the keyboard and eventually a tune would take shape and there would be a cry for the words. A young fellow emptied his glass and stood by the piano:

> Ca' the yowes to the knowes,
> Ca' them where the heather grows,
> Ca' them where the burnie rowes,
>   My bonnie dearie.

> Hark the mavis' e'ening sang,
> Sounding Clouden's woods amang:
> Then a-faulding let us gang,
>   My bonnie dearie. . . .

> Fair and lovely as thou art,
> Thou hast stown my very heart:
> I can die — but canna part,
>   My bonnie dearie.

There was, to me, something infinitely touching in this inevitable cropping up of Burns. It was a Burns concert in spite of itself! Newer songs passed through the air, but always the pianist wandered back to Burns, and always there was somebody, no matter how execrable a vocalist, who knew the words. These men, could they have expressed it, were proud of the association of their 'pub', because apart from the fact that Burns was a great poet everything that they had heard or read about him proved that he was a man very like themselves: a good fellow who would have been the first to call for another round and the first to tell the latest story. But had Burns not been this kind of brotherly Scot they would still have sung his songs in the 'Globe' because they were the songs that they liked best. Is there any poet in the world more intimately associated with ordinary life?

It seemed to me that even Burns's Night with its customary haggis, its time-honoured songs, and its spate of eulogy was not so fine a tribute to the 'immortal memory' as this casual gathering of humble labourers and mechanics in the old 'howff' at Dumfries.

I returned to the little bar. Jock was on his feet. One hand was stretched forth into space. Jock's face was flushed and solemn. He was unconscious of the wild riot of friendly insults that were flung at him as he declaimed:

> As fair art thou, my bonnie lass,
>   So deep in luve am I;
> And I will luve thee still, my dear,
>   Till a' the seas gang dry. . . .

Shouts of laughter and cries of 'Sit doon, Jock!' and 'Aweel, Jock, if a' the seas gang dry, it'll no' interfere wi' ye, so dinna fash yersel'. . . .'

Jock went solemnly on, his eyes fixed on an invisible enchantress:

> Till a' the seas, gang dry, my dear,
>   And the rocks melt wi' the sun;
> And I will luve thee still, my dear,
>   While the sands o' life shall run.

'Jock, sit doon, I tell ye!'

'Jock, will ye sit doon or wull I hae tae pit ye oot o' this?'

'Jock, it's time ye went awa' hame!'

This roused Jock from his sentimental ecstasy. He roared in a tremendous voice: 'It's nae sic thing!' and then, dropping once more into soft, sentimental tones, went on with a wave of his hand:

> And fare-thee-weel, my only luve!
> And fare-thee-well, a while!

And I will come again, my luve,
Tho' twere ten thousand mile!

He kissed his hand deliberately in the direction of the spirit of affection and sat down rather abruptly. Turning to me he said, with a wag of his forefinger:

'That's Rabbie Bur-r-ns for ye! Ye may gang awa' hame tae England and say that ye hae har-rd a Scotsman recitin' his native poetry. Do ye ken? And ye may tell all the Sassenachs ye meet wi' that there's no such vairse in the wide wur-rld. Ye ken that?'

A sudden light of combat replaced the poetic fervour of his expression.

'Do ye agree wi' me?' he asked.

I knew that although we liked one another he would probably have hit me on the jaw had I said 'No'.

'Of course I do, Jock!'

'Well – gie us yer hond!'

Jock was not drunk: he was slightly Olympian. He gazed down from the eminence of his good-fellowship and saw the lovableness of everything and everybody. He was in the mood of knights and baillies and University professors and – dare I say it? – ministers, on a Burns Night.

He became confidential.

'We're all human beings, are we not? Noo I'm askin' ye, are we or are we not?'

'We are.'

Jock drew himself up and brought his hand down on the table.

'And so was Rabbie Bur-rns!'

He looked round triumphantly. It was magnificently final! It was the last word of an orator. He had nothing to add. And it seemed to me at that moment – for I am no prohibitionist – the expression of a great truth. The fact that Jock should have said it – Jock with his great hard hands, his red ex-service face, Jock with his cap tilted over his humorous, glinting eyes – seemed to me at that moment more important than the extensive statements to the same

effect by Stevenson, Henley, Lang, and Lockhart. The very
bottles on the shelves seemed to bow gravely in approval,
the red Spanish mahogany shone in agreement.

'Time, gentlemen!' sang out the innkeeper.

'It's a guid thing Bur-rns is no' alive the noo,' said
someone, 'for he wouldna tak' kindly to this awfu' interfer-
ence wi' the liberty o' the subject. . . .'

'Time, gentlemen!'

'Guid nicht tae ye!'

Jock rose to his feet and sang:

> Should auld acquaintance be forgot,
> And never brought to min'?

'Come awa', Jock, it's time ye were awa' hame!'

'We maun speed the partin' guest,' he cried, pointing to
me, and, gradually, that easiest of all songs to start struck up
in the little bar:

> And there's a hand, my trusty fere,
> And gie's a hand o' thine;
> And we'll tak' a richt guid-willie waught,
> For auld lang syne. . . .
>
> For auld lang syne, ma dear,
> For auld lang syne;
> We'll tak' a cup o' kindness yet,
> For auld lang syne. . . .

'Guid nicht! Guid nicht a'!'

'Guid nicht, Sandy! Guid nicht, Ben!'

We stood in a group outside while the innkeeper came
out and pulled a chain that extinguished the lamp over the
porch of the Globe Inn; and then we knew that the moon
was big over Dumfries. Its clean, soft luminousness fell in
odd squares and angles where the shape of eaves and roofs
was flung downward into the narrow lane.

'Guid nicht, Sandy!'

'Guid nicht, Ben!'

'Guid nicht, Jock!'

Jock took me by the arm.

'Hae ye a minute tae spare?' he asked politely. 'I wouldna wish tae tak up yer time, ye ken?'

We walked up the little lane beside the Globe Inn. We stopped and Jock pointed to a stone step.

'D'ye see yon stane?' he said. 'It's the verra step where poor Rabbie Bur'rns snoozed in the snaw a wee bit before he dee'd. Aye, yon's the verra step, and ye're lookin' at it. Man, ye're lookin' at the verra stane!'

Jock shook his head and sighed, expressing in that sigh the enormous sympathy of the humble for the misfortunes of life.

'Is it true, Jock, or is it just a legend?'

'It's true enough – every wean i' Dumfries can tell ye that! Bur-rns was comin' frae the "Globe" fou' up wi' whusky – it wasna so expensive in his day – and doon he went tae compose himself before he gaed awa hame tae Mistress Bur-rns. But, man, he was awfu' fou', and he begins niddin' and noddin' and – aweel, they found him in the morning stiff and cauld. That was the end o' puir auld Rabbie Burn-rns, for they took him hame and he deid. . . . Aye,' sighed Jock, 'an' he was only thirty-seven! Think o' the buiks he hadna written. . . .'

'Jock,' I said, 'when you work on the roads do you sing these songs to yourself?'

'Aye, I do so,' he said solemnly. 'As I was tellin' ye, it's the humanity o' Bur-rns, and, man – did ye ever see the like o' Bur-rns for a knowledge o' nature? He knew every bir-rd that flies and every flooer that graws; and he couldna go wrang if he tried.'

'And that's why you like him?'

'Och, I'm no' the only yin',' said Jock. 'I'm no' an educated chap like some, and ye may hae thocht tonight that I was a student o' poetry tae hear me recitin' the way I did. Not at a',' cried Jock, hitting me violently on the chest. 'I dinna give a damn for poetry! Bur-rns is different, for he put in his wur-rks a' the things he saw wi' his ain een, and a' the things that happened tae him. Ye ken weel what I mean? Man, it's a' sae true . . . a' sae true! And that's the verra stane whaur puir auld Rabbie Bur-rns laid him doon and dee'd. . . .'

Jock shook hands with me in the wide space of the High Street and walked out across it over the moonlight with his hands in his pockets and his cap pulled down at an angle over one eye. He turned and waved vaguely in my direction, and once he paused as though he had something more to say to me.

There, I thought, goes an ordinary rough Scotsman with certain perceptions and certain qualities found only in gentlefolk. I had a vision of him swinging a hammer to the metre of verse. And before the shadows took him I had also a vision of him swinging a kilt along the roads of Flanders to the same music.

After the desperate friendliness of this evening I felt rather lonely, standing there in the street with a late omnibus cranking up to take the road to Ayr.

It was my last night in Scotland. In the morning I would be going on over the Border to the South. And a hundred memories of the north came crowding to me: of the friendly faces and the friendly voices, of the generous Scottish firesides at which I, a stranger, had been made welcome and happy. I knew that the map of these islands would never again be the same for me. Never shall I look at the far north without a warmth of feeling and a depth of love so great that there will come to me throughout my life, no matter how far I go over the world, some compensating thought of Scotland.

In my pocket at this moment as I stood in the dark square of Dumfries was a letter which said: 'I must tell you that the little bit of your beloved Scotland is growing quite happily in the wood . . .'; and I remembered then a piece of green moss and the primrose roots which I had carried away from the Isle of Skye and sent south with instructions that this living piece of Scotland should take root in an English wood. I knew the very spot beneath a great tree. Sentiment?

I was unashamed! A living link with Scotland among my English trees, a living link with all the lovely things, the kind things, the homely things that I had met over the Border. I thought of the glens and the deep, dark gorges, the white torrents of the slow, brown salmon waters and the way the mountains lie in purple against the sky; and I remembered the little white homes in the hollow of western hills with the flavour of the peet reek over them and round their hearths, stealthy as a little mouse flitting in the firelight, the last memory from an age of swords.

There was a lit window in the dark High Street. There was a burst of laughter, the warm laughter of friends saying goodnight. Then – how often have I heard it from Edinburgh to Aberdeen, from Inverness to Glasgow? – that national anthem which gathers into itself all the sweetness and the friendliness of this dear country:

> *Should auld acquaintance be forgot,*
> *And never brought to min'?*
> *Should auld acquaintance be forgot,*
> *And auld lang syne?*
>
> *For auld lang syne, my dear,*
> *For auld lang syne.*
> *We'll tak' a cup o' kindness yet,*
> *For auld lang syne. . . .*

There was a burst of laughter, a whoop or two, and a volley of goodnights.

Then silence. . . .

In that silence a stranger said goodbye to Scotland.

INDEX